Legislative Style

Chicago Studies in American Politics

A SERIES EDITED BY BENJAMIN I. PAGE, SUSAN HERBST, LAWRENCE R. JACOBS, AND ADAM J. BERINSKY

Also in the series:

WHY PARTIES MATTER: POLITICAL COMPETITION AND DEMOCRACY IN THE AMERICAN SOUTH by *John H. Aldrich and John D. Griffin*

NEITHER LIBERAL NOR CONSERVATIVE: IDEOLOGICAL INNOCENCE IN THE AMERICAN PUBLIC by *Donald R. Kinder and Nathan P. Kalmoe*

STRATEGIC PARTY GOVERNMENT: WHY WINNING TRUMPS IDEOLOGY by *Gregory Koger and Matthew J. Lebo*

THE POLITICS OF RESENTMENT: RURAL CONSCIOUSNESS IN WISCONSIN AND THE RISE OF SCOTT WALKER by *Katherine J. Cramer*

POST-RACIAL OR MOST-RACIAL? RACE AND POLITICS IN THE OBAMA ERA by *Michael Tesler*

LEGISLATING IN THE DARK: INFORMATION AND POWER IN THE HOUSE OF REPRESENTATIVES by *James M. Curry*

WHY WASHINGTON WON'T WORK: POLARIZATION, POLITICAL TRUST, AND THE GOVERNING CRISIS by *Marc J. Hetherington and Thomas J. Rudolph*

WHO GOVERNS? PRESIDENTS, PUBLIC OPINION, AND MANIPULATION by *James N. Druckman and Lawrence R. Jacobs*

TRAPPED IN AMERICA'S SAFETY NET: ONE FAMILY'S STRUGGLE by *Andrea Louise Campbell*

ARRESTING CITIZENSHIP: THE DEMOCRATIC CONSEQUENCES OF AMERICAN CRIME CONTROL by *Amy E. Lerman and Vesla M. Weaver*

HOW THE STATES SHAPED THE NATION: AMERICAN ELECTORAL INSTITUTIONS AND VOTER TURNOUT, 1920–2000 by *Melanie Jean Springer*

Additional series titles follow index

Legislative Style

WILLIAM BERNHARD

TRACY SULKIN

THE UNIVERSITY OF CHICAGO PRESS   CHICAGO AND LONDON

The University of Chicago Press, Chicago 60637
The University of Chicago Press, Ltd., London
© 2018 by The University of Chicago
All rights reserved. No part of this book may be used or reproduced in any manner whatsoever without written permission, except in the case of brief quotations in critical articles and reviews. For more information, contact the University of Chicago Press, 1427 East 60th Street, Chicago, IL 60637.
Published 2018
Printed in the United States of America
27 26 25 24 23 22 21 20 19 18   1 2 3 4 5

ISBN-13: 978-0-226-51014-9 (cloth)
ISBN-13: 978-0-226-51028-6 (paper)
ISBN-13: 978-0-226-51031-6 (e-book)
DOI: 10.7208/chicago/9780226510316.001.0001

Library of Congress Cataloging-in-Publication Data

Names: Bernhard, William, 1966– author. | Sulkin, Tracy, author.
Title: Legislative style / William Bernhard, Tracy Sulkin.
Other titles: Chicago studies in American politics.
Description: Chicago : The University of Chicago Press, 2018. | Series: Chicago studies in American politics | Includes bibliographical references and index.
Identifiers: LCCN 2017028654 | ISBN 9780226510149 (cloth : alk. paper) | ISBN 9780226510286 (pbk. : alk. paper) | ISBN 9780226510316 (e-book)
Subjects: LCSH: Legislators—Professional relationships—United States. | United States. Congress—Officials and employees. | Legislation—United States—Decision making. | Political planning—United States.
Classification: LCC JK1083 .B47 2018 | DDC 331.7/6132873—dc23
LC record available at https://lccn.loc.gov/2017028654

♾ This paper meets the requirements of ANSI/NISO Z39.48-1992 (Permanence of Paper).

Contents

Acknowledgments vii

CHAPTER 1. Legislative Style and Congressional Careers 1

CHAPTER 2. Measuring Legislative Style 16
with Daniel Sewell

CHAPTER 3. The Styles 42

CHAPTER 4. Explaining Freshman Styles 61

CHAPTER 5. Transitions in Style 91

CHAPTER 6. The Electoral Consequences of Legislative Style 124

CHAPTER 7. Styles, Lawmaking, and Legislative Success 153

CHAPTER 8. Career Advancement and Legislative Styles 175

CHAPTER 9. Legislative Styles and Evaluations of Congress 205

Notes 223

Works Cited 241

Index 255

Acknowledgments

The idea to write a book together on legislators' styles developed about five years ago, and, in the intervening time, we have amassed a debt of gratitude to a long list of colleagues and collaborators. It is a pleasure to have this opportunity to thank them.

For helpful conversations and feedback along the way, we thank Bill Bianco, Jim Curry, Justin Grimmer, Christian Grose, Greg Koger, Bryan Jones, David Leblang, Frances Lee, Kris Miler, Jeff Mondak, Chris Mooney, Collin Paschall, Kathryn Pearson, Molly Ritchie, Jen Selin, Gisela Sin, Sean Theriault, Jen Victor, Craig Volden, John Wilkerson, Alan Wiseman, and Laurel Harbridge Yong. Special thanks to Jim Kuklinski, who read the manuscript in its entirety and offered encouragement as we prepared to send it out the door.

We are also grateful to Dan Pemstein, who indulged our early questions about cluster analysis and convinced us that a clustering approach to legislative styles was worth pursuing. That exploration led us to a fruitful collaboration with Dan Sewell and Yuguo Chen of the Department of Statistics at the University of Illinois. Dan, our coauthor for chapter 2 of this book, worked with us for over two years to develop and test a clustering model that adequately captured the reality of long-term congressional careers. After finishing his PhD, he moved on to bigger and better things as an assistant professor of biostatistics at the University of Iowa, and we appreciate his continuing engagement with the project.

We were fortunate to have the opportunity to present the project in its early stages at seminars at the University of Missouri and Ohio State University, as well as here at the University of Illinois. We thank participants in those seminars, as well as at panels at the American Political

Science Association and Midwest Political Science Association for the many useful suggestions that emerged from our discussions.

Our analyses of legislative style rely on a large and varied collection of indicators of MCs' behavior in office, and the project would not have been possible without the generosity of a number of scholars who shared their data with us. In particular, we thank Scott Adler, David Canon, Katie Francis, Brian Gaines, Craig Goodman, Eric Heberlig, Jeff Jenkins, Georgia Kernell, Bruce Larson, Tim Nokken, David C. W. Parker, Michael Rocca, Charles Stewart, Craig Volden, John Wilkerson, Alan Wiseman, Jonathan Woon, and Laurel Harbridge Yong. Their willingness to make their data available (and their good cheer in answering our questions) epitomizes the best of the legislative studies research community.

Kylee Britzman, Victor Hugg, and Collin Paschall all provided expert research assistance at various stages of the project, and we are grateful for their contributions. Collin, in particular, was a major help in collecting last-minute data as we completed the analyses for the final chapters.

It has been a pleasure to work with the University of Chicago Press. We thank John Tryneski for his advice and enthusiasm in the early stages of the process, and for securing careful and thoughtful reviews that shaped in important ways how the book developed. We are grateful as well to Chuck Myers, who shepherded the project through the final steps, and to Holly Smith and the production team for their assistance.

Finally, and most of all, we thank our families.

CHAPTER ONE

Legislative Style and Congressional Careers

There are two kinds of Congressmen—show horses and work horses. If you want to get your name in the papers, be a show horse. If you want to gain the respect of your colleagues, keep quiet and be a work horse. — Senator Carl Hayden's recollection of the advice given to him as a new legislator, as quoted by Matthews (1960, 94)

Upon arriving on Capitol Hill, all new members of Congress (MCs) face a central choice: What kind of legislator will they be? This is not a trivial task, as the available opportunities for investment of time, effort, and resources are numerous. What, for example, is the right balance between working in the district and on Capitol Hill? Will they be policy specialists, focusing on a particular issue; policy generalists, active in a number of areas; or will they avoid investing in policy making altogether? Should they toe the party line or chart their own courses? With whom should they collaborate and form coalitions? Should they seek to develop a national reputation by giving speeches and cultivating the media? What is the "right" amount of time to spend raising money, and what should they do with those funds once they have collected them?

Together, such decisions define an MC's "legislative style." These styles are fundamental to understanding individual legislators' behavior and aggregate dynamics within the House of Representatives. Styles shape the quality of representation constituents receive, the scope and content of the policy legacies legislators leave, and the trajectories MCs' careers take in the chamber and beyond.

We contend that legislators adopt styles that align with their ambitions, past experiences, and personal inclinations, as well as the electoral and institutional constraints they face. Put simply, MCs differ from one another. Some aspire to leadership positions within the chamber, others are content to be part of the rank and file, and still others view the House as a way station en route to other office. Some care intensely about policy and some do not. Some view their primary role as district servants, while others believe that their efforts should be focused on building their party, on promoting a cause, or on passing legislation. These differences shape the choices and trade-offs legislators make in their activities in office, and, hence, in the styles they display as they build their careers.

Consider, for example, the two Ohio Republicans first elected to the House of Representatives in 1990 (the 102nd Congress)—John Boehner and David Hobson. Boehner and Hobson had some similarities—both were born and raised in Ohio, both had military and business experience, and both had served in the state legislature. However, it was apparent from the beginning that their approaches to congressional life were quite different. Hobson was mostly content to use his position to address issues of interest to his district, particularly the concerns of military families (eventually rising to chair of the Military Construction Subcommittee of Appropriations), and he preferred to work behind the scenes on policy matters with the Republican leadership. In describing his choice to bypass press attention and interviews, Hobson said, "That isn't my style. . . . I'm not doing this to build Dave Hobson into a national name" (Barone and Cohen 2001, 1208). That outlook characterized Hobson's long (and largely under the radar) service in the House, from the time of his arrival in January 1991 until his retirement in 2008.

Boehner, in contrast, quickly became known as a "partisan firebrand" (Barone and Ujifusa 1993, 1003) who "in his first term made far more impact than just about any minority party freshman in memory" (1005). Among other initiatives, Boehner pushed for revealing the names of members caught up in the House bank scandal, and he worked with Newt Gingrich on the foundations of what would become the "Contract with America." In 1994, these efforts would help to elevate Republicans to the majority for the first time in decades. Boehner's political skill and ambition were immediately evident; by his third term in office, he had risen in the hierarchy to become House Republican Conference Chairman, the fourth-ranking Republican in the chamber. He would continue to climb the leadership ladder, becoming House Majority Leader, House Minority Leader, and eventually Speaker of the House before resigning from that position, and from his House seat, in 2015.

It is clear from even these brief descriptions that Hobson and Boehner had different goals, different ways of approaching their work, and, hence, different styles. Our goal in this book is to capture legislators' stylistic differences in a systematic way. We argue first that styles extend beyond behavior on a single dimension of congressional activity, and instead are holistic in nature. They reflect the entirety of MCs' choices across the myriad opportunities available to them. Second, we view MCs' individual patterns of behavior as distinctive and characteristic, signaling what they "are like" as legislators. Importantly, though, MCs are not each unique. There are a few common paths to Congress, a handful of different role orientations, and a finite number of possible career goals within and beyond the chamber. As a result, we expect legislators' behavior to cohere into a small set of recognizable styles. In other words, there will be a number of other "Boehners" and "Hobsons" in the House of Representatives. We anticipate that styles will be consistent (though not entirely unchanging) for individuals across time and with a similar distribution across congresses.

Our gestalt view of legislative behavior is not new. The idea of legislative style has its roots in the very earliest empirical work on congressional politics, and it is commonplace among MCs themselves to refer to the various "types" that inhabit the halls of Congress. For example, Tom DeLay (R-TX), the Republicans' Whip and then Majority Leader from 1995 to 2006, often asserted that there were "three kinds of congressmen"—leadership MCs (who "aimed to spend their careers governing the House and their colleagues"), committee MCs (who "took up residence in a particular outpost . . . and made it their fiefdom"), and district MCs (who devoted their time and effort to cultivating their constituencies) (Draper 2012, 15).[1]

However, our approach is in direct contrast to most current research on legislative activity, which tends to focus in depth on a single behavior at a time (e.g., roll call voting or the introduction of legislation or campaign fund-raising). While the benefits of such specialization are many, the downside is that we lack a comprehensive understanding of how MCs approach their jobs as legislators, the manner in which these choices are manifested in their activity in office, and whether this type of strategizing yields electoral, policy, and career dividends for them. In fact, we contend that congressional scholars know more about what MCs are like as *representatives* (building on the work of Fenno 1978, Grimmer 2013, and others) than as *legislators*.

In what follows, we offer an account of congressional careers centering on the origins, evolution, and effects of legislative style. Our analyses focus on MCs who served in the 101st–110th Congresses (1989–2008). We derive styles from the behavior of these legislators (1,011 unique members, and 4,276 MC-congress observations), utilizing a new statistical model for clustering analysis. Our results reveal that MCs' activity clusters into five stable and predictable styles: policy specialists, party soldiers, district advocates, party builders, and ambitious entrepreneurs.

Our analyses explore the distribution of styles across MCs and congresses, the factors that influence why a legislator adopts a particular style in his or her freshman term, the evolution of style over individuals' service in the House of Representatives, and the effects of style on MCs' electoral and legislative success and career advancement. This approach offers new insight into a number of enduring questions in legislative politics. We show, for example, that the path to leadership often begins early. John Boehner was distinct from his peers from the start—among the only 6.5% of MCs who adopt a party builder style by their sophomore terms. We also demonstrate that progressively ambitious legislators—those who desire to move up to higher office—tend to make different stylistic choices than their colleagues planning long service in the House. For some MCs, these stylistic choices are apparent from the beginning of their careers. Bernie Sanders (I-VT), for instance, began his House service as an ambitious entrepreneur, eventually leaving that chamber behind for a run for the Senate and then the presidency. For others, a shift in style accompanies a change in the opportunity structure that makes a run for the Senate or governorship a viable option. Among this latter group are MCs such as Charles Schumer (D-NY), who had been a party builder, but shifted to the ambitious entrepreneur style during the term leading up to his Senate bid.

Legislative style also offers leverage in explaining the effects of macro-level shocks like shifts in majority control and the growth of partisan and ideological polarization on legislative behavior. Changes that make congressional service more attractive to certain types of current or prospective legislators may also influence the distribution of styles within the chamber. As we demonstrate, a congress full of party soldiers looks different from one populated by policy specialists or district advocates, and the styles adopted by MCs have downstream consequences for representation and policy making, ranging from the amount of attention legislators devote to their districts to the volume of legislation passed into law.

A Brief History of Legislative Styles

Style has a long history in the literature on Congress. As far back as the 1950s, political scientists like Donald Matthews (1959, 1960) invoked the famous "work horse versus show horse" distinction when describing differences across MCs (see also Barber 1965; Clapp 1963; Davidson 1969). Such accounts posit two types of members: those who do the heavy lifting legislatively, toiling in obscurity at the mundane work of making law, and those whose primary aim is self-aggrandizement, seeking publicity at the expense of their legislative responsibilities.

Observations by congressional contemporaries of these scholars buttressed the claims of two distinct styles. In his 1947 memoir, *Confessions of a Congressman*, Jerry Voorhis (D-CA) contrasted "prepossessed" and influential "members of long service" with another group:

> At the other extreme in both the House and the Senate are certain members who play regularly to the galleries and to the press. I soon learned that their influence is vastly less than would appear from a reading of either the *Congressional Record* or the morning papers. (1947, 32)

Along the same lines, in his autobiography, *My First Fifty Years in Politics*, former Speaker of the House Joe Martin (R-MA) recalled of his early days in Congress:

> In spite of the great reputations, I soon discovered, as new members probably still do, that whenever a particular subject came up, there was always one or perhaps two members who were expert on it and could address themselves to it far more intelligently than anyone else. And very often, these were members that one had never heard of until he came to Congress. (Martin and Donovan 1960, 47–48)

Underlying these descriptions of legislative types is an argument about advancement and congressional careers. Show horses might receive media and public attention, making it more likely that they rise to a Senate seat or beyond, but the real influence and respect accrues to workhorses, enabling them to attain positions of power (formal and informal) within the chamber. As Mayhew (1974) put it, "The hero of the Hill is not the hero of the airwaves. The member who earns prestige among his peers is the lonely gnome who passes up news conferences . . . in order to devote his time to legislative 'homework'" (147).

However, despite the frequent discussion of the divide between show horses and work horses, few scholars followed up to explore legislative styles in a systematic way. Perhaps this is because it was taken as self-evident that these two types were sufficient to describe important variation in MC behavior. Another likely reason is that styles are difficult to quantify, and by the 1960s and early 1970s, scholars of legislative behavior and representation had turned to large N statistical analysis as the methodology of choice.[2] This contributed to the rise of studies of roll call voting behavior, beginning with the foundational works of scholars like Miller and Stokes (1963), Fiorina (1974), Kingdon (1973), and Matthews and Stimson (1975), and continuing unabated into the 2000s. Indeed, for many years, the study of legislative activity *was* the study of roll call voting, with more gestalt depictions of MCs' behavior falling by the wayside.

A notable exception, of course, is Fenno's (1978) work on legislators' relationships with their districts: their "home styles." Fenno argued that to understand MCs, we must consider where they come from. In particular, how do they think about their constituencies and how do they balance the competing demands they face between their districts and their work on Capitol Hill? In *Home Style: House Members in Their Districts*, he targeted three behaviors of interest—MCs' allocation of resources between the district and DC, their presentations of self, and their explanations of Washington activity—concluding that "each member's amalgam of these three activities—as manifested in the district—constitutes his or her home style" (1978, 33).

For good reason, *Home Style* remains among the most influential books on representation in the United States. Among its many contributions is that it elucidates the role of MCs' perceptions of their constituencies and their relationships with them in explaining legislative behavior. It is also a masterful illustration of the value of the qualitative "soak and poke" approach to research at which Fenno excelled, demonstrating the value of close observation of MCs at work.

From the perspective of our approach to legislative styles, Fenno's identification of the district as the locus of interest is crucial. When he asks "what are members like?" he means what are they like *as representatives*. This focus on style as synonymous with communication with (and to) constituents continues to the present (see, for example, Grimmer 2013; Grimmer, Westwood, and Messing 2014). The result is a rich and nuanced accounting of the causes and consequences of legislators' presentations of self and explanations of their activity on Capitol Hill. However, the question of what MCs are like *as legislators* has received considerably less attention.

There was a brief resurgence of interest in the show horse versus work horse divide in the 1980s, with scholars examining the linkage between media attention and legislative activity. However, evidence largely failed to support the hypothesized inverse relationship between lawmaking and publicity (Langbein and Sigelman 1989; but see Payne 1980). In response, some scholars posited that the growth of television meant that there was no longer a distinction—all MCs were now show horses (Ornstein 1983; Ranney 1983). Others argued that the media had become more sophisticated, granting publicity to those legislators who actually did the heavy lifting (Cook 1988; Hess 1986).

Because these observers were primarily interested in supporting or debunking the show horse/work horse conception itself, or in describing the effects of the media on congressional behavior, they did not seek to offer a new, more accurate, typology of MC style. Meanwhile, scholars of legislative behavior were still largely focused on roll call votes, particularly as measures of MCs' preferences (e.g., Poole and Rosenthal 2007) and, increasingly, on other floor behavior (e.g., Smith 1989). Others, following Fenno, aimed to quantify district attention and constituency service and better understand its effects on MCs' electoral fortunes (Bond 1985; Cain, Ferejohn, and Fiorina 1987; Johannes 1984; Parker 1986).

The 1990s and 2000s saw the expansion of the study of legislative activity beyond roll call voting. This was due in part to the growing recognition that MCs' votes, while important, did not reflect all dimensions of potential interest. Hall (1996), for example, opened his book on participation in congressional committees by noting:

> For every issue that comes before them, there are essentially two decisions that each member of Congress must make: what position to take and how active to be. A rich literature within political science and economics is devoted to the first, exploring the causes and consequences of members' vot-

ing decisions in committee and on the floor. By comparison, almost nothing is known about the decisions that members make every day, issue by issue, regarding how much they will participate in the legislative deliberations in their chamber. (1)

The move beyond voting was aided by advances in data collection and dissemination that made it possible for scholars to access information about MCs that had previously been either unavailable or prohibitively labor-intensive to obtain. Thus, Hall was joined by scholars offering analyses of activities like bill introductions (Rocca and Gordon 2010; Schiller 1995; Woon 2008), cosponsorships (Fowler 2006; Harbridge 2015; Harward and Moffett 2010; Kessler and Krehbiel 1996; Koger 2003; Wilson and Young 1997), committee requests (Frisch and Kelly 2006), floor statements and legislative speeches (Godbout and Yu 2009; Pearson and Dancey 2011; Rocca 2007), media strategies (Kedrowski 1996), member-to-party and member-to-member campaign giving (Cann 2008; Currinder 2009; Heberlig and Larson 2012), and allocation of resources to the home front (Parker and Goodman 2009, 2012).

The effect of this work was to broaden considerably the range of activities of interest to congressional scholars and to counter successfully the argument that behaviors other than roll call voting are solely symbolic and unworthy of sustained attention. However, the tendency toward an activity-by-activity accounting of MCs' behavior means that we have as of yet largely forgone the opportunity to study the relationships among activities. Indeed, recent studies that have utilized multiple behaviors to investigate a particular dynamic, such as legislative entrepreneurship (Wawro 2001), the effects of campaigns on legislators' agendas (Sulkin 2005, 2011), the quality of dyadic representational linkages (Bishin 2009; Burden 2007; Miler 2010; Minta 2011), the role of social class in economic policy making (Carnes 2013), or MCs' rates of activity across their careers (Hibbing 1991), still generally treat activities as independent of one another.

In contrast, we know that in reality legislators view their situations in a more expansive and unified way, with a fundamental goal or goals and an understanding of the context in which they operate that precedes their decisions about how to behave on a particular type of activity (Clapp 1963). MCs use the activities at their disposal to accomplish their broader aims, and this vision about how to approach their jobs shapes their choices on a day-to-day basis. The study of legislative styles captures this dynamic, targeting the common trade-offs legislators make as they build their portfolio of activities.

Trade-Offs and Opportunities

It is a reality of congressional life that legislators must make difficult choices about how to spend their time and prioritize their activities. Given the complexity of the institution and the sheer number of avenues for activity, they simply cannot be highly active on everything.[3] In their book, *American Business and Public Policy*,[4] Bauer, Pool, and Dexter (1963) offer a sampling of the many options available to a legislator, from building a national reputation to becoming a local civic leader to being a party "wheelhorse," but conclude that "the one thing he cannot do is much of all these things. He must choose among them; he has to be a certain kind of congressman" (406–7).

Most often, resources are the limitation, with time being the scarcest of all. MCs commonly lament the many demands on their schedules—more hours on fund-raising means less for lawmaking, developing policy expertise in one issue requires neglecting another, going on the speaker circuit cuts into their days at home in the district, and so on. Former representative Patricia Schroeder (D-CO) equated the job with being "a total juggler. You always have seventeen things pulling on your sleeve" (Davidson et al. 2014, 114). Studies of how MCs spend their time corroborate this conclusion. The Congressional Management Foundation found that members devote, on average, seventy hours per week to work during the congressional session and fifty-nine hours when Congress is out of session, and travel home to the district about forty weekends per year (CMF 2013). Even with these efforts, they are able to satisfy only some of the many requests for their time and attention.

In other situations, the constraint MCs face is not about time limitations, but that choices themselves are incommensurate. For example, a legislator who has just cosponsored a major pro-energy bill on increasing the use of fossil fuels will not also be a speaker at an Earth Day rally. One who decries the show horse approach to congressional life cannot also devote large portions of his or her time to media appearances. One who claims to be a delegate of the district cannot regularly vote against his or her constituents' expressed interests. In short, legislators are constrained in their abilities to have their cake and eat it too.

At the end of the day, all MCs must make decisions to pursue some opportunities and forgo others. They do not do so haphazardly, as there is much riding on their choices. How, then, do they make their decisions? We argue that legislators consider the incentives and restrictions they face, particularly as these relate to their immediate and long-term ambitions. Fortunately, MCs have at least some leeway to build their careers as they see fit. As political-scientist-turned-representative David Price (D-NC) put it, "most members, most of the time, have a great deal of latitude as to how they define their roles and what kind of job they wish to do" (1973, 146).

To illustrate, imagine four newly elected legislators, each of whom arrives on Capitol Hill with a different combination of goals, constraints, and views about his or her role as representative.

> **Legislator A:** Believes that he was elected to serve the people of his district, and thus chooses to spend time and resources there. The district is heterogeneous, making him potentially electorally vulnerable, so he prioritizes raising money and has to choose between being a party loyalist (in the hopes of obtaining financial support from the party) or steering a more bipartisan course and enlarging his reelection constituency.
>
> **Legislator B:** Wants to one day be a party leader, so she needs to demonstrate visibility, a commitment to the party, and prowess at lawmaking and fundraising. She has less to gain from building a reputation for policy expertise in a specific area and, given the other demands on her time, devotes only as much attention to the district as is necessary for reelection.
>
> **Legislator C:** Comes to Congress with an interest in a particular policy area, based on his expertise from a previous career, or from experiences as a state legislator. He seeks a relevant committee assignment and devotes his efforts to it, but will not emphasize party-building or constituency-oriented activities.
>
> **Legislator D:** Harbors a desire to be president one day (but might settle for a Senate seat or a governorship). She needs to make a splash and thus will seek public visibility. Focused more on her goals than those of the party, she is not a loyalist in her voting, although she may curry favor by raising and redistributing funds.

These are just a few archetypes, but they highlight the point that MCs are strategic actors and behave in a way that helps them to reach their goals. Legislators operating within similar milieus and with similar policy, career, and electoral ambitions should therefore adopt similar patterns of behavior. These patterns, in turn, correspond to distinct legislative styles.

The Nature of Legislative Styles

We conceive of style as fundamental to who MCs are as legislators, a function of the context in which they operate, their role orientations, and their long-term vision of the path their careers will take. Accordingly, we predict that legislative styles will be relatively stable features of individuals, with most MCs demonstrating consistent styles across time. We do not anticipate, for instance, that legislators will careen from being party builders in one term to district advocates in the next to ambitious entrepreneurs in the next, and then go back to being party builders.[5] The distribution of styles should also be relatively invariant at the aggregate level, with similar proportions of each style from congress to congress. However, MCs' styles may change with their individual circumstances or as their career goals evolve, and macro-level "shocks" such as redistricting or a majority shift may lead to more widespread changes.

Given our theory about the origins of style, we also expect that MCs' styles will be predictable. Their initial styles (i.e., the stylistic choices they make in their freshman terms as representatives) are likely to be a result of their prior political experiences and ideological leanings, as well as their personal characteristics and institutional status. For instance, MCs who had previously served in a state legislature bring different skills and perspectives to the job than those without political experience, and this affects their behavior, and, perhaps, their styles (Francis 2014). Characteristics of MCs such as their ideological extremity, age, gender, and race may matter as well, shaping their level of interest in policy, their views about representation, and their career ambitions. Features of the district, such as its level of heterogeneity (ideological or demographic), can also influence style by presenting MCs with varying levels of constraint on their activity. Finally, legislators' relative power and status upon arrival in Washington may interact with their goals to affect their stylistic choices. For instance, majority and minority MCs face different opportunity structures, as do those with prime committee assignments and those without. These factors all come together to shape new MCs' styles.

Once MCs establish a style, we predict that it will be relatively "sticky." Many of the constraints legislators face are unchanging, their role orientations are relatively fundamental, and they develop habits of behavior from which they are unlikely to diverge. Nonetheless, we do not expect style to be a constant, particularly across a long career. We anticipate some natural evolution as MCs gain seniority, learn from their experiences, and gain influence within the chamber. Beyond that, we predict that it will take fairly major shocks to induce a shift in style. For example, an MC who is newly electorally safe or vulnerable may find herself with new freedom to behave as she wishes, or with new constraints that affect how she spends her time. Along the same lines, a switch in majority status or obtaining (or losing) a position of power within the chamber may change MCs' decision calculus[6] and the styles they display going forward.

In turn, these styles will themselves contribute to MCs' electoral and legislative success, as well as their career trajectories. Disentangling the direction of causality is complicated, as the same factors that lead an MC to take on a given style may also affect his or her success in a particular realm. For instance, legislators who are strong partisans may be more likely to adopt a style that prioritizes party building *and* be more likely to attain leadership positions within the party. Nonetheless, it is possible to take these factors into account, and, after doing so, we expect to see relationships between style and MCs' success at building coalitions, passing legislation, and obtaining preferred committee assignments; at winning support from voters and warding off potential challengers; and at rising to positions of power within the chamber and successfully moving beyond the House to win Senate seats and governorships.

Our Approach

To evaluate these expectations requires that we first identify each MC's style in each congress. This is easier said than done, as there are numerous options for proceeding. The two basic questions to consider are, first, whether we should impose an a priori categorization of styles or let the classifications emerge from the analyses, and, second, whether we should rely on quantitative or qualitative evidence in making the assignments.

The advantage to beginning with a set of styles and then assigning MCs to those styles is that it ensures that one has a small set of categories that resonate with current popular and/or scholarly understandings of differences in legislative behavior. However, the biggest risk to such an approach is that it could lead us to impose a distinction that we believe exists but in reality does not. We think of this as the work horse/show horse problem. Avoiding the "if you look for it, you will find it" dynamic is of central importance to us, so we opt instead to take an inductive approach, allowing the styles to emerge from our data.

What, then, should be the source of our information about MCs' behavior? One option would be to ask legislative scholars and/or staffers to identify styles and assign MCs to those categories. This has the advantage of drawing on their expertise, but it presents problems in categorizing lesser-known MCs, and few respondents would have the historical memory to characterize the behavior of legislators who served in the earlier congresses in our sample. In addition, knowledge of the current behavior of an MC might lead respondents to mischaracterize his or her earlier activity as consistent with later behavior, even if there were differences.

Instead, we opt to collect data on a large number of activities engaged in by MCs and then to use a statistical technique called clustering analysis to generate a single indicator of style for each MC in each congress. We discuss our approach to data collection and modeling in depth in the next chapter. The advantages to our method are that it allows us to identify stylistic categories without imposing classifications and to objectively and reliably assign each legislator in each congress to a specific style. It also enables other scholars to easily transport our method to different time periods in US history or to different contexts (e.g., state legislatures or comparative national legislatures).

Plan of the Book

In what follows, we explore in detail the dynamics of legislative style. Chapter 2 develops the theoretical foundations for our hypotheses about the relationships between MCs' goals and their legislative styles and provides specifics about our data collection and modeling strategies. In chapter 3, we present the five styles that emerge from our clustering analysis—policy specialists, party builders, district advocates, party soldiers, and ambitious entrepreneurs. We describe each cluster in depth, discussing what distinguishes that style overall and relative to the other groups. We also show the distribution of styles across parties and congresses, demonstrating the overall stability of style and offering hypotheses about the dynamics of style within and across MCs' careers.

Chapters 4 and 5 establish the causes of variation in style across and within MCs. In chapter 4, we focus on where MCs begin—their styles in their first terms in office. We demonstrate that legislators' freshman styles are a function of characteristics of MCs and their districts, as well as the context in which they find themselves in that term. Chapter 5 explores the question of transitions in style across time: under what conditions will an MC adopt a new legislative style? Our results show that changes in electoral security and institutional status affect the propensity to shift style, but that the effects of these variables differ depending on an MC's current style. For example, if an MC is already a party builder, then gaining a leadership position is unlikely to result in a change in style. If, however, that legislator has a different style, a transition is more likely. In both chapters 4 and 5, we supplement our statistical analyses with case studies of MCs to offer nuanced assessments of the dynamics of style.

Chapters 6 through 8 investigate the consequences of style for MCs' success. In chapter 6, we explore the electoral implications of style. We argue that legislative styles are most likely to result in electoral success if they map well onto the district. The competing demands of heterogeneous constituencies, for instance, may be better managed by some styles than others. All else equal, the failure to adopt one of these styles is likely to produce stronger electoral challengers, lower vote shares, and potentially defeat. We also compare the legislative styles of MCs elected from the same district to determine how electoral context shapes legislative style. All else equal, we expect that MCs who arrive in office having unseated an incumbent are likely to adopt styles that differ from those of their predecessor, while those who replace a retiring incumbent are more prone to continuing that style.

Chapter 7 targets the legislative outcomes associated with style. We demonstrate that style is indeed related to MCs' accomplishments in lawmaking, but that there are multiple paths to such achievement (i.e., styles associated with legislative stature and with expertise both yield success in the legislative realm). We also show that some payoffs are relatively immediate consequences of style, while others accrue more slowly, as MCs build reputations across time.

Chapter 8 investigates the longer-term implications of style for MCs' careers. We argue that legislators' trajectories are a function of individuals' decisions, as well as strategic choices on the part of the existing party leadership about which MCs to support and promote. For example, many future leaders distinguish themselves early, adopting styles that are more common among senior MCs than those of their freshman and sophomore colleagues. We also explore the linkages between style, retirement, and progressive ambition, explaining who leaves the House voluntarily, who runs for higher office, and how MCs from different styles think about strategy when planning their futures.

Finally, in chapter 9, we draw out the normative consequences of style for effective governance. We conclude by discussing the effects of possible congressional reforms on the distribution of party builders, ambitious entrepreneurs, party soldiers, policy specialists, and district advocates within the House of Representatives. We argue that such reforms may have unintended, and unwelcome, consequences for representational and policy-making outcomes.

CHAPTER TWO

Measuring Legislative Style

with Daniel Sewell

The sheer busyness in Washington, as well as at home, surpasses what almost all members experienced in their previous careers and requires specific survival techniques. Most important, you must set priorities—separate matters in which you want to invest considerable time and energy from those you wish to handle perfunctorily or not deal with personally.
— David Price (D-NC), *The Congressional Experience* (2004, 72)

The most critical choices legislators make are how to spend their time and prioritize their activities. The opportunities are many and at times overwhelming. As a newly elected legislator interviewed by Fenno put it: "It was like being dropped into the jungle and having to learn how to survive. Gradually, you cut out a little place for yourself, a clearing in which you can live" (1986, 142).

The job undoubtedly grows easier with the passage of years, but MCs always find themselves facing many more demands than they can reasonably accommodate. Fortunately, however, they have useful heuristics and strategies for choosing among the options that come their way. The various activities at their disposal are not ends in and of themselves. Instead, MCs engage in them to promote their more general goals and their vision of what "type" of legislator they are and want to be.

What are these goals? In *Congressmen in Committees*, Fenno (1973) offered three—reelection, influence within the House of Representatives, and good (from the perspective of the legislator) public policy.[1] Following soon after, Mayhew (1974) famously reduced MCs' calculations to a single goal, arguing that they can be usefully depicted as "single-minded seekers of reelection" (5).

In what follows, we assume that MCs harbor multiple goals and that they make trade-offs between them. The particular balance of these goals varies across legislators, and, at the level of individual MCs, across careers, depending on their personal inclinations and the context in which they find themselves. It is these balances and trade-offs, manifested in MCs' activity, that define their legislative styles. For some legislators, the balance of goals is a sincere reflection of their personal preferences and ambitions. For others, it is induced by constraints they face, as when a legislator who wishes to be prominent on the national scene is instead compelled by constituency considerations to focus on her district, or when an MC who would like to one day be Speaker of the House knows that his unwillingness or inability to be a loyal partisan will be a stumbling block and so chooses an alternate path. Regardless of their origins, though, these motivations shape the decisions MCs make on a day-to-day basis.

At first glance, our views about legislators' goals might seem consistent with Fenno's conception and inconsistent with Mayhew's. Neither assessment is quite accurate. While Fenno acknowledges that "all Congressmen probably hold all three goals," (1973, 1) at least to some extent, he posits that each has a primary goal, and, in his formulation, each seeks a committee assignment where that goal is also dominant.[2] Accordingly, he treats each of the goals as separate. In contrast, we do not presume that MCs have a dominant goal (although some might), and instead are interested in capturing the ways in which legislators balance their goals and ambitions.

Like Fenno, Mayhew assumes that legislators are largely motivated by a single goal, but posits that it is the *same* goal for all. Reelection is at the center, the most proximate motivation of MCs, "the goal that must be achieved over and over if other ends are to be entertained" (1974, 16). However, this formulation is not quite as limiting as it might seem at first glance. It does leave open the possibility that relatively electorally secure MCs will choose, at least occasionally, to pursue goals that contradict the reelection imperative (see also Arnold 1990), or, perhaps more realistically, that reelection-focused legislators will be willing to sacrifice a small amount in vote share for a big payoff in other realms.[3] On this point, we concur with Fenno's assertion in *Home Style* that "all want reelection in the abstract, but not all will pay any price to achieve it; nor will all pay the same price" (1978, 221).

Mayhew also explicitly notes that pursuing reelection need not necessarily mean forgoing other ends (1974, 15–16; see also Mayhew 2000). It is an oversimplification of his argument to claim that every behavior can be categorized as either reelection oriented or not, and that strategic MCs always take the reelection option at the expense of other goals. Most of what legislators do does not approximate a forced dichotomous choice wherein one option promotes reelection prospects and the other harms them.[4] More often, the decision is about *which* reelection-oriented behaviors to pursue. As Bauer, Pool, and Dexter (1963) note, "It is a cliché that the main job of a congressman is to be re-elected. There is much truth to it, but there are various ways of getting re-elected" (406).[5]

MCs can and do choose activities that support their electoral efforts and enable them to achieve other goals. For example, a legislator from a rural district may be able to promote both policy and reelection by specializing her lawmaking agenda on agriculture; an MC with a highly partisan constituency can engage in visible party-building activities that enhance the likelihood of rising to a position of power within the chamber without sacrificing his or her electoral prospects; and a House member with ambitions for higher office and an interest in a policy issue of national importance may be able to promote the former by taking leadership on the latter.

In short, legislators face a complicated environment, with dozens of choices to be made on a daily basis. They structure their activity to achieve their particular profile of electoral, policy, and career goals. Their actions in these domains are not independent of one another, but neither are they always zero-sum. Indeed, the central strategic task of all MCs is to develop a set of activities that enables them to achieve multiple goals. As Bauer, Pool, and Dexter (1963) described it: "A rational congressman who has decided what kind of congressman he wants to be would then use his resources according to strategies consisting of whole packages of related acts" (407).

These "packages" of activity, while distinctive, are not unique to individual MCs. Because there are a finite number of goals and career paths in the House, many legislators find themselves subject to similar incentives and constraints. In response, these legislators will adopt common patterns of behavior, and, as such, we predict that MCs' activity will coalesce into a relatively small number of styles.

In the next sections, we discuss our measurement of legislators' activity and their resulting styles. Two caveats are worthy of mention.

First, we cannot directly assess MCs' goals, as these are necessarily latent. Thus, we cannot know for sure that Legislator A values policy but also wants to be elected to the Senate, or that Legislator B is concerned about her security in the district and would be happy staying as a rank-and-file member of the House. We can only assume that MCs are goal-oriented and infer their motivations from their overall patterns of activity and the observable decisions they make about their careers. From our perspective, this is not problematic because our ultimate aim is not to identify MCs' goals, but to categorize legislators by their behavior and to assess the correlates and consequences of the resulting styles.

Second, although there is a tendency in the literature to identify particular activities as specific to a given goal, we caution against doing so. A behavior may accomplish multiple goals, so simply observing the activity does not always reveal the motivation. Introducing a bill could aid reelection, it could promote policy, it could help an MC to gain influence within the chamber, or it could do all three. Relatedly, the *same* activity can have different effects for different MCs. For instance, some districts (or subconstituencies within those districts) may reward MCs who are players on the national scene, while others may punish this behavior, wanting their representatives to spend time on the home front (Harden 2016; Sulkin, Testa, and Usry 2015). Accordingly, in our discussion in the next sections about the motivations for particular activities, we are necessarily imprecise in making matches between MCs' actions and the broader aims of reelection, good public policy, and careerism (within and beyond the chamber). Indeed, it is the *combination* of activities that is telling in explaining MCs' styles. These patterns of activity serve as proxies that give us insight into legislators' underlying styles.

The Choices

To assess legislative style, our first step was to identify the set of relevant activities in which legislators engage. In doing so, we imposed several requirements. First, we are interested here in the "everyday" behaviors of MCs as they go about their jobs in the House.[6] Our most important rule of thumb was that a behavior or activity has to be directly within the control of legislators—actions or decisions that they have the power to make. So, for example, the number of bills an MC introduces or the number of district offices he or she operates counts, but whether he or she becomes a committee chair does not, since that is a position appointed by others. We view attaining leadership positions as a cause and consequence of style, but not as a component of style itself. Similarly, although MCs' actions can influence their success, levels of legislative effectiveness are a result of activity, not a measure of it.

More practically, an activity has to be measurable for all MCs in all congresses in the sample (the 101st–110th Congresses, 1989–2008). This means that some behaviors cannot be included. For example, ideally we would incorporate MCs' participation in their committees (i.e., how often they attend committee and subcommittee meetings, how active they are in markup of bills), but this is not feasible to collect for all legislators in a single congress (see Hall 1996), much less for ten congresses.[7] Fortunately, though, we are able to gather data on a wide swath of activities undertaken by MCs. We focus on eight different domains of behavior—attention to the district, lawmaking, public visibility (aka "showboating"), fund-raising, party loyalty (in contributions and voting), bipartisanship in coalitions, and policy focus.

District Attention

The division of representational resources between the district and Washington, DC, is a central choice for MCs. Under current House rules, each MC receives a Member Representational Allowance (MRA)[8] to spend as he or she so decides. As a result, some legislators choose to devote more of this allocation to the district than do others. We include two indicators of relative district attention—the number of district offices operated by the MC and the proportion of legislative staff assigned to the district rather than to Capitol Hill. There is substantial variation in these measures across legislators. Two-thirds of MCs in our sample operate just one or two offices, but others establish more—up to a maximum of eight for Representative Robert Davis (R-MI) in the 101st Congress. The average MC has about half of his or her staff in Washington and half at home, though about 10% devote less than one-third of their staff to the district and a handful devote two-thirds or more.[9] For instance, Joseph Gaydos (D-PA) regularly assigned over 75% of his staff to one of his district offices, while Jim McDermott (D-WA) allocated only 20% of his. We argue that these differences in resource allocation reflect variation in MCs' goals and trade-offs, and hence bear on their styles.

Lawmaking

Given our focus on MCs' *legislative* styles, we also target a number of other activities, starting with those that occur within the halls of Congress. These include roll call voting and introducing, cosponsoring, and amending legislation.

We begin with roll call voting, typically viewed as the defining job of legislators. For obvious reasons, most MCs make it a point not to miss votes. Local newspapers often report representatives' attendance records,[10] and a sure way to draw ire from constituents and potential challengers is to fail to perform this duty. Not surprisingly, rates of absenteeism are generally very low—the median "present on vote" figure is 97%, and fewer than 10% of MCs miss more than one-tenth of their roll calls.[11] However, there remains meaningful variation in roll call rates across MCs, as the congresses in our sample each presented MCs with about 1,500 opportunities to vote. A one or two percent difference in absenteeism thus reflects a relatively large number of votes. As others have shown, variation in voting rates is linked to MCs' broader decisions to prioritize Washington, DC versus district concerns (see Grimmer and Powell 2013).

Similarly, nearly all MCs are involved in introducing and cosponsoring legislation,[12] though for both of these activities, there is considerably more variation across legislators than there is for attendance rates on roll call votes. In contrast to the reactive nature of voting (i.e., MCs are presented with a bill and choose whether to vote yea or nay), these activities are proactive. Legislators decide when and how often to engage in them, and there is no defined norm about the appropriate volume of activity. Introducing a bill or resolution is the rarer of the two because it requires more effort, with the MC responsible for drafting the legislation (though, in reality, this task is most often accomplished with the substantial assistance of staffers and representatives of friendly interest groups) and building a coalition to support it and move it through the legislative process. The median MC in the sample introduces ten bills in a congress, with the most prolific (the top 10%) introducing twenty-five or more. The top introducer in our sample is Robert Andrews (D-NJ), who, in the 109th Congress, sponsored 119 bills on topics ranging from campaign finance to defense to welfare.[13] The choice to introduce legislation indicates a commitment to lawmaking (albeit a noisy one) and so contributes to MCs' styles (see Schiller 1995).

Cosponsorship requires somewhat less of MCs, as it entails signing on in support of bills that are introduced by others. Legislators may learn about cosponsorship opportunities on their own or because the sponsor writes them a "Dear Colleague" letter asking for their support. Not surprisingly, cosponsorships outpace introductions. The median number of cosponsorships per congress for MCs in our sample is 220, with some MCs undertaking many more. In the 101st Congress, for example, Cardiss Collins (D-IL) signed on in support of 1,045 different bills, over 15% of all measures introduced in that congress. She is clearly an outlier on this activity, but even so about one in ten MCs cosponsor more than 400 bills.

The importance of cosponsorships has been a source of some disagreement in the literature. Early observers noted that cosponsorship is relatively undemanding and that most cosponsors are attached to bills that do not progress very far in the legislative process. As a result, it was once common to conclude that it was a mostly symbolic activity (see, for example, Mayhew 1974). In recent years, however, a number of scholars have established that cosponsorships can be influential in a number of ways—affecting the likelihood of bill progression (Browne 1985; Krutz 2005; Wilson and Young 1997), signaling to other legislators the ideological content of a measure (Aleman et al. 2009; Harbridge 2015; Kessler and Krehbiel 1996), shaping future legislation (Koger 2003), and serving as a commitment mechanism for coalition building (Bernhard and Sulkin 2013). Accordingly, MCs' involvement in this activity is important to take into account when measuring styles.

Compared to cosponsorships and even introductions, participation in the amending process is more constrained, particularly in the House, where many rules exist about the timing and content of amendments. Nonetheless, two-thirds of the MCs in our sample do introduce an amendment during a particular congress, with most introducing just one or two, but ranging up to sixty (for Jeff Flake [R-AZ] in the 110th Congress). Indeed, there are two hundred instances in our sample of MCs introducing more than ten amendments in a term. Thus, this behavior serves as an additional reflection of legislators' engagement with the lawmaking process.

Showboating

Of course, MCs do not limit themselves to lawmaking and district service, and they can also devote their efforts toward other ends, such as public visibility. This visibility may help them with their current constituents and/or to build a state or national reputation. We highlight two indicators of attempts at public visibility—counts of MCs' floor speeches and the number of editorials/opinion pieces they write.

The congressional schedule provides limited options for nonlegislative debate, so many MCs avail themselves of one minute speeches, usually given at the beginning of the legislative day. MCs can use their time to discuss any matter of their choosing—about pending legislation, about the party's "daily message," or something more mundane or even silly (Schneider 2013).[14] Four-fifths of the MCs in our sample make at least one of these speeches in a term, and for those who do, the median number of speeches is four. There is a long tail to this distribution though, with 10% making more than twenty-five speeches. Among the most active speechmakers is Jim Traficant (D-OH), who, in each of three congresses (the 103rd, 104th, and 106th) gave almost two hundred speeches. The top spot, though, belongs to Jim Gibbons (R-NV), who gave 207 such speeches in the 106th Congress.

MCs who wish to get into the public eye have other options available to them as well, such as penning editorials and opinion pieces for state and national newspapers.[15] An MC who engages in such activity is able to extend his or her name recognition beyond the House chamber. To measure this behavior, we searched Lexis-Nexis for all articles during a particular congress that were authored or coauthored by an MC (i.e., had his or her name in the byline). A little more than half of legislators have at least one article per congress, with three-quarters of those authoring between one and three stories. Some MCs, of course, are much more prolific. The top spot belongs to Newt Gingrich (R-GA), who penned twenty-nine editorials and opinion pieces in the 104th Congress. However, he is not alone in being particularly active in this realm—there are nearly fifty cases of MCs with ten or more articles in a congress, spread across all congresses and both parties, with legislators such as Ray LaHood (R-IL), John Lewis (D-GA), Butch Otter (R-ID), William Pascrell (D-NJ), James Saxton (R-NJ), Lamar Smith (R-TX), and Tom Tancredo (R-CO) doing so in multiple congresses.

Fund-Raising

In addition to choices about lawmaking and visibility, MCs also face the decision of how much time and effort to devote to fund-raising. Legislators may choose to raise funds because their immediate electoral prospects are threatened (see Jacobson 1978, 1990), as an offensive measure to build up a "war chest" to deter potential opponents at some point in the future (Ansolabehere and Snyder 2000; Box-Steffensmeier 1996; Goodliffe 2001, 2007), or to have funds to redistribute to their party and copartisans (Cann 2009; Currinder 2008; Heberlig and Larson 2012). Regardless of the purpose of the fund-raising, hours devoted to these efforts generally means time taken away from other endeavors.

While we cannot assess the time spent on raising funds, we can measure the amount of money each legislator raises. Our indicator is the Federal Election Commission's "total receipts" variable. The mean amount raised by MCs in the sample is $785,545, though there is considerable variation in these figures, with a standard deviation of $623,406. As expected, many of the top fund-raisers are congressional leaders aiming to raise money to promote their party and colleagues—Dennis Hastert (R-IL), Newt Gingrich (R-GA), and Richard Gephardt (R-MO) all appear in the top ten. On the flip side, MCs who are electorally vulnerable also tend to raise more than their secure peers,[16] likely in an effort to run strong campaigns and/or ward off potentially formidable challengers.

Not surprisingly, the average amount of money raised per congress rises across time (from a mean of $446,132 in the 101st Congress to a mean of $1,315,465 in the 110th). This is due both to inflation across the twenty-year time period we examine, as well as to the increasingly important role that money has played in congressional politics. Accordingly, in the analyses that follow, we standardize this (and indeed all of our indicators) by congress in order to make for meaningful comparisons across congresses. More details are provided on these procedures below.

Party Giving

Overall fund-raising is a central component of legislators' styles. However, by itself it does not capture a particularly important choice MCs face, which is how much money to redistribute to the party organization and to copartisans. Over the congresses we examine, fund-raising efforts became fundamental to parties' strategies to boost their numbers in Congress (see Heberlig and Larson 2012). MCs are encouraged and even "required"[17] to donate portions of their own funds to party campaign funds, with rewards (both tangible and intangible) for those who give the most (Pearson 2015).

For this reason, we view the redistribution of funds as an indicator of an MC's level of party advocacy or loyalty. Campaign finance rules enable legislators to make contributions from their own campaign funds (personal campaign committees and PACs) to their "hill committees" (the Democratic Congressional Campaign Committee, or DCCC, and the National Republican Congressional Committee, or NRCC) and directly to the campaign committees of fellow legislators. With the former, the MC adds to the party coffers and enables the leadership of the hill committee to redistribute the money as it sees fit, and with the latter, the MC him- or herself can target particular colleagues for assistance.

We include both of these measures as indicators of "party giving."[18] Such giving is widespread among MCs. We find that about two-thirds of legislators make some contribution to their hill committee during a particular congress, ranging from about $100 up to $1.8 million (with a mean of about $50,000). The top givers include John Boehner (R-OH), Nancy Pelosi (D-CA), James Clyburn (D-SC), Richard Gephardt (D-MO), Steny Hoyer (D-MD), and Jerry Lewis (R-CA). However, that leaders give generously should not obscure the fact that rank-and-file members do so too. Indeed, one-quarter of the MCs who make a hill committee contribution give more than $100,000.

Even more legislators (about 80% per congress) give to fellow colleagues, in total amounts ranging from $50 to $1.6 million, with a mean of about $38,000. The top spots are once again occupied by senior leadership MCs, though a somewhat different constellation of them. Eric Cantor (R-VA), Charles Rangel (D-NY), Rahm Emanuel (D-IL), and Tom DeLay (R-TX) join Pelosi, Boehner, Hastert and Hoyer as the most generous givers on this measure, with Cantor (in the 109th Congress) and Hoyer (in the 110th Congress) coming in as the greatest contributors. Again, however, giving is widespread—about one-quarter of MCs give more than $10,000 in a congress.

Party Voting

Of course, financial contributions are not the only, or even most obvious, way that legislators can demonstrate party loyalty. Most commonly, such loyalty is measured via MCs' voting on roll calls. In other words, how often can a legislator be counted on to vote with his or her copartisans? Two indicators commonly used in the literature are the percentage of the time a legislator votes with his or her party on "party votes" (where a majority of one party votes against a majority of the other) and the percentage of the time he or she votes with the party leadership (on votes where one party's top leaders all vote yay and the other party's top leaders all vote nay) (Cox and McCubbins 1993).

On both of these measures, most MCs demonstrate high levels of loyalty (averaging about 87% for each), but, as with other activities, there is substantial variation across legislators. There are forty-two instances (out of 4,276 MC-congress observations) of perfect fealty to the leadership, though only one instance of an MC never breaking from the party on a party vote—Dick Cheney (R-WY), in the 101st Congress. However, about 5% of legislators vote against their party and 10% against the leadership at least one-quarter of the time.

More notably, a small proportion of MCs even votes *against* the party more than with it. For example, in the 104th Congress, Ralph Hall (D-TX), described by David Broder as "a deep-dyed conservative, [who] bolts the party with impunity" (1993), voted against his fellow Democrats 76% of the time (and against the leadership 74% of the time). This lack of loyalty is only slightly higher than in the next three congresses, where he averaged 67% disloyalty in voting. Perhaps unsurprisingly, Hall eventually formally switched his affiliation to the Republican Party. Other MCs who diverged the most frequently from the party line include Constance Morella (R-MD) and Silvio Conte (R-MA), well known for their moderate stances, and the iconoclastic James Traficant (D-OH).

Coalition Bipartisanship

We supplement these voting and giving-based measures of party loyalty with an indicator of the extent to which MCs participate in partisan versus bipartisan coalitions. In particular, of their cosponsorships, what proportion are of bills introduced by a member of the opposite party? There are many reasons why an MC might choose to cosponsor an outpartisan's bill—to contribute to the efforts of his or her state delegation to pass policies that aid the state,[19] to soften the appearance of partisanship, or to express his or her sincere preferences on legislation. And, indeed, bipartisan cosponsorship coalitions are considerably more common than the current rhetoric about polarization might lead one to believe (Harbridge 2015).

The choice to cross the aisle (or not) in cosponsorships is undoubtedly driven by similar factors as the decisions to vote or give with the party are, but we view them as slightly different phenomena. The latter reflects attentiveness to the leadership's request (i.e., that members contribute to party coffers and vote the party line), while the former is a measure of what MCs do when given more leeway. And there is no reason why MCs might not mix and match strategies—for example, by contributing to party coffers to make up for a lack of loyalty in voting or cosponsorship. As such, we include all of these indicators as components of legislative style.

We find that, on average, about 70–75% of the bills MCs cosponsor are introduced by a copartisan, and indeed there are only five instances of legislators who *never* cosponsored an outpartisan's bill in a congress, with two of these (Tom Foley [D-WA] in the 101st Congress and Nancy Pelosi [D-CA] in the 110th Congress) leaders who did not cosponsor many measures. Thus, it is common to cross the aisle at least some of the time, although again, there is considerable variation across MCs. Most focus their cosponsorship efforts primarily on measures introduced by copartisans, but about 15% devote at least half to those introduced by members of the opposition.

Policy Focus

Our final indicators relate to MCs' level of policy focus. More specifically, in their introduction of legislation, do they pursue a wide range of policies inside and outside of their committee jurisdictions, or do they limit their efforts to a few well-defined areas? In the House, there has been a traditional norm of specialization, although many argue that this has eroded across time (Hibbing 1991; Rohde 1988; Schneier 1988; Sinclair 1986). Specialization enables MCs to build reputations for expertise, and some may arrive in Congress with well-developed interests in a particular area. On the other hand, there are opportunity costs to focusing narrowly, and it is not clear from the literature that expertise yields dividends for MCs' career advancement.

We employ two measures of policy focus—the size of MCs' introduction agendas (i.e., the number of issues in which they introduce) and the proportion of their introductions that are referred to a committee on which they sit. We assume that MCs who introduce in more areas and/ or whose activity extends beyond their committee assignments display more generalist tendencies.

To identify the issue area of bills, we coded all introductions (56,968 measures introduced by our sample) into one of nineteen issue categories.[20] Our scheme is adapted from the Policy Agendas and Congressional Bills Project categories and is designed to be exhaustive and mutually exclusive, such that each bill receives one, and only one, code (see Sulkin 2011). Using this scheme, we find that the size of MCs' agendas ranges from zero (for the thirty-nine MCs in the sample who did not introduce any measures in a congress) to seventeen issues, with a median of five. The size of the agenda is, of course, correlated with the number of introductions made by an MC. However, our model takes that into account as well (i.e., by including the count of introductions as a measure of activity), and in addition, there is substantial variation in concentration among MCs who introduce the same number of bills. For example, among the seventy-five MCs who introduced twenty bills, the scope of their agendas varies from two issues (Lane Evans [R-IL] who, in the 107th Congress, introduced only on defense and education) to thirteen issues (John Duncan [R-TN], who, in the 102nd Congress, introduced on the budget, campaign finance, corporate regulation, crime, defense and foreign policy, education, environment, government operations, health, jobs and infrastructure, Medicare, Social Security, and taxes).

For our second measure, the proportion of introduced bills referred to a sponsor's committee, we used Adler and Wilkerson's Congressional Bills Project data (see Adler and Wilkerson 2013) to identify the referrals for each bill (i.e., the committee or committees to which it was assigned). If at least one of those committees was one on which the sponsor sat, we coded that as a bill referred to the sponsor's committee. Of course, sponsors do not determine where a bill is referred, but the issue content and framing of the measure enable them to predict with accuracy whether their committee(s) will see it. The median score for MCs on this measure is 30%, so close to one-third of their introductions are on issues related to their committee jurisdictions. Of those who introduce, three-quarters have at least one measure referred to their committees, and about 3% have *all* of their measures referred to a committee on which they sit.

Summarizing Legislative Activity

In all, then, we have sixteen measures of legislative behavior that encompass a variety of domains of legislative activity. Table 2.1 presents descriptive statistics and sources.

We expect that differences in activity levels emerge between MCs due to variation in their aims and constraints. For instance, legislators who are concerned about cultivating their constituencies will allocate more of their staff to their districts and operate more offices there (Cain, Ferejohn, and Fiorina 1987; Parker 1986; Parker and Goodman 2009); those who want to enhance their public visibility will give speeches and pen editorials (Maltzman and Sigelman 1996; Morris 2001; Rocca 2007; Pearson and Dancey 2011); those who want to show their loyalty to the party will vote with it, raise and redistribute money to copartisans, and/or focus their coalition-building efforts on fellow Democrats or Republicans (Cann 2008; Carson 2008; Carson, Koger, et al. 2010; Heberlig and Larson 2012; Poole and Rosenthal 2007); those who want to demonstrate legislative energy will introduce and cosponsor legislation and participate on the floor by offering amendments and being present to vote on roll calls (Burden 2007; Koger 2003; Rothenberg and Sanders 2000; Wawro 2001); and those who want to specialize in a particular policy area will have a focused agenda (i.e., will introduce bills in relatively few policy areas), most likely dealing with issues under the jurisdiction of their committees (Volden and Wiseman 2014).

These aims can be thought of as intermediate-level goals that MCs piece together to achieve their broader aims. As discussed above, some of these require direct trade-offs of time, attention, or money. MCs have a set budget for staff, so funds allocated to the district cannot also be allocated to DC. The decision to devote oneself to the lawmaking process means less time for other activities. Investing attention in one policy area makes it less likely that an MC will be able to become an expert in another. And so on. Other choices do not force trade-offs, at least not directly. Being a party loyalist does not take more time than charting one's own course, so an MC can match high or low levels of party loyalty with activity in any of the other realms. It is also not clear that policy focus cuts into fund-raising or penning editorials, though it may be that specialists, in general, care more or less than generalists about raising money or public visibility and/or face more or less success in these realms.

TABLE 2.1 **Components of legislative styles**

Activity	Mean and standard deviation	Range	Source
Number of district offices	2.1 (1.10)	0–8	*Almanac of American Politics* (collected by authors)
Proportion of staff in district	46.7% (9.7%)	0–78.5%	Parker and Goodman (2009) for 104th–108th Congresses; collected by authors from *Congressional Staff Directory* for other congresses
Introductions	13.1 (11.0)	0–119	Congressional Bills Project for bill introductions; Library of Congress THOMAS site for joint resolutions
Cosponsorships	241.6 (130.6)	0–1045	THOMAS
Amendments	2.1 (3.8)	0–60	THOMAS
One-minute speeches	7.9 (15.8)	0–207	Rocca (2007) for 101st–106th Congresses; collected by authors from *Congressional Record* for other congresses
Percentage of roll calls present for	95.3 (6.5)	0–100	Jenkins and Nokken (2008) for 101st Congress; collected by the authors for other congresses
Bylines (editorials and opinion pieces authored)	1.4 (2.2)	0–32	Collected by authors from Lexis-Nexis
Money raised (total receipts)	$785,545 ($623,406)	0–$8.1 million	Collected by authors from FCC data
Money to Hill committee	$49,721 ($111,622)	0–$1.8 million	Heberlig and Larson (2012)
Money to colleagues	$37,069 ($115,947)	0–$1.6 million	Heberlig and Larson (2012)
Percentage of party vote	87.2% (10.6%)	24–100%	Calculated by the authors from Poole and Rosenthal's roll call data
Percentage of leadership vote	87.0% (10.2%)	26–100%	Calculated by the authors from Poole and Rosenthal's roll call data
Agenda size (number of issue areas in which an MC introduces measures)	5.6 (2.8)	0–17	Calculated by the authors from Sulkin's (2011) data
Percentage of introduced measures referred to own committee	33.1% (30.1%)	0–100%	Calculated by the authors from Congressional Bills Project
Percentage of bipartisan coalitions (proportion of an MC's cosponsorships that are of bills introduced by the other party)	30.1% (17.5%)	0–100%	Calculated by the authors from Fowler's (2006) and Harbridge's (2015) data

Note: This table presents the indicators of legislative activity that serve as measures of MCs' style.

We expect, therefore, that MCs combine these different sorts of activities in a variety of ways. Moreover, variation across legislators should be one of degree rather than a qualitative difference. MCs display different levels of party loyalty, lawmaking activity, etc., but as shown above, the distribution of any given activity is not bimodal (i.e., that some legislators place all their staff resources in the district and the rest place them all in DC). Instead, MCs attempt to balance these activities into a coherent whole that accomplishes multiple goals, aiming for a synergy that defines what they are "like" as a legislator.

Take, for example, the five MCs who comprised the Iowa delegation in the 110th Congress (2007–2008)—Democrats Bruce Braley, David Loebsack, and Leonard Boswell and Republicans Tom Latham and Steve King. These MCs were all moderately active in introducing legislation (sponsoring between nine and eighteen bills or joint resolutions each), but otherwise illustrate well the differences that emerge in MCs' activity profiles. For instance, as shown in table 2.2, which summarizes these MCs' activity, none of Latham's bills were referred to a committee on which he sat, while one-third of Boswell's were. Loebsack's bills were spread across four (of nineteen) issue areas, while King introduced in eleven. King cosponsored a relatively modest 165 bills, while Braley and Boswell each cosponsored close to four hundred. Only one-third of Latham's cosponsorships were of bills introduced by copartisans, while Braley and Loebsack stuck to the party line, with about 90% of their cosponsorships of bills introduced by fellow Democrats. When it comes to voting with the party, however, King was the most loyal, "cheating" on the party only 1% of the time, as compared to Boswell and Latham, who did so 6% of the time (with Braley and Loebsack falling in between). Braley was by far the most prolific speech giver of the group, making twenty-six one-minute speeches on the floor of the House, whereas his colleagues all gave three or fewer. He and Boswell both raised the most money—$2.1 million (about $1 million more than Latham, and $1.5 million more than Loebsack and King). However, while Braley redistributed about $275,000 to copartisans and the Democratic Congressional Campaign Committee, Boswell only devoted about $7,000 of his funds to this purpose. Finally, these MCs differ substantially in their allocation of resources to the district, with King and Boswell both placing over half of their staff there, and Braley, Latham, and Loebsack devoting one-quarter to one-third of theirs.

When we consider the sum total of each MC's behavior, particularly in comparison to his colleagues, some patterns begin to emerge. Braley, for example, appears to be a party loyalist with an interest in lawmaking and public visibility. King, in contrast, shares the focus on party loyalty, but is less intent on participating in lawmaking and allocates more resources to the constituency. Boswell and Latham both diverge the most from their parties on voting, but for Latham this also translates into bipartisan cosponsorship coalitions, and for Boswell it does not. Boswell is

TABLE 2.2 **Summary of Iowa delegation activity, 110th Congress**

Activity	Boswell	Braley	King	Latham	Loebsack
Number of district offices	1	3	5	3	2
Proportion of staff in district	56%	25%	53%	31%	29%
Introductions	18	17	15	9	10
Cosponsorships	375	383	165	223	298
Amendments	3	1	20	0	1
One-minute speeches	3	26	1	1	2
Percentage of roll calls present for	94.9%	95.0%	97.9%	99.1%	97.1%
Bylines (editorials and opinion pieces authored)	0	1	1	0	0
Money raised (total receipts)	$2.1M	$2.5M	$61K	$1.1M	$522K
Money to Hill committee	0	150,000	30,000	100,000	25,000
Money to colleagues	6900	124,300	39,500	66,100	1000
Percentage on party vote	94%	95%	97%	87%	95%
Percentage on leadership vote	92%	94%	96%	84%	95%
Agenda size (number of issue areas in which an MC introduces measures)	9	9	11	5	4
Percentage of introduced measures referred to own committee	33%	6%	7%	0%	20%
Percentage of coalitions that are bipartisan	15%	11%	28%	72%	10%

Note: This table presents the variation in activity undertaken by the five members of the Iowa delegation in the 110th Congress.

more focused on legislative activity and the constituency than Latham. Loebsack falls between the extremes on almost all measures, though he emerges as the most focused of the five in the content of his policy making.

Our goal in what follows is to codify these differences in a systematic way, by using patterns in MC behavior to identify legislative styles and then to explain the causes and consequences of those styles, as well as their dynamics across legislators' careers. For example, Bruce Braley and David Loebsack, both first-term representatives in the 110th Congress, appeared to make quite different choices about how to approach their jobs. Do these indeed reflect different legislative styles? If so, can we explain why they might have adopted different styles?

Style may also offer insight into the different paths these MCs' careers have taken. In 2014, seven years into his service in the House, Braley threw his hat in the ring for the Senate seat left open after Tom Harkin's retirement. He became the Democratic nominee, though he eventually lost to Republican Joni Ernst. Loebsack declined to run for the seat[21] and chose instead to endorse Braley, concluding that "there is not a better choice in the Democratic Party or the state to succeed Senator Harkin" (Hoyle 2013). In a report on Harkin's announcement of his retirement, a journalist noted that Loebsack's decision not to enter the race was "not a surprise. Loebsack hasn't been seen as positioning himself for higher office" (Tibbetts 2013). As we show in chapter 8, stylistic differences can help us to understand progressive ambition, as well as what becomes of MCs more generally as they navigate the various opportunities available to them in the House.

Identifying Legislative Styles

To derive styles from MCs' patterns of activity, we opt to use a clustering approach. Cluster analysis is a statistical technique that identifies groups of observations that are similar to one another and distinct from those in other groups (for an overview, see Rui and Wunsch 2005 or Gan, Ma, and Wu 2007).[22] For example, a marketing researcher could use these methods to identify different types of consumers (i.e., with regard to brand loyalty or price consciousness) to determine how best to reach them (see Mooi and Sarstedt 2011), and in medical research, these techniques are employed to develop categories of patients or presentations of diseases (McLachlan 1992).[23] Clustering is also used regularly in other social science disciplines, but has been employed more rarely in political science. However, in the past few years, scholars have demonstrated the value of applying clustering to political data, developing typologies of democracies (Gugiu and Centellas 2013; Jang and Hitchcock 2012), varieties of capitalism (Ahlquist and Breunig 2012), parliamentary voting blocs (Spirling and Quinn 2010) and cabinet appointments (Krook and O'Brien 2012), and communication styles in senators' press releases (Grimmer 2013).

In implementing a cluster analysis, the first task is to decide on the inputs. One option would be to include each of the sixteen measures of legislative activity described above. However, this presents two possible complications, both related to the fact that we often have multiple indicators for the same general concept. For instance, if we were to enter the variables separately, we would probably find that MCs who contribute to their party hill committees at high rates cluster with those who contribute the most to their colleagues.[24] This is not at all surprising, since these are both viewed in the literature as money-based party-building activities (see, for example, Heberlig and Larson 2012). What we really want to know is what *categories* of behavior cluster together. For example, is party loyalty associated (positively or negatively) with efforts at lawmaking, or district attention, or public visibility? This highlights the value of some initial categorization of the input variables into indices.[25]

Creating indices also avoids the problem of over- or underweighting some categories in the clustering. For example, since we have four measures of how much attention legislators devote to lawmaking activities (e.g., introductions, cosponsorships, amendments, and presence or absence on roll call votes), but just two measures of district attention (number of district offices and proportion of staff), including all of these indicators separately might weigh lawmaking too heavily.

As discussed above, we looked to the literature on legislative activity as well as our own intuitions to classify our raw indicators into common indices. Table 2.3 presents the eight indices and their constituent variables.[26] These indices—home front activity, showboating, lawmaking, policy focus, party voting, party giving, money (aka fund-raising), and bipartisanship in coalition-building—reflect a wide swath of legislative activity. The variables that constitute the indices are measured on different scales, so to provide standardization, we calculated a z-score for each MC for each variable for each congress,[27] with these calculations split by

TABLE 2.3 **Indices of activity**

Index	Components
Home front	Number of district offices
	Percentage of staff in district
Showboat	One-minute speeches
	Bylines
Party voter	Percentage on party vote
	Percentage on leadership vote
Party giver	Money to Hill committee
	Money to colleagues
Policy focus	Agenda size
	Percentage of introduced measures referred to own committee
Money/fund-raising	Total receipts
Bipartisan	Percentage of coalitions that are bipartisan
Lawmaker	Number of introductions
	Number of cosponsorships
	Number of amendments
	Percentage of roll calls present

Note: This table presents the eight indices of activity and their component parts.

party. Then, for each MC, we averaged these z-scores for all of the variables in each index. These averages are the input variables in the clustering analysis.

The relationships between the indices define the clusters. For example, legislators with aspirations to be movers and shakers in their party will likely distinguish themselves as high scorers on the "showboat," "lawmaker" "party voter," and "party giver" indices, but will not necessarily devote much time to the district. In contrast, those most focused on cultivating their constituents will score highly on the "home front" index, and will steer a more bipartisan course in their roll call voting and coalition building. The clustering analysis reveals whether there are, in fact, distinct groups of MCs, what indices are associated with each cluster, and how common each of the clusters is.

The longitudinal nature of our data presents some unique challenges and opportunities in implementing the clustering. Since we examine a twenty-year time span (101st–110th Congresses, 1989–2008), many legislators appear in the sample multiple times. However, most extant algorithms are for clustering independent objects, not time-dependent data.

As such, we employ a variant of the longitudinal clustering model developed by Sewell et al. (2016) to address these issues. To account for the dependence in observations across time, the model assumes that the expected cluster assignment at a particular time point depends on the cluster assignment at the previous time point (i.e., the cluster assignments follow a Markov process). Additionally, the expected indices are modeled not only as a function of the cluster to which the MC belongs, but also as a function of the MC's indices at the previous time point. This accounts for temporal dependence induced by individual effects and leverages our large N to provide for more precise estimates. Details of the model and support for our assumptions are provided in the appendix to this chapter.[28]

It is important to underscore that the clustering is solely a function of MCs' behavior—their scores on the indices of legislative activity. In the chapters to come, we explore the correlates of style (i.e., those characteristics of individual legislators and their districts that shape stylistics choices) and its consequences for legislators' success and their career trajectories. These, however, are not components of style itself.[29]

In any clustering analysis, an important decision is how many clusters/groups to use. This choice includes elements of both art and science. As Filho et al. explain it:

> The choice of number of clusters is fundamental in cluster analysis and should be theoretically guided. For example, if previous studies suggested the existence of three groups, an analytical possibility is to replicate the number of groups.... In absence of theoretical guidance, the research can adopt an exploratory approach and run different analysis varying the number of groups. Different solutions should be compared with the literature searching for substantive explanation. (2014, 2411)

Here we are in a bit of a gray area. Our theory and the literature point us toward expecting a small number of clusters, though not a precise number. Therefore, we opted for a hybrid approach, running the model multiple times, specifying a different number of clusters each time (between two[30] and seven clusters), and, for each, calculating a variety of fit statistics. These include the average silhouette statistic (which considers how close an observation is to other observations in its cluster and compares that to how close the observation is to the observations in the nearest cluster), the marginal likelihood (which compares the relative performance of the model as a whole), and information criteria such as the AIC and BIC (which assess a best fit after taking into account the number of parameters in the model).

For all of these tests, a model with five clusters emerges as a particularly good fit. As we show in the next chapter, it also yields clusters that are intuitive matches with what we know of legislative behavior. Again, this external validity criterion is an important one. The advantage of cluster analysis is that the approach is data driven, and hence, atheoretical—the researcher allows the clusters to emerge from the data. In choosing among particular models, however, researchers need to draw on their substantive knowledge of the phenomenon under consideration to make the best choice (Filho et al. 2014, Romesburg 2004).

Conclusions

In the next chapter, we take up each of the five clusters—district advocates, party builders, ambitious entrepreneurs, party soldiers, and policy specialists—describing each in depth, discussing what distinguishes each style from the others, and demonstrating the distribution of styles across individuals, parties, and time. These results confirm that our styles capture meaningful differences in MCs' activity, enabling us to offer a gestalt view of legislative behavior. We contend, therefore, that this approach, combining both deductive and inductive reasoning, offers the distinct advantages of not imposing an a priori categorization (which may not, in actuality, reflect meaningful differences across legislators) and enabling us to examine a large number of MCs across many congresses. To demonstrate these contributions, we turn now to the styles.

Appendix: The Model

To cluster MCs over time, we implement the longitudinal model-based clustering algorithm proposed by Sewell et al. (2016). This gives us a framework with which we can appropriately model the time dependence inherent in our data. The model can be thought of as an extension of the multivariate normal mixture model (a commonly used clustering approach for more traditional static contexts) to clustering multivariate time series of varying lengths. This approach captures temporal dependence through both the observations and through the evolving cluster assignments. It also has the flexibility to account for extreme special cases, such as a normal random walk (no cluster effects), or temporally independent events.

Before giving the details of the model, we first provide the notation to be used. Let K be the fixed number of groups/clusters. Let X_{it} and Z_{it} denote the p behavioral variables (observed) and the cluster assignment (latent) respectively of the ith MC during his/her t^{th} term, for $i = 1, \ldots, n$ and $t = 1, \ldots, T_i$, where T_i is the number of terms served for the ith MC. For ease of notation, we will use χ_i to denote the set $\{X_{it} : 1 \leq t \leq T_i\}$.

The dependence structure of the model relies on two assumptions. First, given the entire history of cluster assignments, the current cluster assignment only depends on the previous cluster assignment (i.e., the cluster assignments follow a Markov process). Second, given the history of both the cluster assignments and behavioral values, the current behavioral values only depend on the previously observed values and the current cluster assignment (i.e., the behavioral values follow a Markov switching model). More formally, we have

$$Z_{it} | Z_{i1}, \ldots, Z_{i(t-1)} \stackrel{\mathcal{D}}{=} Z_{it} | Z_{i(t-1)}$$

and

$$X_{it} | X_{i1}, \ldots, X_{i(t-1)}, Z_{i1}, \ldots, Z_{iT_i} \stackrel{\mathcal{D}}{=} X_{it} | X_{i(t-1)}, Z_{it}.$$

The cluster assignments are assumed to have initial cluster probabilities given by

$$\mathbb{P}(Z_{i1} = k | \Psi) = \alpha_k$$

and transition probabilities given by

$$\mathbb{P}(Z_{it} = k | Z_{i(t-1)} = h, \Psi) = \beta_{hk},$$

where Ψ is the vector of the model parameters. That is, the α_k's give the probability that a freshman MC will belong to cluster k, and given that a MC belonged to cluster h the previous time point, β_{hk} gives the probability that the MC will currently belong to cluster k. Furthermore, we have the following distributional assumptions:

$$X_{i1} \mid Z_{i1}, \Psi \stackrel{ind}{\sim} N(\mu_{Z_{i1}}, \Sigma_{Z_{i1}})$$

$$X_{it} \mid X_{i(t-1)}, Z_{i1}, \Psi \stackrel{ind}{\sim} N(\lambda \mu_{Z_{it}} + (1-\lambda)X_{i(t-1)}, \Sigma_{Z_{it}})$$

The kth cluster mean is given by μ_k, that is, the "typical" behavior of a MC belonging to cluster k, and Σ_k is the covariance matrix corresponding to the cluster k, that is, how the different behaviors of a MC belonging to cluster k relate to each other; the cluster means and cluster covariances are temporally constant structures which allow us to interpret the clusters in a meaningful way. The parameter λ can be thought of as a blending coefficient that determines the impact of the cluster assignments on the behaviors X_{it}, and considerably extends the flexibility of the model. For example, if $\lambda = 1$, then all the information contained in the previous history of the observations and cluster assignments is contained in the current cluster assignment, whereas if $\lambda = 0$, then there is no clustering structure and the X_{it}'s follow a normal random walk. In our context, λ represents the measure of how much an MC's behavior can be attributed to having a specific legislative style versus the variation due to the individual. A high λ value, for example, would imply that MCs of the same legislative style all act extremely similarly to one another, whereas a low λ value would imply that MCs of the same legislative style act similarly but with much more individual variability in behavior.[31]

Also note that the absence of temporal dependence of any kind can also be captured in this model. Specifically, letting the transition cluster probabilities equal the initial cluster probabilities, that is, $\beta_{hk} = \alpha_k$ for all h and k and letting $\lambda = 1$, is equivalent to using the commonly encountered static normal mixture model for clustering, treating the observations across time points as independent.

When estimating the cluster assignments and unknown model parameters, we immediately run into a computational issue, in that the computational cost of evaluating the likelihood grows exponentially with the number of time points, which we will denote by T. However, this can be overcome by utilizing the following recursive relationships (we drop the subscript i for ease of notation):

$$\pi(X_1,...,X_t) = \pi(X_1,...,X_{t-1}) \sum_{Z_t=1}^{K} \sum_{Z_{t-1}=1}^{K} \pi(Z_{t-1}|X_1,...,X_{t-1})\beta_{Z_{t-1}Z_t}\pi(X_t|X_{t-1},Z_t)$$

$$\pi(Z_t|X_1,...,X_t) \propto \sum_{Z_{t-1}=1}^{K} \pi(Z_{t-1}|X_1,...,X_{t-1})\beta_{Z_{t-1}Z_t}\pi(X_t|X_{t-1},Z_t)$$

where

$$\pi(Z_1|X_1) \propto \pi(X_1|Z_1)\alpha_{Z_1}$$

and

$$\pi(X_1) = \sum_{Z_1=1}^{K} \pi(X_1|Z_1)\alpha_{Z_1}.$$

Utilizing these recursive relationships reduces the computational cost to be linear with T.

We aim to fit the model by finding the maximum likelihood estimators for the model parameters. This is accomplished via implementing a generalized EM algorithm (Dempster, Laird, and Rubin 1977; Wu 1983). This simultaneously allows us to estimate the posterior probabilities of cluster assignments. However, we again run into the issue of computational complexity growing exponentially in T. To overcome this we note that

$$\mathbb{P}(Z_t|Z_{t-1},\chi) \propto q(Z_t|Z_{t-1})$$

where

$$q(Z_T|Z_{T-1}) = \beta_{Z_{T-1},Z_t}\pi(X_T|X_{T-1},Z_T),$$

for $2 \leq t < T$

$$q(Z_t|Z_{t-1}) = \beta_{Z_{t-1}Z_t}\pi(X_t|X_{t-1},Z_t) \sum_{l_{t+1}=1}^{K} q(Z_{t+1}=l_{t+1}|Z_t),$$

and

$$\mathbb{P}(Z_1 | \chi) \propto \alpha_{Z_1} \pi(X_1 | Z_1) \sum_{l_2=1}^{K} q(Z_2 = l_2 | Z_1).$$

Thus by working backward we can compute the conditional posterior distributions of the cluster assignments, and as a straightforward extension their marginal posterior distributions. The computational cost is once again linear with respect to T.

The remainder of the generalized EM algorithm involves sequentially updating each parameter according to the following:

$$\alpha_k = \frac{1}{n} \sum_{i=1}^{n} \mathbb{P}(Z_{i1} = k | \chi_i),$$

$$\beta_{hk} = \frac{\sum_{i=1}^{n} \sum_{t=2}^{T_i} \mathbb{P}(Z_{i(t-1)} = h | \chi_i) \mathbb{P}(Z_{it} = k | Z_{i(t-1)} = h, \chi_i)}{\sum_{i=1}^{n} \sum_{t=2}^{T_i} \mathbb{P}(Z_{i(t-1)} = h | \chi_i)},$$

$$\lambda = \frac{\sum_{i=1}^{n} \sum_{t=2}^{T_i} \sum_{l_t=1}^{K} \mathbb{P}(Z_{it} = l_t | \chi_i)(X_{it} - X_{i(t-1)})' \sum_{k}^{-1} (X_{it} - X_{i(t-1)})}{\sum_{i=1}^{n} \sum_{t=2}^{T_i} \sum_{l_t=1}^{K} \mathbb{P}(Z_{it} = l_t | \chi_i)(\mu_{it} - X_{i(t-1)})' \sum_{k}^{-1} (\mu_k - X_{i(t-1)})},$$

$$\mu_k = \frac{\sum_{i=1}^{n} \{\mathbb{P}(Z_{i1} = k | \chi_i) X_{i1} + \lambda \sum_{t=2}^{T_i} \mathbb{P}(Z_{it} = k | \chi_i)(X_{it} - (1-\lambda) X_{i(t-1)})\}}{\sum_{i=1}^{n} \{\mathbb{P}(Z_{i1} = k | \chi_i) + \lambda^2 \sum_{t=2}^{T_i} \mathbb{P}(Z_{it} = k | \chi_i)\}}$$

and

$$\Sigma_k = \frac{\sum_{i=1}^{n} \{\mathbb{P}(Z_{i1} = k | \chi_i)(X_{i1} - \mu_k)(X_{i1} - \mu_k)' + \sum_{t=2}^{T_i} \mathbb{P}(Z_{it} = k | \chi_i) H_{it} H_{it}'\}}{\sum_{i=1}^{n} \{\mathbb{P}(Z_{i1} = k | \chi_i) + \sum_{t=2}^{T_i} \mathbb{P}(Z_{it} = k | \chi_i) H_{it} H_{it}'\}},$$

for $k = 1, \ldots, K$, where $H_{it} = X_{it} - \lambda \mu_k - (1-\lambda) X_{i(t-1)}$.

Thus the generalized EM algorithm iterates between estimating the conditional and marginal posterior distributions of the Z_{it}'s and the updating of the parameter values. This iterative algorithm proceeds until convergence is achieved.

CHAPTER THREE

The Styles

The mix of actual member activities is, in one sense, determined by the Constitution's job description for House and Senate members, but in another sense it is empirical. You have to look and see. — David Mayhew, *America's Congress* (2000, 10)

The first step in understanding legislative style is to describe the five styles that emerge from our clustering analysis: What characterizes the MCs who fall into each style, and what distinguishes a particular style from the others? Such descriptions assist us in determining whether the styles we uncover are valid—that is, if our analysis yields meaningful groupings of MCs—and also set the stage for theorizing in more detail about congressional careers and testing our hypotheses about the causes and consequences of style.

There exists no universally accepted standard for describing the results of cluster analyses, but most scholars begin by comparing the average scores for each cluster on the input variables (Burns and Burns 2008; Romesburg 2004). In our case, this means examining how each of the five styles falls relative to the others on each of the eight indices of legislative activity discussed in the previous chapter (i.e., home front, showboating, lawmaking, policy focus, party voter, party giver, money, and bipartisan). A heat map provides a useful visual representation of the results, illustrating how strongly each style is associated with each index. In the heat map in figure 3.1, black indicates low values and white indicates high values. So, for example, MCs in the first style raise the least money and those in the fifth style raise the most, with the other styles falling in between. We can also use these values to offer overall characterizations of the styles, summarizing where they stand on all of the indices of activity.

THE STYLES 43

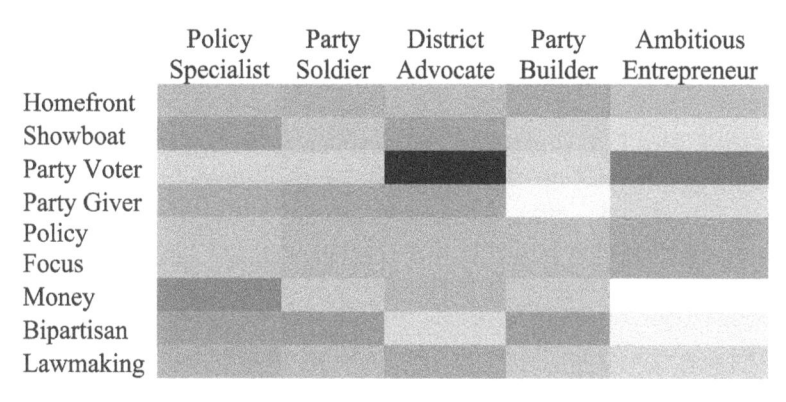

	Policy Specialist	Party Soldier	District Advocate	Party Builder	Ambitious Entrepreneur
Homefront					
Showboat					
Party Voter					
Party Giver					
Policy Focus					
Money					
Bipartisan					
Lawmaking					

FIGURE 3.1 Heat map of cluster means
Note: Heat map of each cluster's mean for each of the indices. Black indicates low values and white high.

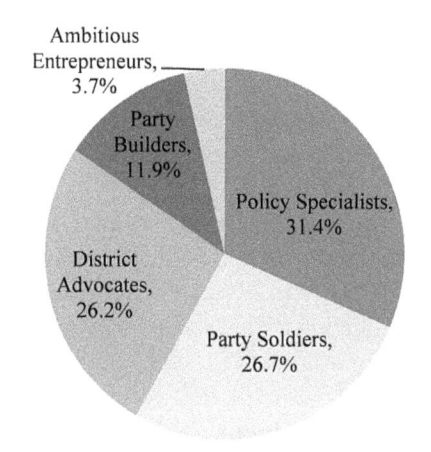

- Ambitious Entrepreneurs, 3.7%
- Party Builders, 11.9%
- Policy Specialists, 31.4%
- District Advocates, 26.2%
- Party Soldiers, 26.7%

FIGURE 3.2 Distribution of legislative styles
Note: Proportion of observations (an MC-congress) that fall into each of the five legislative styles. $N = 4276$

The distribution of the five styles is presented in figure 3.2. As shown, there are three relatively large clusters (comprising about one-quarter to one-third of MC-congress observations each) and two smaller clusters.[1]

Policy Specialists

The largest cluster, at 31.4% of observations, is distinguished by representatives who have the highest scores of any group on the policy focus index (i.e., they have focused agendas, generally targeting issues within the jurisdiction of their committee assignments), and who vote and cosponsor regularly with their parties. They have the lowest score of any cluster on the showboat index and hence do not engage in much speechmaking or other publicly visible activities, and they do not raise or redistribute much money. We call this cluster the "policy specialists."

To illustrate how this policy specialist style manifests itself, consider a few of the 158 MCs with this style in the 110th Congress (2007–2008), the congress from which all of our examples in this chapter will be drawn. Some of these legislators have reputations for concentrated investments in a particular issue. Carolyn McCarthy (D-NY), for example, who first took office in 1996, was motivated to run for the House on a gun control platform after her husband was killed and her son injured in a mass shooting on a Long Island Railroad commuter train in 1993. Once in office, she devoted the majority of her legislative efforts to gun violence, becoming known as "the fiercest gun-control advocate in Congress" (Toeplitz 2011).

Similarly, Henry Waxman (D-CA) is best known for his career-long interest in health and environmental issues, including pesticides, clean air, food and drug safety, and tobacco regulation. These issues fall largely within the jurisdiction of the Energy and Commerce committee, which, in the 110th Congress, was chaired by Waxman. Waxman held a seat on this committee since his first election to Congress in 1974, where he was one of the lucky few freshmen to receive a first-choice assignment to a relatively prestigious committee. His interests in these issues date back to his service as a member of the California State Assembly. As Waxman himself describes it:

> Early on, I decided that in order to become an effective legislator, I should develop an area of expertise, which would enable me to exert outsized influence whenever that subject arose. Because my district was home to a large elderly population, health policy struck me as a good specialization. (Waxman and Green 2009, 20)

Accordingly, the decision to specialize was, for Waxman, largely a strategic one, enabling him to carve out a niche for himself as a policy expert.

Paul Ryan (R-WI), who explicitly identified as a specialist, claiming, "I've always been one of the House policy wonks" (Wallace 2012), also falls into this style in the 110th Congress. Like Waxman, Ryan's interests developed early—his first job on the Hill was as a staff economist to Senator Bob Kasten (R-WI). Upon entering Congress in 1999, he quickly earned a reputation for his interest and expertise in fiscal issues, rising, by 2007, to the ranking member of the House Budget Committee. He became the voice of the Republican Party on budget issues, serving as chief author of its budget proposals, and eventually achieving even greater national prominence as Mitt Romney's vice presidential running mate in 2012 and then, in 2015, becoming Speaker of the House.[2]

While McCarthy, Waxman, and Ryan devoted themselves to particular issues, other policy specialists in the sample are distinguished by a more general focus on policy making. For example, Rosa DeLauro (D-CT) and Thaddeus McCotter (R-MI), chairs of their parties' steering and policy committees in the 110th Congress, are both policy specialists in that congress. And, of course, many other MCs who go (relatively) quietly about their business, attending to their committee assignments and doing their jobs as MCs, fall into this style.

What, then, makes policy specialists distinct from MCs with other styles? The differences in patterns of behavior become most clear when we draw direct comparisons with the activity of those MCs who fall into one of the other four clusters.

Party Soldiers

The second-largest cluster, comprising 26.7% of observations, consists of MCs we refer to as "party soldiers." These legislators vote regularly with their parties and only rarely cross the aisle to cosponsor bills introduced by the other party (the bipartisan index). They engage in considerably more showboat activity than do policy specialists, and they raise a fair amount of money, but they do not redistribute it. In short, these MCs are loyal backbenchers and members of the party team who can be counted on to toe the party line and participate in the legislative process, but who do not appear to be particularly invested in policy specialization or in fund-raising activities that would help them rise through the hierarchy.

This cluster includes several of the longest-serving MCs, such as Edward Markey (D-MA) and Dale Kildee (D-MI), both elected in 1976, and Dan Burton (R-IN), elected in 1982. As expected, all are party stalwarts, with Burton, for example, described by the *Almanac of American Politics* as "an active and enthusiastic Republican" (Barone and Cohen 2007, 614). All three of these MCs accumulated records of legislative accomplishment, though perhaps with less focus than many of their policy specialist colleagues, and also without the positions of power of some of their colleagues with other styles. However, this did not keep them from seeking and attaining visibility. Indeed, several hold reputations as gadflies. The same holds true of many of the midcareer party soldiers, such as Dennis Kucinich (D-OH), described by the *Almanac* as "unrepentant" about pushing Cleveland into default when he was mayor in the 1970s (2008, 1302); Mike Pence (R-IN), who "quickly made his mark as one of the House's more outspoken conservative members" (2008, 617); and Jim Moran (D-VA), "known for his short temper and quick tongue" (2008, 1685).

The real heart of the party soldiers group, however, is relative newcomers to Congress. In fact, in the 110th Congress, half of the eighty-five MCs with the party soldier style were in their first or second terms, and 63% of the newly elected representatives in that congress adopted the party soldier style. This suggests that this style may be a way station of sorts for many new MCs, who begin as party soldiers and then move on to other styles. We return to this puzzle later in this chapter and again in chapter 4.

District Advocates

The third cluster, with 26.2% of observations, includes those MCs we call "district advocates." These legislators have a high mean score on the home front index (edged out just slightly by the ambitious entrepreneurs), and the lowest on the party voting index. Indeed, they also often cosponsor with members of the opposite party. They also receive low scores on the showboat index and are the lowest of the five clusters on the party giving and lawmaking indices. In sum, these MCs are not a part of the party fold and operate largely beneath the radar. Instead, they devote their energy and resources to cultivating their districts.[3]

Included in this cluster are a number of long-serving MCs whose partisan leanings run against those of their states, such as Southern Democrats Bud Cramer (D-AL) and Gene Taylor (D-MS) and New England Republicans Christopher Smith (R-NJ) and James Walsh (R-NY).[4] It also includes some MCs known for their focus on pork projects and earmarks for their districts, such as Stephanie Herseth Sandlin, included as a "top earmarker" in 2008 by the Center for Responsive Politics, and Alan Mollohan (D-WV), named "Porker of the Year" by Citizens Against Government Waste in 2006. In response, Mollohan proudly noted:

> The founding fathers gave Congress the power of the purse recognizing that the people's representatives were in a far better position than the executive branch to be responsive to the needs of people and communities. . . . I am pleased to receive recognition for my efforts to support West Virginia, which is as deserving as any other state to receive federal assistance for community and economic development. (Barone and Cohen 2007, 1749)

The district advocates cluster also includes a number of early career MCs ensconced in what Fenno (1978) referred to the "expansionist" stage of their careers (i.e., wherein they attempt to expand their base of support within the district), including, in the 110th, freshmen such as Gabrielle Giffords (D-AZ) and Heath Shuler (D-NC).

Party Builders

MCs in the fourth cluster share with their party soldier and policy specialist colleagues a focus on party loyalty. They vote at the highest rates with their parties and do not often cosponsor measures introduced by the other party. However, their loyalty is not limited to their legislative actions—they also redistribute campaign contributions to their party organizations and to copartisans, receiving the highest score of any group on the "party giving" index. In addition, they are quite active in the lawmaking process and are publicly visible, scoring highly on the showboat index. However, they have the lowest score of any of the groups for home front attention. We name this cluster the "party builders." They comprise 11.9% of observations in the sample, and they include many movers and shakers—those MCs who are strong party supporters, serve as its public face, and engage in heavy lifting legislatively.

In the 110th Congress, this cluster includes nearly all of the legislative leaders and whips (Nancy Pelosi [D-CA], Eric Cantor [R-VA], Steny Hoyer [D-MD], James Clyburn [D-SC]); the financiers (Chris Van Hollen [D-MD] and Tom Cole [R-OK], who chaired the Democratic and Republican campaign committees); and some long-serving members such as John Conyers (D-MI). However, this cluster is not limited to senior MCs, and it also includes some relative newcomers, such as up and coming sophomores Debbie Wasserman Schultz (D-FL) and Tom Price (R-GA). Schultz's efforts on behalf of the party in her first term in office in the 109th Congress earned her a seat on the Appropriations Committee and a position as Chief Deputy Whip in the 110th, and she went on to become chair of the DNC. Price quickly established himself in the conservative wing of the Republican Party, joining the Republican Study Committee and Republican Policy Committee (both of which he would later chair), and rising to prominence in the 111th Congress as the main sponsor of the Empowering Patients First Act, the Republican competitor to Obamacare (i.e., the Affordable Care Act).

Ambitious Entrepreneurs

The fifth and smallest cluster, with just 3.7% of observations in the sample, consists of MCs we label "ambitious entrepreneurs." These legislators score the highest of any of the five clusters on money raised, showboating, and in the volume of lawmaking activity. They edge out district advocates on the home front index and come in second to them on voting against their parties, but are the most likely of the five groups to cross the aisle in their cosponsorship coalitions. However, this behavior does not necessarily indicate that they are moderate. Instead, some are part of idiosyncratic coalitions, either steering their own individual course or trying to build reputations in the chamber and beyond to enable them to rise to positions of power. In the 110th, this group includes progressively ambitious MCs such as the newly elected Kirsten Gillibrand (D-NY), who would serve just one full term in the House before being appointed to a Senate seat and then winning reelection for that seat, and Bobby Jindal (R-LA), who was in his second term in the House following a failed run for the governorship in 2003, but who would run again for governor, this time successfully, during the 110th Congress.

Importantly, this style is not just the province of the (imminently) progressively ambitious. In the 110th, it also includes more senior iconoclasts such as John Murtha (D-PA), Ralph Hall (R-TX), and James Obserstar (D-MN). In earlier congresses, Newt Gingrich (R-GA), Ron Paul (R-TX), Dan Rostenkowski (D-IL), Bernie Sanders (I-VT),[5] and James Traficant (D-OH) occupied this cluster.

Aggregate Patterns in Legislative Styles

These patterns all reveal that our clustering analysis yields meaningful styles that accord with our intuitions about the nature of legislative style. As predicted, we observe a small set of styles, and these map well onto scholarly and popular understandings of the trade-offs MCs make in their behavior. Before proceeding to analyze the causes and consequences of style, however, more background work is needed. To assess the robustness of our clustering approach and to build more nuanced theory about the dynamics of legislators' style, there are three things we need to show about styles. First, we must demonstrate that there is a relatively even distribution of styles across parties and across time. If, for example, the patterns in figure 3.2 are a function of Democrats mostly falling into two or three clusters and Republicans mostly falling into the others, then we are not really tapping into decisions about activity that are universal across legislators. Second, we need to establish how *well* the clusters group MCs. Put another way, do most MCs fall solidly within a single style, or do many have styles that are difficult to characterize, a hybrid of two or more different categories?[6] Third, we need to investigate the stability of styles for individuals across time. Our theory of style suggests that styles should be "sticky," and that shifts in style from one congress to the next will be relatively rare.[7] To the extent that this is the case, it provides further support for our approach. However, if our results suggested that most MCs changed styles every congress, then one might reasonably question the validity of our method.

Patterns in Style across Parties and Congresses

We begin by exploring partisan patterns in legislative styles. The contemporary Democratic and Republican parties do differ on some important dimensions that could bear on their styles. The Republicans, for example, display less ideological dispersion than do the Democrats (see Bonica 2013), and, under Newt Gingrich, began increasing centralization of power in the leadership (Davidson et al. 2014, 137). However, the resurgence of partisanship in voting and as an organizing force in Congress has affected both Democrats and Republicans. Moreover, we view style as more fundamentally about individual differences in how to approach the job of MC. We expect these differences to precede party, occurring for both Democrats and Republicans. Accordingly, we hypothesize that differences in the distribution of style across parties will be small in magnitude.

The results in figure 3.3 confirm this expectation. To assess overall party differences, we compared the mean proportion of each of the five styles for Democrats and Republicans. We find that styles are relatively evenly distributed across the parties. Slightly more Republicans than Democrats are ambitious entrepreneurs (4.5% vs. 3.0%, $t = 2.5$) and

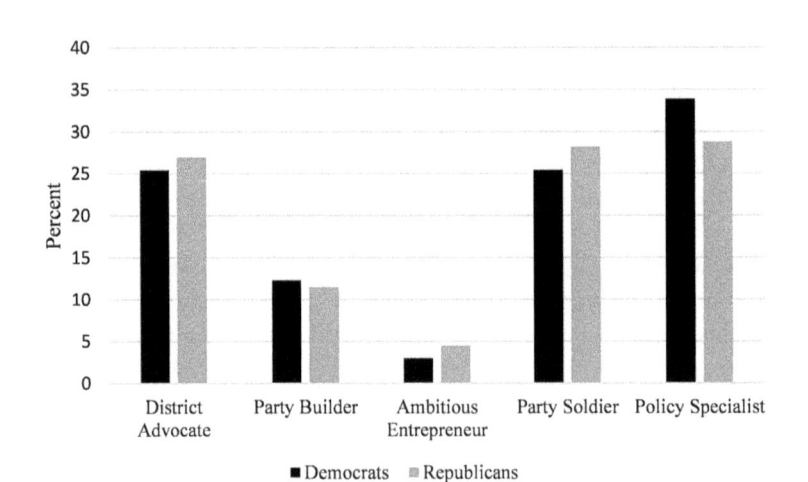

FIGURE 3.3 Distribution of styles by party
Note: Proportion of Democrats and Republicans (where the observation is the MC-congress) who adopted each of the styles. $N = 4276$

THE STYLES   51

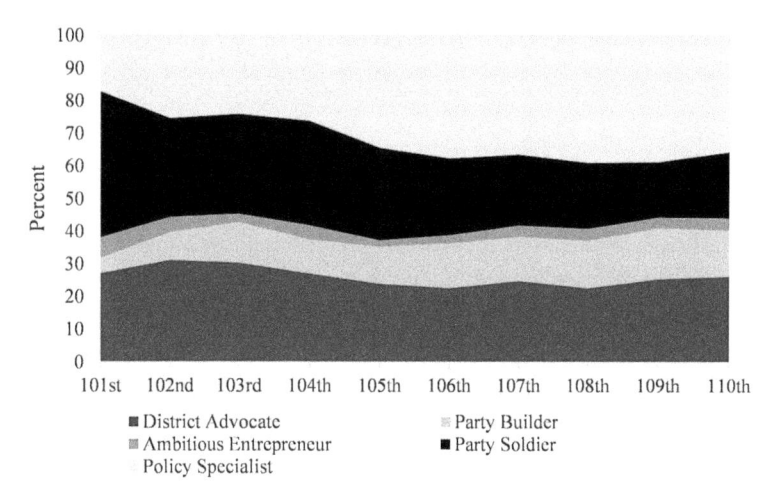

FIGURE 3.4 Distribution of styles across congresses
Note: Proportion of MCs in each congress between the 101st and 110th who adopted each of the styles. $N = 4276$

party soldiers (28.2% vs. 25.3%, $t = 2.1$); and a larger proportion of Democrats than Republicans are policy specialists (33.4% vs. 28.8%, $t = 3.6$), but these differences are not large in magnitude, and the rank ordering of the styles by relative size is the same for both parties. Thus, partisanship does not drive cluster assignments.

We would be similarly concerned about our approach if there were major differences in the distribution of styles across congresses. If, for example, all of the party builders fell within a single congress, or if there were no district advocates in some congresses, or if all of the ambitious entrepreneurs were grouped in the first or second half of the timeframe, then we might conclude that we had failed to identify enduring patterns in style. To assess this, figure 3.4 plots the percentage of MCs who fall into each cluster in the 101st–110th Congresses. As shown, there is some movement, but the congress-to-congress shifts are not dramatic. The only change that stands out is an increase in policy specialists (and a concomitant decrease in party soldiers) across time.[8] This may be due to increasing party competition and ideological polarization during this period. The more congressional politics is driven by a sense of competing party teams (Lee 2016), the less distinct a "team-oriented" style is. As a result, fewer MCs may rely on that alone to define their style, and hence, more may gravitate to the policy specialist style.[9] We conclude, nonetheless, that our styles "work" well across all congresses we study.

Styles and Goodness of Fit

Our next question turns our focus to individual MCs. How cleanly do they fall into their assigned clusters/styles? Are most legislators clearly a fit for a single style, or are many a mixture of different styles? Fortunately, our algorithm enables us to address this. To this point we have focused on the "hard" cluster assignments (i.e., whether, in a given congress, an MC is a policy specialist, a party soldier, a district advocate, a party builder, or an ambitious entrepreneur), but these assignments are determined by the relative probabilities of an MC falling into each of the five clusters (i.e., the "soft" assignments). Thus, based on an MC's scores on each of the eight indices of legislative activity in a particular congress, the algorithm estimates the probability for each MC of being a policy specialist, party soldier, district advocate, party builder, or ambitious entrepreneur. MCs are then assigned to the cluster with the highest probability.

Take, for example, Eric Cantor (R-VA). In the 110th Congress, based on his patterns of behavior, the algorithm assigns him a 1.0 probability of falling into the party builders cluster, and zero probability of falling into the policy specialist, party soldier, ambitious entrepreneur, or district advocate clusters. Thus, there is no doubt that Cantor should be classified as a party builder.

Other MCs have an unambiguous stylistic leaning, but with probabilities lower than 100%. For instance, our results indicate that Dennis Kucinich (D-OH) has a .72 probability of falling into the party soldiers cluster and a .28 probability of being an ambitious entrepreneur. Accordingly, he is clearly a party soldier, though with some tendency toward the entrepreneurial style. This combination fits well with Kucinich's public persona and with his pattern of expressed ambition, having run for President in 2004 and 2008. Overall, MCs with patterns of soft assignments that approximate Kucinich's are straightforward to categorize by style.

In contrast, other MCs are more difficult to classify. In the 110th Congress, C. W. "Bill" Young (R-FL) has a .52 probability of being a policy specialist, a .28 probability of being a party builder, a .19 probability of being a district advocate, a .01 probability of being a party sol-

THE STYLES 53

dier, and zero probability of being an ambitious entrepreneur. This hybrid style is explicable, as his was clearly a career in transition. Young arrived at the House in 1973 (at his death in 2013, he was the longest-serving Republican in the chamber) and had been a career-long member of the Appropriations Committee, serving as its chair in the 107th and 108th Congresses.[10] However, with the Democrats gaining the majority in the 110th, he had lost some of that influence and was acclimating to a changed context. He also faced a district that, while once solidly Republican, had been trending toward the Democrats in recent years.

Thus, while Young is classified as a policy specialist in the 110th Congress (i.e., because that is the cluster for which he had the highest probability), he certainly is not "as much" of a specialist as an MC like Henry Waxman (D-CA), who had a .94 probability of falling into that style. Obviously, it would point to very different assessments about the nature of style and the quality of our approach to classifying MCs if more legislators in the sample look like Young than like Cantor, Kucinich, or Waxman.

Fortunately, as shown in figure 3.5, our clusters do a good job of describing and categorizing MCs. For each MC in each congress we identify the value of the "maximum soft probability" corresponding to the cluster to which they were assigned. For example, in the 110th Congress,

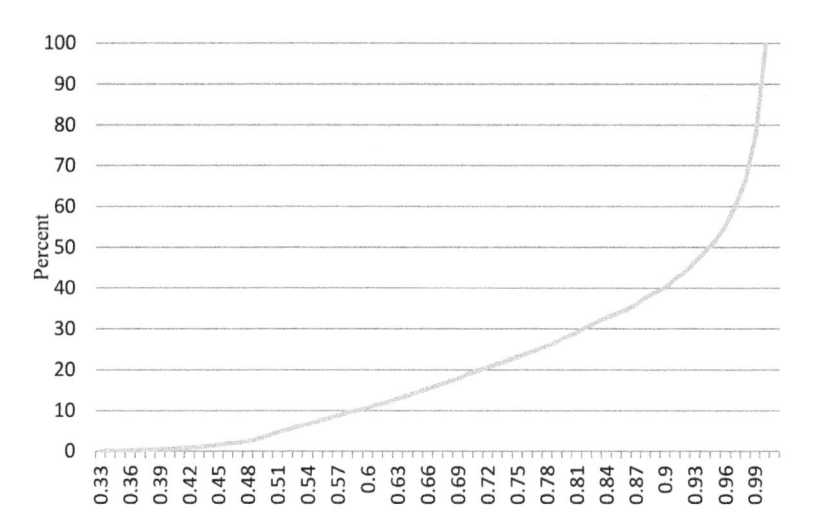

FIGURE 3.5 How well do MCs fit into their styles?
Note: Distribution of the "maximum probability" for each observation. $N = 4276$

Waxman had a maximum soft probability of .94 and Young had one of .52. The figure presents the cumulative percentage of these maximum soft probabilities. Thus, for example, we can see that the median maximum soft probability (where the curve crosses the 50% line) is very high—about .94. Indeed, 22% of the observations in our sample have a 100% probability of falling within a single cluster, and for only 3% of the observations is the maximum soft probability less than .50.

We also observe a reasonable amount of consistency across clusters. For all five styles, the median maximum soft probability for MCs is greater than .90, with the medians (and means) slightly lower for party soldiers and policy specialists than for party builders, district advocates, and ambitious entrepreneurs. Thus, MCs in all five styles generally fall neatly into that style, which underscores both that the styles we uncover are meaningful in the aggregate (i.e., none are simply a grab bag of relatively unclassifiable legislators) and that they are useful descriptors of individual MCs' activity.

Accordingly, in the analyses to come, we choose to focus largely on the "hard" cluster assignments—whether one is a policy specialist, a party soldier, a district advocate, a party builder, or an ambitious entrepreneur. However, the soft probabilities do come back into play, particularly in our investigations of transitions in style across time. For example, they enable us to ascertain whether changes in style from one congress to the next generally reflect a major shift in behavior, or whether these are more often a function of slow evolution across time (i.e., as when an MC who was almost a policy specialist in one congress has a maximum soft probability in the next term that makes him or her a true policy specialist).

Stability and Change in Individual Styles

Despite this discussion of change in styles, we expect that overall, individual MCs' styles should be relatively stable. Research on legislative behavior shows that dimensions of activity such as roll call voting patterns (Poole and Rosenthal 2007), bill introductions and cosponsorships (Ragsdale and Cook 1987), and presentational styles (Fenno 2000; Grimmer 2013) tend to display consistency across time. Thus, if most MCs were in different clusters in every congress, or if they were regularly moving between clusters that were largely incompatible with one another (e.g., from party builder to district advocate), then we might question the validity of our approach and of the styles we uncover. On the other hand, we do not expect style to be constant, especially over the long term. As we discuss below, much can happen to MCs across a period of years that could lead to a shift in goals, capacity, and priorities, and hence a transition in style.

Table 3.1 presents the proportion of MCs by cluster who maintained or shifted style in the next congress. To calculate these figures, we take MCs' styles in each congress (time t) and examine their distribution of styles in the next (time $t + 1$). Thus, the diagonal in the table reveals the amount of consistency for each style (for example, the proportion of party builders in congress t who remained party builders in congress $t + 1$).

There is an impressive amount of stability. It is highest for district advocates, 92% of whom remain so from one congress to the next. This makes sense, as the decision to be a district advocate is likely a function of (unchanging) constituency constraints. Policy specialists and party builders follow closely after (at 83% and 79% respectively). Party soldiers and ambitious entrepreneurs lag behind, with consistency rates of 58% and 50%. Since ambitious entrepreneurs often have their sights set on career goals outside the chamber, they may be likely to shift their patterns of activity to accommodate changing circumstances.[11] Similarly, the party soldiers cluster, occupied by many freshman and sophomore legislators, likely serves as a starting point for many new MCs who then settle into different styles.[12]

To further explore these dynamics, we examine the proportion of styles by seniority (i.e., by first termers, second termers, and so on). As figure 3.6 shows, close to 60% of MCs begin as party soldiers, followed by a precipitous drop in this style in the second and third terms before

TABLE 3.1 **Transition patterns from cluster to cluster (%)**

	Ambitious entrepreneur	District advocate	Party builder	Party soldier	Policy specialist
Ambitious entrepreneur	**50.0**	18.3	22.1	9.6	0
District advocate	2.0	**91.5**	1.3	2.4	2.9
Party builder	7.2	4.2	**79.2**	2.0	7.4
Party soldier	1.0	5.1	6.5	**58.1**	29.3
Policy specialist	0	5.1	6.6	4.9	**83.4**

Note: This table presents the proportion of MCs that belonged to one cluster (the rows) and then transitioned to another cluster (the columns). The diagonals (in bold) indicate the proportion of MCs who maintained a consistent style from one congress to the next. $N = 3298$

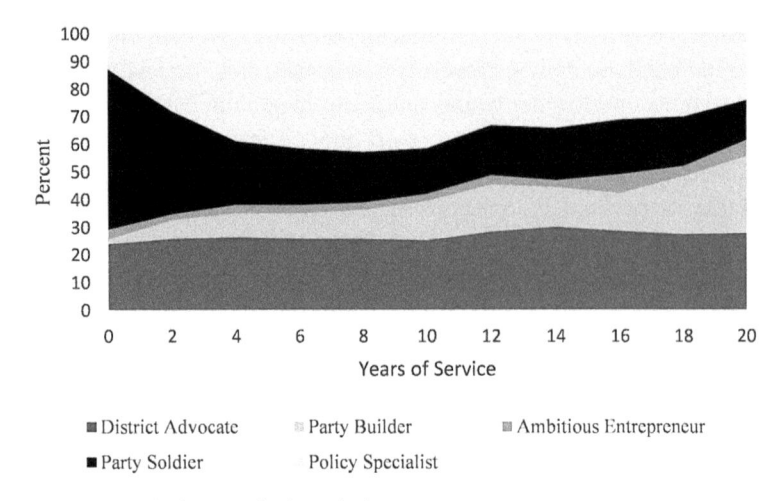

FIGURE 3.6 Distribution of styles by seniority
Note: Proportion of MCs by seniority (i.e., those who have served two years, four years, six years, up through twenty years) who fall into each style. $N = 4276$

stabilizing at about 18–20% for fourth termers and beyond. Over time, an increase in policy specialists and party builders accompanies these decreases in party soldiers, with a quick jump for policy specialists and a slower one for party builders. In fact, the policy specialist style peaks among midcareer legislators, dropping off for those with more than four terms in office and eventually being overtaken by the party builder style among the most senior MCs. The proportion of ambitious entrepreneurs moves slightly up and down by seniority, but with little discernible pattern, and the percentage of district advocates never changes by more than a point or two.

Styles and Careers

Together, these patterns indicate that our approach to measuring style is valid. We uncover meaningful and stable styles that accord with intuitions about differences across legislators. Having established that these styles exist, we now turn to the real goal of this book, and the focus of the chapters to come—to use style as a lens for understanding congressional careers.

For this, we return to our theory of legislative styles. We view styles as a function of individual inclinations and the interaction between those inclinations and the context in which MCs find themselves. While styles have a strategic element, with goal-oriented legislators adopting patterns of behavior to help them achieve their aims, they are also "sticky." Once established, we expect that MCs will only veer from their habitual ways of doing things when there is reason to do so. When change does occur, it may be gradual or abrupt, may mark a permanent shift in the type of legislator one is or a brief foray into a new pattern of activity, and can reflect sincere shifts in an MC's approach to congressional work, be induced by environmental factors, or be a combination of both.

Of course, "a career" is not a variable, and so linking styles to careers is not always straightforward. Moreover, style is endogenous to careers—the choices MCs make shape the paths their careers take and vice versa—and it is not possible to separate them cleanly from one another. In what follows, we adopt an approach that reflects this complicated reality, while also enabling us to study styles and careers in a systematic and rigorous way. Specifically, we dip in and out of MCs' careers, approaching them from different angles and at different points in time. This enables us to explore critical career junctures as well as the evolution of style across time; to investigate how MCs adopt initial styles and how styles are associated with what becomes of them in the end; and to understand how stylistic choices shape what individual legislators and the House of Representatives as a whole are able to accomplish in the electoral and lawmaking arenas.

To illustrate, we return to the 110th Congress Iowa delegation (Democrats Leonard Boswell, Bruce Braley, and David Loebsack and Republicans Steve King and Tom Latham). As we expected, the differences in patterns of behavior displayed by these MCs translate into differences in legislative style. In the 110th, first termers Braley and Loebsack were a party soldier and policy specialist, respectively, returnees Boswell and Latham were district advocates, and King a party soldier.

These assignments accord well with the descriptions of the styles above. Compared to Loebsack, for example, Braley was a prolific speech giver and fund-raiser, but had a much less focused agenda (introduced in nine areas vs. four, and only 5% of his bills were referred to a committee on which he sat, compared to 20% of Loebsack's). Similarly, Boswell and Latham demonstrate well the characteristics of district advocates, breaking from the party more often on roll call votes (about 6% of the time, compared to only 1% of the time for King) and devoting more staff to their districts.

However, while Boswell and King had maintained their styles since entering Congress (Boswell in the 105th Congress and King in the 108th), Latham had demonstrated two shifts in style, beginning in the 104th at a party soldier, transitioning to a policy specialist in the 105th–107th Congresses, and again to a district advocate in the 108th–110th Congresses. As expected, these changes in style correspond to shifts in behavior; Latham decreased his speechmaking as his career progressed, increased and then decreased his lawmaking activity, and shifted away from the party in his roll call voting. We discuss reasons for transitions in style in chapter 5, but the shift to the specialist style may have been driven by his gaining an exclusive committee assignment (Appropriations) in the 105th Congress, and the move to the district advocate style in the 108th may have been precipitated by drop in vote share (from 70–100% in the 1994–2000 elections to 56% in the 2002 election).

The Iowa delegation's careers also took different paths in the years after the 110th Congress. As we write this in 2017, King and Loebsack are still serving in the House of Representatives. Neither holds formal positions of particular power or influence, but both have enjoyed some legislative victories. King has received his share of media attention as an outspoken conservative, defending Todd Akin (R-MO) in the aftermath of his controversial statements about rape and pregnancy,[13] and making waves as a vocal critic of immigration.

Braley, as discussed in chapter 2, ran for an open Senate seat in 2014 (being vacated by fellow Democrat Tom Harkin), but lost to Republican Joni Ernst in the general election and is now back to practicing law. Boswell was defeated in 2012 after redistricting forced him to run against fellow incumbent Tom Latham, who emerged victorious in the general election. Boswell retired to his family farm in Iowa, and Latham himself retired shortly thereafter, announcing in December 2013 that he would not run for another term.

While we could tell stories or offer journalistic accounts about why these MCs started out where they did, why they did (or did not) shift styles during this time period, and how their styles are related to their career choices and outcomes, with such a small group of legislators our explanations would be necessarily overdetermined. Instead, in what follows, we take a multimethod approach, combining statistical analyses and case studies to illuminate the dynamics of style and careers at various junctures.

Critical Junctures

In the next chapter, we highlight the freshman term as a particular focus of interest. Upon entering Congress, MCs make initial choices about how to behave and what type of legislator to be. These decisions, we argue, are a function of their prior career experiences (political and otherwise), their own personal characteristics, the nature of their constituencies, and the context in which they find themselves in their first terms—in particular, the standing of their party and their status within that hierarchy. What, then, accounts for the prevalence of the party soldier style among freshmen, and why do some MCs deviate from this style?

Following that, we explore the dynamics of style at a number of important career junctures, beginning in chapter 5 with an investigation of transitions in style across careers. Some of the phenomena of interest to us are what political sociologists would call "lifecycle effects"—potentially influencing all MCs at particular stages of their careers. For example, the aggregate patterns in figure 3.6 suggest that we see a substantial proportion of shifts in style in MCs' second and third terms (largely away from the party soldier style). Can we explain what distinguishes those MCs who maintain their freshman styles as they settle in to legislative life from those who shift to other patterns of behavior?

Other questions of interest in explaining transitions in style center on "period effects"—changes in the environment that affect all MCs who are serving at a particular time. Most notable among these is a shift in the control of the House majority party (which occurs twice during our time of study, from the Democrats to the Republicans in the 104th Congress, and back to the Democrats in the 110th Congress). Do most MCs stay the course after a majority shift, or do these tend to produce changes in activity patterns that translate to shifts in style?

Other career junctures of interest are more targeted—they happen for some MCs but not for all. These include the gain or loss of institutional positions, such as prestigious committee assignments or a spot in the leadership, and electoral shifts, whether due to changing support from constituents, changes in the level of political competition within the district, or changes in the composition of the constituency itself (i.e., as occurs with redistricting). Which of these developments affect transitions in style, and are the effects constant across MCs, or are those in some styles influenced more by these types of contextual changes?

In explaining transitions in style, much of our focus will be on congress-to-congress changes (i.e., as when an MC who is a party soldier in one congress becomes a party builder or policy specialist in the next). However, we are also interested in the processes underlying these changes. Is a shift in style the result of a gradual movement in behavior over time that eventually "pushes" an MC from one category to another, or does it reflect an abrupt change in activity?

Finally, we target the reciprocal relationships between style, success, and career trajectories. What types of MCs are most successful at gaining their preferred committee assignments, at building coalitions among their peers, or at pushing legislation through the House? Which successes accrue immediately with style, and which emerge over a longer time period? In the electoral arena, how are styles related to performance in primary and general elections or in the ability to ward off challengers? How early in MCs' careers can we predict who will rise to positions of power within the chamber? What do styles tell us about who will demonstrate progressive ambition and run for higher office? Or about who will voluntarily retire from Congress, opting out of public life?

Conclusions

In this chapter, we have demonstrated the potential value of a clustering approach to understanding legislative styles. Based on readily observable measures of MCs' activity, which, in combination, serve as signals about legislators' underlying tendencies, we derived five distinct legislative styles. These styles align with scholarly understandings of differences across MCs and enable us to assign all MCs who served in the 101st–110th Congresses to styles. Most MCs fall solidly within a single style and, as predicted, styles are relatively stable for individuals across time. We also observe consistency in the distribution of styles across parties and across congresses, suggesting that these styles do a good job of capturing fundamental and enduring differences in legislators' approaches to their jobs. We turn now to exploring the dynamics of legislative style in MCs' freshman terms, as they embark on their Washington careers.

CHAPTER FOUR

Explaining Freshman Styles

> Freshman senators have more time and resources, but House members do not. They need to craft three to five strategic goals and stick with them. If they don't, they'll end up becoming one of two kinds of members of Congress. If they're from a safe district, they'll become an ineffective member; if they're from an unsafe district, they'll be a former member.
> — Bradford Fitch, *Roll Call*'s "The Cures to Freshman Office Headaches," May 26, 2015

Between the 1988 and 2006 elections, 649 new MCs joined the House of Representatives. Some of these legislators would go on to become chamber leaders. Some would move up to the Senate or the State Capitol.[1] Others would serve just a term or two before losing their seats. And many others would quietly build long-term careers in the House of Representatives.

We contend that MCs' stylistic choices are linked to these career trajectories, affecting what they accomplish as legislators in the House and the type of representation they provide to their constituents at home. As we will show, these phenomena all have their roots in MCs' earliest days in Congress. To understand style and careers, we therefore start at the beginning, with legislators' initial styles as freshmen.

The Transition to Congress

After winning their general election battles, newly elected legislators, like freshmen everywhere, attend orientation. In the House, New Member Orientation, organized by the Committee on House Administration, takes place in the weeks after the election and covers the basics of life in the House of Representatives. New MCs receive tours of the Capitol, are invited to briefings on the logistics of running an office (including hiring staff and managing their Member Representational Allowances) and on House rules, participate in workshops on security and ethics, meet with their party leadership, mingle at receptions, pose for a class photo, and participate in the assignment lottery to select their office spaces (Bowman 2014; Dumain 2012). Following this official orientation, many new members attend other, more policy-oriented sessions. Some, such as those offered by the Kennedy School of Government at Harvard University, are bipartisan in nature, while others, such as those sponsored by the Heritage Foundation, have a more ideological bent.

These weeks leading up to the start of the term are a heady time for incoming freshmen, but also a potentially confusing one. As David Price (D-NC) wrote in his journal after his initial election to office in 1986:

> The orientation process has emotional ups and downs that compare fully with the campaign. Most new members seem to come in with euphoria from election night still lingering, full of campaign stories. But a sense of satisfaction at simply being here quickly becomes mixed with anxiety about all there is to be done and about one's own status in the unfolding order of things. (2004, 64)

Immediate decisions about office location and staff may consume much of their attention, but newly elected MCs are also concerned with the broader questions of how to approach the job, what to prioritize, and what type of legislator to be.

Of course, legislators do not arrive in Washington, DC, as blank slates. All come with prior career experiences that bring with them a skill set and, perhaps, a world view (Berkman 1994; Francis 2014). Most have been in politics before. The vast majority (about 83%) of new MCs during this time period had prior elected office experience (with about 60% of those having had a state legislative background), and one in ten had been, like David Price, a staffer on Capitol Hill. Such legislative background brings familiarity with the procedures of lawmaking, as well as with the perils and possibilities of congressional politics.

Prior political backgrounds are not the only career experiences that may shape activity. Nonpolitical jobs can be equally important. Legislators commonly refer to how their lives as doctors or farmers or teachers or small business owners or lawyers affect their behavior in Congress (Burden 2007). In many cases, career paths influence the substance of their activity. Former medical professionals pursue health care policy at high rates, former teachers are interested in education, and so on (Francis 2014).[2] However, these experiences may also have broader implications for how MCs organize their staffs, collaborate with colleagues, and delegate responsibilities, and for whether they seek out the limelight or prefer to operate beneath the radar.

For instance, David Price argued that his temperament and his previous experiences as a college professor shaped his transition to Congress and the decisions he made, from the issues that he pursued (education and research) to the way he managed his communications (choosing to do much correspondence and speechwriting himself rather than delegating to his staff), to his choices as a lawmaker—in his words, to adopt "an activist, but selective and specialized, legislative style." As he explained:

> In my early terms, I concentrated on a limited number of initiatives, mostly in my committee areas, on which I could work in a concerted fashion. This was a sensible strategy for a junior member, but it also stemmed from my preference, rooted in prior experience, to focus on a manageable number of projects and operate from a substantial base of knowledge. (2004, 73)

Thus, it seems clear that MCs' histories have the potential to influence their activity in office. Of course, more proximate sources matter as well. These include lessons learned and promises made in the previous campaign (Sulkin 2005, 2011). Freshmen who offered pledges to pursue a particular policy area, to devote time to the home front, or to support (or buck) their parties will benefit from following through on those appeals. A failure to do so gives ammunition to future challengers, a situation that electorally risk-averse legislators are keen to avoid.

The preferences and demands of the constituency will also affect behavior. We know that some constituencies (those that are politically interested, highly educated, and policy-focused) expect more of their MCs than others (see, for example, Griffin and Flavin 2007; Harden 2016), and savvy representatives will be aware of this and respond accordingly. It is also the case that some districts, due to their ideological and/or demographic heterogeneity, are more challenging to represent. MCs from those districts must calibrate their activities to appeal to a broad set of constituents with different ideas about what a representative should do (Sulkin, Testa, and Usry 2015). The realm of possibilities open to legislators will therefore be influenced by the nature of their districts and the composition of their constituencies.

Finally, new MCs will be attentive to the inducements and consequences meted out by the party leadership. In some congresses, freshmen find themselves asked to take sides in battles over leadership positions or other policy or procedural matters, and the choices they make shape their reputations and connections in the party in ways that affect the opportunities that come their way. In the 104th Congress, for example, newly elected MC Lindsey Graham chose to challenge Newt Gingrich and the party leadership by pushing for retroactive term limits for committee chairs and to extend these term limits to include the Speaker of the House. As Fenno (2007) described it:

> He was plunging in and drawing lines of division as he charted his course. He could not be understood, as the Washington press would have it, as a Gingrich "robot" or "foot soldier." . . . Predictably, Graham received none of the early preferment accorded his colleague. "Did you get the committee you wanted?" I asked him. "No," he said. (210)

Facing similar circumstances, other MCs choose to follow the preferences of the party leadership, sometimes to their benefit, and sometimes at their peril. Famously, Marjorie Margolies-Mezvinsky (D-PA) became the deciding vote on Bill Clinton's 1993 budget act when entreaties from the chamber leadership and from Clinton himself led her to reverse her opposition. When she cast her vote, Robert Walker, a Republican member of her Pennsylvania delegation, called out "Goodbye, Marjorie!" (Sarlin 2009). Walker was prescient, as Margolies-Mezvinsky was defeated by a substantial margin in the next election.

However, despite the influences of experience, constituency, and party, MCs also enjoy considerable freedom to chart their own course as legislators. Many observers have noted that there is something about moving to the Capitol—"inside the beltway"—that leaves legislators unencumbered by their former lives and able to take on new identities and new challenges. As Meg Greenfield, the renowned *Washington Post* and *Newsweek* columnist, described it in her memoir, *Washington*: "The professional value system of political Washington entices those who came to it from elsewhere; most adopt Washington-centered behavior patterns" (2001, 8), leaving behind what came before. Thus, MCs can and do create themselves anew. Although not unconstrained, the choice of style is ultimately just that—a choice.

This point is perhaps truer now in the contemporary period than in congresses past. Fenno (2007) describes the emergence in the 1970s and 1980s of "a new group of elected politicians—more self-starting, more self-propelling, less dependent on party than before, and, therefore, not easily portrayed in familiar, standardized ideological or partisan categories" (15). This is in accord with the common argument that the traditional norms of deference and apprenticeship in Congress have been replaced by a new entrepreneurialism. Even in an era of increasing ideological polarization, legislators are less defined by their parties (though most remain loyalists in voting, and, as we will see, a party-oriented style remains common among freshmen) and more by their individual choices.

Freshman Styles

It is in this context of past experiences and new opportunities that freshman MCs adopt patterns of behavior that comprise their initial styles. Formally, all of the dimensions of activity we study (home front attention, showboating, raising and redistributing funds, lawmaking, party voting, policy focus, coalition-building) are as accessible to freshmen as to their senior colleagues. Informally, new MCs' relative lack of experience means that some doors will be closed to them, and they may be more reliant on cues from the leadership about what to do (Stratmann 2000). As a result, we do not expect the distribution of styles for freshman MCs to approximate that of their senior colleagues. Most freshmen will take some time to come into their own.

The patterns in figure 4.1 confirm these expectations. As shown, compared to the full sample of MCs, among freshmen there are many more party soldiers, considerably fewer policy specialists and party builders, and about the same proportion of district advocates and ambitious entrepreneurs. By the sophomore term, however, the distribution more closely approximates the overall division of styles, with about one-third party soldiers and policy specialists, one-quarter district advocates, 5% party builders, and 2% ambitious entrepreneurs.[3]

In the next chapter, we explore shifts in style from the freshman to sophomore term and beyond. For purposes of this chapter, the patterns in figure 4.1 raise two questions of interest. First, why are there so many party soldiers among freshmen, especially relative to their more experienced colleagues?[4] Second, can we account for variation in styles across freshmen, explaining where MCs start out and why?

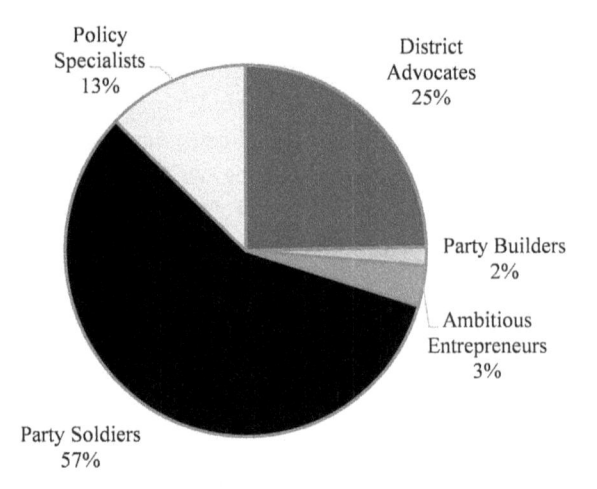

FIGURE 4.1 Distribution of freshman style
Note: Proportion of freshman MCs who fall into each of the five legislative styles. $N = 567$

COMPARING FRESHMEN AND EXPERIENCED LEGISLATORS To answer the first question, it helps to begin with a brief review of what party soldiers as a group are like as MCs. As discussed in chapter 3, soldiers are characterized by party loyalty in roll call voting and cosponsorship coalitions. They raise a lot of money, but they do not redistribute much to copartisans. They are legislatively active, but not particularly specialized in policy, and pursue opportunities to be publicly visible. They tend to focus more on Washington and less on the home front.

How, then, does this map on to the experiences of freshmen versus more senior members? First, freshmen are, in general, more reliant on the party, and they want to impress the higher-ups in order to obtain prime committee assignments and other positions. They may also come in with a higher sense of loyalty to the idea of a party "team," especially if they attribute their victory in part to the efforts of their copartisans.

New MCs also tend to arrive in Congress more electorally vulnerable than their senior peers—they are less likely to have been unopposed in the previous race (2.3% of new MCs faced no general election challenger versus 15% of returning legislators; $t = 8.4, p < .05$), and, among those with opposition, earn a lower proportion of the vote share (59% for freshmen vs. 67% for returnees; $t = 19.2, p < .05$). Thus, they often feel a need to raise funds to shore up their prospects in the next election.

They also may be hesitant about redistribution of campaign money until their own needs are met, and they face less pressure from the party to contribute (Cann 2008; Heberlig and Larson 2012).

Legislatively, freshmen are eager to make their mark through their presence in DC. They miss fewer votes than do their senior colleagues (present for 97.4% of roll calls, as compared to 95.1% for sophomores and above; $t = 9.0, p < .05$) and make more speeches on the floor (11.4 vs. 7.5; $t = 5.5, p < .05$), though, as they learn the ropes, they are less active in introducing and cosponsoring legislation (8 vs. 14 introductions; $t = 13.2, p < .05$ and 229 vs. 249 cosponsorships; $t = 3.3, p < .05$).

Compared to their more experienced peers, freshmen have less specialized agendas—for example, a lower proportion of their introduced legislation is referred to a committee on which they sit (26% vs. 34%; $t = 6.8, p < .05$). This is likely due to a combination of not having settled into their committees and/or not yet attaining their preferred assignments. David Price describes in his memoir his failure to achieve a seat on Energy and Commerce in his first term, settling for Banking and Science, Space, and Technology, and setting his sights on an eventual slot on Appropriations. It is clear from his discussion that his aim as a freshman was not to begin a career-long specialization in his initial committee assignments, but to leverage these assignments to achieve his broader goals:

> I concentrated on securing compatible committee assignments, preferably under young, aggressive subcommittee chairmen who would pursue an expansive agenda and would welcome my participation. Such criteria are often more important than the subcommittee's precise jurisdiction, for the subject matter lines are rather ill defined and an aggressive chairman generally has wide latitude in exploring policy questions of interest. (2004, 80–81)

Finally, although freshmen typically report feeling a pull from the constituency and express a commitment to spending time "at home," they also get swept up in the newness of Washington life and the need to focus there, and they also may lack the experience or budget to operate full-fledged operations both in DC and in the district. Indeed, freshmen in our sample devote less of their staff to the district than do their experienced peers (45% vs. 47%; $t = 4.3; p < .05$) and have fewer district offices (1.9 vs. 2.2; $t = 4.4, p < .05$).

As indicated, these differences in activity are generally not large in magnitude, but they do suggest that freshmen are, on average, drawn more toward patterns of activity that correspond to the party soldier style. However, it is important to reiterate that we see style as more than just the sum of its parts. Because style is necessarily latent, we view MCs' patterns of activity as signals about their underlying type. If our measures of style are valid, they should tap into this gestalt sense of what MCs are "like" as legislators—what motivates them and how they see their job in Congress.

For example, we contend that being a party soldier is about more than just voting with the party—lots of MCs from all the styles do this. Instead, it stems from something more intangible—a sense of being a dyed-in-the-wool "man (or woman) of the party," for whom the party and its leadership is the central organizing force. In *Congressional Travels*, Fenno (2007) offers an extended account of the early career of David McIntosh (R-IN), who was swept into office in 1994 as part of Newt Gingrich's Republican Revolution. What emerges from this depiction, in McIntosh's own words, is an MC who orients himself around the party team with a "broad, party-centered attitude" (193). Indeed, McIntosh, selected by Gingrich as a part of the Republican transition team, identified strongly as a member of the freshman class and successfully ran for the position of class liaison with the leadership (190).

These choices may have been strategic, but they were also a function of who McIntosh was and the experiences that had shaped his professional outlook. After graduating from law school at the University of Chicago, McIntosh had moved to Washington, first to work in the Reagan Administration as Special Assistant to the Attorney General and as Special Assistant to the President for Domestic Affairs, and then, under the George H. W. Bush Administration, as Executive Director of Vice President Dan Quayle's Council for Competitiveness. As Fenno described it:

> He came, also, as a product of mentoring and protégé systems. In law school, there had been Professor Antonin Scalia (who, as a Supreme Court justice, swore him in privately before the ceremony in the House), and, in Washington, there had been Vice President Dan Quayle. Prior experience had helped him to fit easily into a similar relationship with Newt Gingrich, the man who invited him to join in making the decision to adopt the contract as the party's legislative agenda. Party leaders acknowledged his preparation, they

co-opted him, and they treated him as a now and future Republican Party leader. (2007, 190–91)

As a result, McIntosh fit the mold of a party soldier, and his behavior aligned with what one would expect of such an MC. As expected, our results reveal that McIntosh was indeed a party soldier in the 104th Congress.[5] Although he also sought to cultivate his constituency and had interests in policy, his style was far from that of a district advocate or policy specialist.

As a comparison, McIntosh was significantly different stylistically from the MC who had preceded him in Indiana's 2nd district, Democrat Phil Sharp. Sharp had represented the traditionally Republican constituency since 1974 (among a group of Democrats who rode the Watergate scandal into office) and had cemented his victories by working hard to connect with his constituents, orienting himself away from the party and toward the needs of his district. This was manifested both in how he spent his time and in the nature and content of his behavior in Washington, DC. As Sharp put it:

I always tried to be nonpolitical, to emphasize my small-town background. I did not come on as a politician with loud or strong positions. . . . That was my strength in Congress, too. Maybe I was too passive; but I don't think so. I didn't come in and say "We've got to have a deal now." I let things work themselves out. (Fenno 2007, 206)

Like McIntosh, Sharp chose a legislative style that fit who he was, how he thought about the job of MC, and what he was able to accomplish given the constituency he represented. Unsurprisingly, in the congresses for which we have data for Sharp (his last three terms in office—the 101st–103rd), he is a district advocate.

PREDICTIONS ABOUT FRESHMAN STYLE As argued in chapters 1 and 2 and highlighted by the examples above, MCs adopt styles that align with their goals as well as the incentives and constraints they face. While we cannot measure goals, and it is impossible to collect data on all factors that might contribute to style (e.g., an MC's personality), we can identify a number of possible covariates that should explain freshman style. In line with our expectations, we target three sets of predictors: the political experiences and leanings new legislators bring to the job, MC and district demographics and characteristics, and legislators' electoral and institutional status in their first terms. Given the very small numbers of party builders and ambitious entrepreneurs among freshmen (nine and twenty MCs, respectively), we focus our hypotheses on distinguishing party soldiers from their district advocate and policy specialist colleagues.

We begin with the effects of political experience. New MCs come to Congress with a variety of backgrounds, with about 50% of the freshmen in our sample having served in the state legislature. These MCs enter with a base of knowledge that should make them less reliant on the party and, perhaps, with a developed interest in a particular policy area.[6] Thus, we predict that experienced freshman legislators are less likely to be party soldiers and more likely to be policy specialists, or, possibly, district advocates. In addition, although there are few party builders among freshmen, we expect that they will be disproportionately drawn from those with state legislative experience.

Ideology, particularly ideological extremity (as measured by the absolute value of the common space NOMINATE score),[7] should also be an important predictor of initial style. Moderates are, almost by definition, considerably less likely to toe the party line and be party soldiers. They may also recognize that certain paths within the chamber will be blocked to them because of their moderation, and so choose to build niches for themselves by adopting a district advocate style, or by pursuing a policy specialist style.

A second category of potential influences on freshman style is MCs' demographic characteristics. In making predictions about these factors, we are guided by the literature on race, gender, and representation and by work on political ambition. In particular, research on women, African Americans, and Latinos as representatives demonstrates that, relative to their white male counterparts, they focus their agendas more intently on racial and women's issues, and they see themselves as providing collective representation on these issues to constituents beyond just those who happen to live in their districts (see, for example, Canon 1999; Fenno 2003; Grose 2011; Rocca and Sanchez 2008; Swers 2002, 2013; Tate 2003). Accordingly, we hypothesize that this desire to provide descriptive and substantive representation may lead women and representatives from minority racial/ethnic groups to be less likely to adopt a party soldier style and more likely to be a policy specialist or, perhaps, a district advocate.[8]

New MCs' age upon arriving in Congress may also matter for their styles, as it affects their time horizons, and hence how they view their career trajectories. Those who enter the chamber at a young age and are looking ahead at long service in the chamber may be prone to start as party soldiers or even party builders (or, if they plan to move up and out quickly, ambitious entrepreneurs). It is also less likely that a very young legislator has had time to build up a policy focus that would lead him or her to the policy specialist style as a freshman. Older MCs, in contrast, may come with a strong policy focus related to their previous careers, and so be more likely to be policy specialists, or bring with them a lifelong commitment to the district and its people, leading them to be district advocates.

Characteristics of new MCs' districts may also shape what patterns of activity are feasible. For example, ideologically or demographically heterogeneous districts make it challenging for MCs to toe the party line without risking electoral defeat. A party-centered style like David McIntosh's would not have worked for him had he hailed from a district that was not solidly Republican. Thus, we anticipate that legislators from relatively heterogeneous districts will be more likely to begin as policy specialists[9] or district advocates than as party soldiers. Our analyses utilize Kernell's (2009) estimates of district ideological heterogeneity and our version of the "Sullivan Index" (1973) of constituency diversity, including the racial and economic composition of districts.

The place of an MC's district within the state may matter as well for his or her style. Legislators who come from states dominated by a single party, with a relatively homogenous political culture, are likely to face less need to cultivate the constituency or develop policy specialization, and, instead, can benefit from associating in a visible way with the party team. It is also the case that a potentially progressively ambitious new freshman from such a state will see that linking him or herself to the party could pay dividends down the line. As a result, we predict that a high degree of copartisanship within the state delegation (measured as the percentage of the delegation that are of the same party as an MC) will increase the probability of that legislator adopting a party soldier style.

It is also possible that the distance of the district from DC affects style. MCs who represent districts far removed from Washington may face more pressure to show that they are remaining faithful to the needs of their constituents and maintaining their "outside the Beltway" credentials, and so may be more likely to diverge from the soldier style to be district advocates. On the flip side, however, those with shorter commutes can more easily spend time at home, so any effect may wash out in the aggregate. However, is important to remember that being a district advocate is about more than just allocating resources to the district. As with all styles, it is a broader orientation. For instance, advocates also break from the party on voting and do not seek out media visibility, and it is less clear how distance might affect these patterns of behavior.

We expect that MCs' relative electoral security (i.e., their vote shares) upon entering Congress may also affect their styles. Again, though, there are potentially competing expectations about the direction of this effect. All else equal, more secure MCs should be freer from constraints and more able to steer their own course, making them less likely to be party soldiers. However, if their initial safety was a function of having campaigned as a good partisan (and/or having received financial support from the party), they might feel compelled to adopt a soldier style. Relatively secure MCs will also face less need to adopt a district advocate style to appeal to constituents, though depending on the nature of their districts, such a choice may best promote their safety over the long run.

Our last category of predictors of freshman style relate to the status of the MC in his or her first term. We anticipate that majority party freshmen will be more likely than minority MCs to be party soldiers, since the stakes for party loyalty are higher for the majority, and because its leaders have more enticing rewards to dole out. We also expect that freshmen who obtain an exclusive committee assignment (Appropriations, Energy and Commerce, Financial Services, Rules, Ways and Means) will have a greater probability of adopting a party soldier style[10] because these assignments are both a cause and consequence of being (or potentially being) a good partisan.[11] Across the time period we examine, the parties were increasingly involved in distributing such benefits to promote their goals (see, for example, Meinke 2016; Pearson 2015), so we may see effects beginning as soon as the freshman term.

Beyond just majority status, the size of the partisan cohort may also shape style. Across the time period we examine, new freshmen are members of incoming party classes ranging from fourteen members (for Democrats in the 107th Congress) to seventy-three (for Republicans in the 104th Congress). Their stylistic choices may be related to these cohort sizes, affecting their desire or need to stand out from the pack and, relatedly, the likelihood of attaining plum positions as freshmen. A large freshman cohort pulls in two directions, though. It is easier to stand out if one is part of a smaller group, but a sizable cohort of freshmen makes it more likely that newcomers will be a powerful force and that some of their number will receive good positions. Therefore, large cohorts could encourage the party soldier style, or MCs elected in such cohorts could choose to differentiate themselves via a policy specialist or district advocate style.

Explaining Initial Styles

As a first step in assessing these hypotheses, we compare freshman party soldiers, district advocates, policy specialists, party builders, and ambitious entrepreneurs on the various characteristics of MCs, districts, and political context described above. Table 4.1 presents the mean values for

TABLE 4.1 **Comparing characteristics of freshman MCs by style**

	Party soldiers $N = 326$	District advocates $N = 140$	Policy specialists $N = 72$	Party builders $N = 9$	Ambitious entrepreneurs $N = 20$
Experience and inclinations					
Former state legislator	.48	.46	.58	.78	.40
Ideological extremity	.39	.20	.41	.42	.27
Democrat	.44	.58	.47	.44	.50
MC demographics					
Woman	.20	.08	.14	.33	.20
Underrepresented group	.12	.07	.28	0	0
Age	46	45	46	46	44
Under 35	.10	.12	.06	0	.10
Over 55	.13	.12	.14	.11	.05
District characteristics					
Sullivan Index	.40	.40	.40	.41	.39
Demographically diverse?	.55	.56	.69	.56	.45
District heterogeneity	687.5	671.8	651.2	737.1	714.2
Miles from DC	1167	1097	940	1197	1092
Copartisan delegation percentage	.61	.54	.56	.54	.54
Delegation size	17	16	18	24	22
Vote share	.60	.57	.65	.65	.59
Political context					
In majority?	.62	.58	.64	.67	.55
Exclusive committee	.33	.24	.24	.67	.50
New copartisans	41	41	48	42	38

Note: This table presents the mean value for each independent variable across each of the five styles. The analyses are limited to the 567 freshmen in our sample.

each style for each variable. For example, we find that 48% of party soldiers come to Congress with state legislative experience, compared to 47% of district advocates, 58% of policy specialists, 78% of party builders, and 40% of ambitious entrepreneurs. In what follows, we focus our comparisons primarily on soldiers, advocates, and specialists, since the raw numbers of party builders and ambitious entrepreneurs are low. We return to a more detailed discussion of party builders and ambitious entrepreneurs later in the chapter.

These descriptive statistics provide some initial support for our hypotheses. We see, for example, that among the three large stylistic groups, policy specialists are more likely than party soldiers and district advocates to have had state legislative experience, and that district advocates are more ideologically moderate than soldiers and specialists. There also look to be some demographic differences; a lower proportion of women are district advocates and a substantially higher proportion of MCs from underrepresented groups are policy specialists. While there are no discernible differences in average age of freshmen across styles, party soldiers and district advocates are more likely to fall into the "young" group (under thirty-five years of age).

There are also important differences in district characteristics, particularly for soldiers versus the other categories. Soldiers hail from more distant locales and come from districts that are moderately ideologically heterogeneous, but relatively demographically homogenous.[12] Soldiers also come from the most homogenous states in terms of congressional delegation partisanship (though there are no differences across soldiers, advocates, and specialists in state size). In their initial vote shares, they arrive more electorally secure than district advocates, but not as safe as policy specialists.

We also see some variation in political context for the different freshman styles. Soldiers and specialists are more likely than advocates to come from the majority, specialists tend to arise from larger partisan cohorts, and soldiers are more likely than their advocate and specialist peers to attain an exclusive committee assignment in the first term.

Although our focus here is not on party builders and ambitious entrepreneurs, they differ in important ways as well, and are perhaps the most distinct groups. Builders are the most likely to come to Congress with legislative experience (78% of them were state legislators) and ambitious entrepreneurs the least (just 40%). Across all five groups, both also come from the most ideologically heterogeneous districts. Compared to the three larger styles, they contain the highest proportions of women and the lowest of underrepresented minority groups, hail from the largest states, and are the most likely to receive exclusive committee assignments.[13]

To draw firmer conclusions requires that we test these initial findings in a more rigorous way. To do so, we estimate a multinomial logit model. These models are appropriate in situations where there is a categorical dependent variable (in our case, each freshman MC's legislative style), and they allow one to estimate the effects of a set of independent variables on the probability of an observation falling into each category of the dependent variable relative to a baseline category. Our independent variables are the characteristics of MCs and their districts described above, and we also include controls for party and for congress. Given the nature of our hypotheses, we choose the party soldiers category as the baseline, and, due to their low numbers, omit party builders and ambitious entrepreneurs.

The results of the model are presented in table 4.2. They indicate that even after controlling for a variety of factors, our hypothesized covariates still serve as significant predictors of initial styles. In particular, freshman party soldiers differ in important ways from their peers who adopt other styles. Compared to both district advocates and policy specialists, soldiers are more likely to come from states that have homogenously partisan congressional delegations, and they are more likely to receive exclusive committee assignments in their first terms.[14] They are also more likely than advocates to be ideologically extreme, and they are more likely to be women and less likely to be young. Compared to policy specialists, they are less likely to have state legislative experience, come from less demographically diverse districts, and are elected to office with lower vote shares.

Equally important are what do *not* seem to matter. In these multivariate analyses, we see no independent effect of race on styles. The size of the partisan cohort in which MCs find themselves does not matter either, nor does majority status. Below, we give some of these dynamics a more nuanced investigation to ascertain whether there may be more subtle relationships between these variables and style. For present purposes, we focus on those covariates that emerge as significant predictors of freshman style.

Importantly, while the coefficients in table 4.2 enable us to ascertain which independent variables are significantly associated with styles, they

TABLE 4.2 **What explains freshman style?**

	District advocates	Policy specialists
Experience and inclinations		
Former state legislator	.02 (.32)	.49 (.29)*
Ideological extremity	−22.97 (2.29)**	.67 (1.37)
MC demographics		
Woman	−.91 (.48)*	−.60 (.41)
Underrepresented group	.63 (.61)	.49 (.46)
Under 35	1.46 (.56)**	.53 (.52)
Over 55	−.37 (.49)	.12 (.43)
District characteristics		
Demographically diverse?	.52 (.34)	.66 (.34)**
District heterogeneity	.00 (.00)	−.00 (.00)
Miles from DC	−.00 (.00)	−.00 (.00)
Copartisan delegation percentage	−2.65 (.98)**	−1.86 (.93)**
Delegation size	.00 (.01)	−.00 (.01)
Vote share	−.00 (.02)	.04 (.02)**
Political context		
In majority?	−.25 (.45)	−.01 (.38)
Exclusive committee	−.58 (.35)*	−.67 (.33)**
New copartisans	.03 (.02)	.01 (.01)
101st Congress	1.56 (.90)	−.01 (.98)
102nd Congress	1.47 (.85)*	−.53 (.99)
103rd Congress	.87 (.77)	.60 (.72)
104th Congress	1.90 (.80)**	.71 (.78)
105th Congress	.13 (.84)	.50 (.67)
106th Congress	1.76 (.87)**	.13 (.81)
107th Congress	2.99 (.89)**	.03 (.86)
108th Congress	1.89 (.83)**	.81 (.70)
109th Congress	3.11 (.92)**	−.35 (.99)
Constant	4.68 (1.76)	−3.42 (1.61)
N		538
Pseudo R^2		.38

Note: The table presents multinomial logit coefficients with standard errors in parentheses. The dependent variable is each MC's style in the freshman term, and party soldiers are the baseline category. ** = $p < .05$; * = $p < .10$. N is less than 567 due to some unavailable data on covariates for some MCs.

cannot themselves directly tell us the magnitude of the effects. For example, how much does state legislative experience matter in explaining styles? To estimate these effect sizes, we use software called CLARIFY (see Tomz, Wittenberg, and King 2003) to calculate the probability of a freshman falling into each of the five styles when characteristics of the MC, his or her district, and the political context are varied. In doing so, we target those variables that distinguish district advocates and/or policy specialists from party soldiers, as this maps on to the hypotheses we developed above. These variables include state legislative experience, ideological extremity, district diversity, delegation partisanship, vote share, and having a seat on an exclusive committee.[15]

In our first set of calculations, we aim to set these variables at values that will maximize the probability of an MC being a party soldier. Recall that the assignment of MCs to styles is solely a function of their actual legislative behavior, so what the multinomial logit model does is to assess the extent to which characteristics of MCs and their districts are associated with their patterns of activity, and, hence, their styles. For our first scenario, we set experience at 0, ideological extremity at the 66th percentile, district diversity at 0 (i.e., a Sullivan Index score below the median), delegation partisanship at the 66th percentile, vote share at the 33rd percentile, and exclusive committee assignment at 1. All other variables in the model are set at their means. As shown in figure 4.2, a freshman MC with those characteristics has a 94.1% probability of being a party soldier (and a 1.6% probability of being a district advocate and a 4.2% probability of being a policy specialist). It is important to underscore that these probabilities are different from the "soft cluster proba-

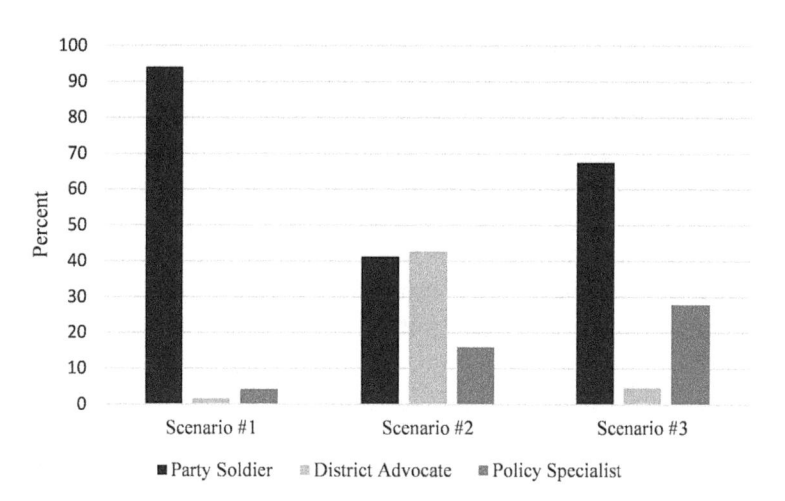

FIGURE 4.2 The effects of MC and district-level covariates on legislative styles
Note: This figure illustrates the magnitude of the effects uncovered in table 4.2. It demonstrates the likelihood of an MC adopting each of the three large styles when the characteristics of MCs and their districts are varied as described in the three scenarios in the text.

bilities" discussed in chapter 3. Those reflected how well an MC's pattern of activity fit into a particular style. These probabilities reflect how strongly characteristics of MCs and their districts are associated with their "hard" cluster assignments (i.e., the styles).

For our second scenario, we calculate the probabilities of falling into each stylistic category when these independent variables are flipped (i.e., switching the 0s to 1s and vice versa and the 33rd percentile values to the 66th percentile and vice versa). Here, we find that the probability of being a soldier drops by more than half—to just 41.3%. In this situation, a new MC has an about equal probability of being a district advocate (42.7%), and a 16% probability of being a policy specialist.

In essence, these scenarios compare an inexperienced, ideologically extreme MC from a demographically homogenous district and a homogenously partisan state who is moderately electorally secure and in possession of an exclusive committee assignment to an experienced, moderate MC from a heterogeneous district and state who is electorally secure and has relatively unprestigious committee assignments. These are not unrealistic combinations of characteristics. In the 106th Congress, for example, Lee Terry (R-NE) has scores on the independent variables equal to those in the first set of calculations, and based on his patterns of legislative activity, the clustering algorithm assigned him a 99% probability of being a party soldier (i.e., to use the language of chapter 3, his hard cluster assignment was a soldier, and his "maximum soft probability" value was .99 party soldier). In the 104th, Charles Bass (R-NH) has scores identical to those in model two, and based on his behavior in his first term, was classified as a district advocate (with a 46% soft probability of being an advocate, a 44% probability of being a soldier, and a 10% probability of being a policy specialist).

One point that jumps out from these comparisons is that, in setting the independent variables at values to minimize the likelihood of being a soldier, most of that probability is shifted to the district advocates category rather than the policy specialists category. As suggested by the results in tables 4.1 and 4.2, advocates and specialists tend to differ from one another in their ideological extremity. Advocates are generally moderates and specialists, like soldiers, tend to be more ideologically extreme. If we modify the second scenario slightly to set ideological extremity back to the 66th percentile, there is, as shown for scenario three, a 27.9% probability of an MC being a policy specialist (vs. a 67.5% chance of being a party soldier and just a 4.6% probability of being a district advocate).

EXPLAINING FRESHMAN STYLES 79

Therefore, we conclude that MCs' backgrounds and characteristics, and the context in which they find themselves, help to explain whether they adopt a party soldier, district advocate, or policy specialist style during their freshman terms. These factors also account for the rarer styles among freshmen—party builders and ambitious entrepreneurs. Table 4.3 presents these legislators.

The MCs who fall into these styles align well with our discussion from chapter 3 of the nature of the various types. The party builder group includes legislatively active party loyalists, many of whom embarked on long congressional careers and rose to positions of influence in their parties and chambers. To cite just a few examples, Janice Schakowsky (D-IL) became Chief Deputy Whip; Debbie Wasserman Schultz (D-FL),

TABLE 4.3 **Freshman party builders and ambitious entrepreneurs**

Name	Freshman congress	Style
Anna Eshoo (D-CA)	103rd	Party builder
Tom Coburn (R-OK)	104th	Party builder
Gerald Weller (R-IL)	104th	Party builder
Janice Schakowsky (D-IL)	106th	Party builder
Mike Thompson (D-CA)	106th	Party builder
Mike Rogers (R-MI)	107th	Party builder
Edward Schrock (R-VA)	107th	Party builder
Tom Price (R-GA)	109th	Party builder
Debbie Wasserman Schultz (D-FL)	109th	Party builder
Tom Campbell (R-GA)	101st	Ambitious entrepreneur
Charles Luken (D-OH)	102nd	Ambitious entrepreneur
Bernard Sanders (D-VT)	102nd	Ambitious entrepreneur
Dick Zimmer (R-NJ)	102nd	Ambitious entrepreneur
Michael Huffington (R-CA)	103rd	Ambitious entrepreneur
Thomas Davis III (R-VA)	104th	Ambitious entrepreneur
Jon Fox (R-PA)	104th	Ambitious entrepreneur
Enid Waldholtz (R-UT)	104th	Ambitious entrepreneur
Virgil Goode (D-VA)	105th	Ambitious entrepreneur
Darrell Issa (R-CA)	107th	Ambitious entrepreneur
Adam Schiff (D-CA)	107th	Ambitious entrepreneur
Rahm Emanuel (D-IL)	108th	Ambitious entrepreneur
Katherine Harris (R-FL)	108th	Ambitious entrepreneur
Dan Boren (D-OK)	109th	Ambitious entrepreneur
Bobby Jindal (R-LA)	109th	Ambitious entrepreneur
Allyson Schwartz (D-PA)	109th	Ambitious entrepreneur
Vern Buchanan (R-FL)	110th	Ambitious entrepreneur
Joe Donnelly (D-IN)	110th	Ambitious entrepreneur
Kirsten Gillibrand (D-NY)	110th	Ambitious entrepreneur
Ron Klein (D-FL)	110th	Ambitious entrepreneur

Note: This table lists those legislators who adopted a party builder or ambitious entrepreneur style in their freshman terms.

chair of the Democratic National Committee; Tom Price (R-GA), Chair of the Republican Study Committee, Republican Policy Committee, and now Budget Committee; and Mike Rogers (R-MI), Chair of the Permanent Select Committee on Intelligence. And, although Nancy Pelosi (D-CA) is not included in this list of new members, as her career began when she was elected mid-100th Congress in a special election (right before our data collection begins), in her first full term, the 101st, she was also a party builder.[16]

The ambitious entrepreneurs group includes a number of MCs known for their ambition and "outside-the-box" entrepreneurial activity, such as Rahm Emanuel (D-IL), who came to Congress after having served as Senior Advisor to Bill Clinton, and whose three terms in the House would include stints as Chair of the Democratic Congressional Campaign Committee and House Democratic Caucus. Emanuel would later leave Congress to serve as White House Chief of Staff to Barack Obama, and then would run, successfully, for mayor of Chicago. Katherine Harris (R-FL), who came to national attention in the 2000 election when as Secretary of State of Florida she oversaw the presidential election recount there, would serve two terms in the House before running (unsuccessfully) for Senate. Bobby Jindal (R-LA), as described in chapter 3, came to the House on the heels of a gubernatorial loss, and would serve just three years before running again for the governorship and securing a win.

The ambitious entrepreneurs group also includes its share of iconoclasts, such as Bernard Sanders (VT), who ran as an independent but caucused with the Democrats and became the runner up for the 2016 Democratic presidential nomination; Virgil Goode (VA), who entered Congress as a Democrat, but over the course of his career switched to an Independent and then, again, to the Republican party; and Michael Huffington (CA), businessman turned legislator turned film producer, who would serve just one term in the House before spending 28 million dollars (at the time, the most money spent in any nonpresidential campaign) in a failed bid for the US Senate (RealClearPolitics 2009).

These patterns all suggest that where MCs start out stylistically is both informative to scholars and potentially consequential for the trajectory of MCs' careers. Of course, not all freshman party builders (or ambitious entrepreneurs) go on to positions of great influence, and not all legislators who become influential start out as party builders. In the chapters to come, we explore the dynamics of style, success (electoral and legislative), and these career paths. Before doing so, however, we backtrack a bit to explore in more detail the relationships between MCs' prepolitical careers, their race and gender, and their status in the majority or minority party on their freshman styles.

Precongressional Careers and Style

In our analyses of freshman style in table 4.2, we focused on the effects of a single measure of MCs' precongressional careers—whether they had served in the state legislature. This was done both for the sake of parsimony and because the literature on congressional careers points to such experience as a particularly important factor driving MCs' behavior in their early years in DC (e.g., Berkman 1994). However, it is possible that other, nonpolitical career experiences also have a legacy in MCs' styles. For example, all else equal, MCs whose precongressional careers focused on a particular public policy area (e.g., medicine, education, or agriculture) might be more likely to be specialists. Similarly, those from military or business backgrounds, with experience working within a clear hierarchy, might be more likely to be party soldiers, as might MCs with the desire and aptitude for visibility that comes from a career in entertainment or the media. It is also possible that MCs with careers that were intimately linked to the district and its geography (e.g., farming) could be more likely to be district advocates.

As Francis (2014) explains, analyzing the effects of careers is made complicated by the fact that many, if not most, MCs have had more than one type of job in their precongressional lives. In exploring the links between style and careers, one could target the most proximate job experience, the longest-held one, all experiences, and so on. For simplicity, we consider all MCs who have any experience in a particular career category to have had that experience. Figure 4.3 presents the breadth of precongressional nonpolitical career experiences for freshmen in our sample. We focus on those occupations held by at least five percent of the sample. As shown, there is a wide range of such experiences, with the most common being the congressional "feeder occupations" of business and law (see Lawless and Fox 2005).

The question of interest is whether this variation in experience translates into differences in legislative style. We are agnostic about causality (i.e., do experiences themselves shape style, or are certain types of

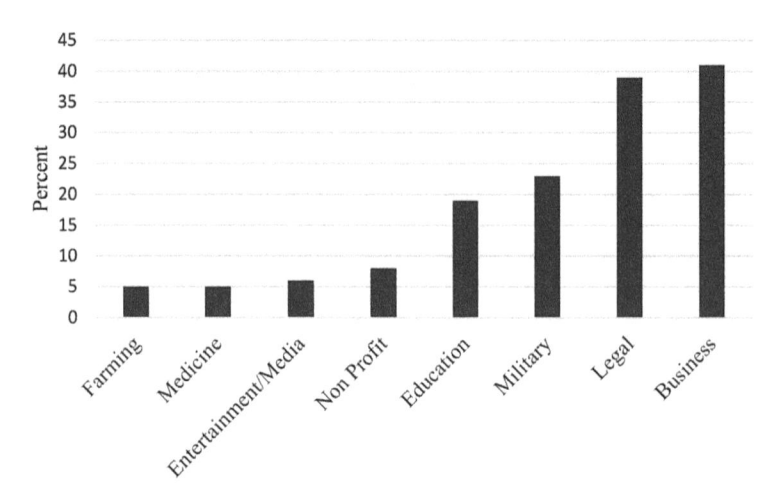

FIGURE 4.3 Nonpolitical career experiences of freshmen
Note: Proportion of freshman MCs in our sample who had experiences in each career area prior to entering Congress. The totals sum to more than 100 because most MCs have had experience in more than one area. We present only those occupations held by at least five percent of the sampled freshmen.

future MCs drawn to particular careers and, then, particular styles?) and instead are focused on ascertaining whether associations exist between experiences and style. As shown by the results in table 4.4, estimated using multinomial logit, the answer is largely no. As in earlier analyses, the dependent variable is each new MC's cluster assignment (i.e., his or her style). The independent variables are the nonpolitical experiences from figure 4.2 and a control for former state legislative experience, since that effect may swamp the influence of other nonpolitical experiences. We see that there are some differences for the district advocates category (relative, once again, to the party soldiers baseline). MCs with a background in entertainment and the media are, as expected, less likely to be beneath-the-radar district advocates. Contrary to our initial predictions, however, those with military experience are actually less likely to be soldiers and more likely to be advocates. Upon further investigation, this is due in large part to the fact that those freshmen with military backgrounds are more ideologically moderate than their nonmilitary peers (mean absolute value of NOMINATE scores of .31 vs. .35; $t = 3.0$, $p < .05$), a result that holds even when the sample is split by party. If we

TABLE 4.4 **Nonpolitical career experiences and freshman style**

	District advocates	Policy specialists
Farming	.60 (.47)	.51 (.63)
Medicine	−.40 (.52)	−.64 (.79)
Entertainment/media	−1.02 (.56)*	−.25 (.57)
Nonprofit	.23 (.38)	.20 (.49)
Education	−.25 (.28)	−.54 (.40)
Military	.54 (.24)**	−.03 (.35)
Legal	−.07 (.26)	−.07 (.34)
Business	−.08 (.25)	−.24 (.33)
Former state legislator	−.13 (.21)	.26 (.28)
Constant	−.70 (.27)	−1.48 (.35)
N	518	
Pseudo R^2	.02	

Note: The table presents multinomial logit coefficients with standard errors in parentheses. The dependent variable is each MC's style in the freshman term, and party soldiers are the baseline category. The analysis is limited to the three major styles among freshmen (i.e., omitting party builders and ambitious entrepreneurs). ** = $p < .05$; * = $p < .10$

include a control for ideological extremity, the relationship between military experience and adopting a district advocate style disappears.

For policy specialists, we see no relationships with nonpolitical careers, a pattern that holds no matter how we conduct the analyses (e.g., at the bivariate level, multivariate analyses with different sets of controls, and so on). Accordingly, we feel comfortable concluding that nonpolitical careers have little direct influence on style.[17] This does not mean that they have no relationship with the *content* of MCs' activity. For example, in their first terms, former teachers introduce more bills on education (.72 introductions on average, compared to .39, $t = 3.5$, $p < .05$), and those with medical experience introduce more on health (1.15 intros vs. .39, $t = 4.1$, $p < .05$). However, this does not translate into broader differences in the propensity to be, say, a policy specialist. Instead, these overarching stylistic choices are more a function of factors such as ideology, political context, and the nature of MCs' districts.

Race, Gender, and Freshman Style

Another dynamic that warrants further investigation is the relationship between MCs' demographic characteristics and their stylistic choices. Table 4.2 demonstrates that, after controls are taken into account, freshman styles have no relationship with race and limited relationship with gender. In the raw data, however, we observed substantial differences across men and women and members of different racial and ethnic groups. Because these differences bear on our understanding of the nature of constituent representation, we explore them here in more detail.

Between the 101st and 110th Congresses, seventy new MCs from underrepresented groups were elected to Congress, including forty-two African Americans, twenty-three Latinos, and five Asian Americans. Across this time span, ninety-two women were elected as well, three-quarters of them Caucasian and one-quarter from racial/ethnic minority groups. These overall numbers represent a substantial increase in the presence of both women and people of color during the congresses we study. In the 101st (1989–1990), women comprised just 6% of representatives and minority MCs held 9% of seats. By the 110th Congress (2007–2008), those proportions had risen to 16% and 15%, respectively. Thus, while these groups do not enjoy levels of representation that are proportional to their percentage of the voting population, the patterns reflect a slow move in that direction.

The arrival of more women and people of color in Congress spawned a large literature in political science that sought to explore whether these MCs represent and legislate differently than their white male colleagues. The general conclusion to come from this research is that, for all MCs, party and ideology are the most important factors driving behavior, but that race and gender influence the content of the policies legislators pursue and their orientation toward representation (Fenno 2003; Grose 2011; Swers 2002; Tate 2003). While large differences did not emerge between the styles of men and women and underrepresented minorities and others in the multivariate analyses earlier in this chapter, we may see such patterns emerge at lower levels of aggregation, as is done in figure 4.4. This figure presents the proportion of men and women and members of various racial/ethnic groups who fall into each of the five styles as freshmen.

The biggest difference to jump out from this figure is that there are substantially fewer women and MCs from underrepresented groups in the district advocates category—12% of women and 14% of minority MCs start out as advocates, as compared to 27% of men and 27% of Caucasian MCs. The overall difference for race is driven by the gap between African Americans and Caucasians—just 7% of new African American representatives adopt a district advocate style.[18]

EXPLAINING FRESHMAN STYLES

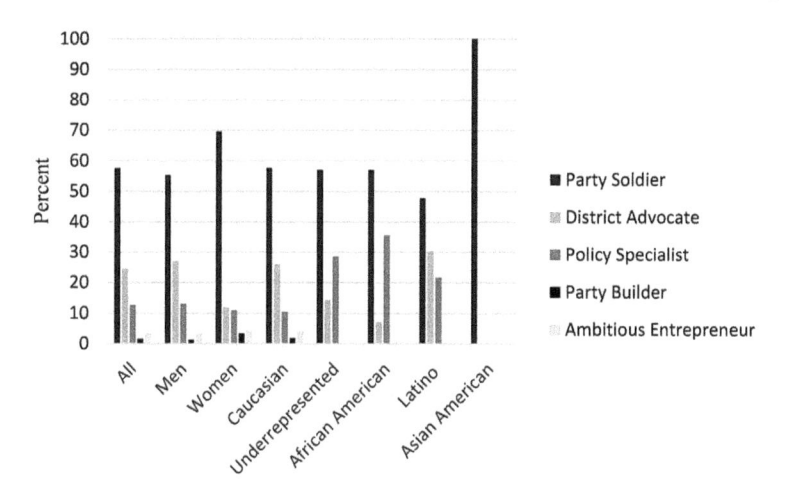

FIGURE 4.4 Freshman styles by race and gender

Where, then, do the women and African American freshmen who are not district advocates go? We find that women and men are policy specialists at about the same rate, but there are considerably more party soldiers among women (70% vs. 55%; $t = 2.5, p < .05$).[19] For African Americans, it is the opposite, with significantly more policy specialists—36% of African American freshmen are specialists, compared to just 13% of Caucasians ($t = 4.7, p < .05$).[20] Latino freshmen are also more likely to be specialists—22% of them start out in that style ($t = 1.7, p < .10$). Importantly, these differences do not go away over the course of MCs' careers. Among the full sample, African American MCs are less likely than Caucasians to be district advocates (9.7% vs. 28.0%; $t = 7.4, p < .05$) and African Americans and Latinos are more likely to be policy specialists (49.9% vs. 28.9%; $t = 9.8, p < .05$). The same pattern holds for women—they are less likely than men to be district advocates (19.4% vs. 27.1%; $t = 3.6; p < .05$) and, when we look beyond just the freshman term, are more likely to be policy specialists (38.1% vs. 30.6%; $t = 3.4; p < .05$).

Importantly, these differences disappear once we include controls, so race and gender do not themselves exert an independent effect on style. Instead, the most likely scenario is that women and members of underrepresented groups differ from men and white MCs on other variables that also affect style. Ideology, and its interaction with party affiliation, is the most obvious culprit. As background, it is important to note that there are substantial differences in the numbers of women and MCs of color by party. Among the freshmen in our sample, there are sixty-two Democratic women versus thirty-two Republican women and sixty-two Democratic African Americans, Latinos, and Asian Americans, compared to just eight Republicans from underrepresented groups.

If we split the sample by party and investigate differences in ideology, we find that, among Democrats in our sample, women and minority MCs are considerably more ideologically extreme (i.e., liberal) than their male and white copartisans. On average, women receive scores about .04 higher than men, and MCs from underrepresented groups have scores about .14 higher (where the mean absolute value NOMINATE score is .31 and the standard deviation is .14). We know from the results earlier in this chapter that district advocates are less likely to be ideologues, and so it therefore makes sense that fewer Democratic women and minority MCs adopt that style.

For Republicans, the pattern is different—women are more likely to be moderates (with scores about .07 lower than men), but there is no difference between minority and white MCs. And among Republicans, there are fewer differences in the distribution of style by group. Male and female freshmen adopt the various styles at the same rates, and new Republican MCs of color are actually more likely to be district advocates—four of the eight adopt this style.[21] These two points—that there are fewer Republican women and minority MCs, and that those who do win seats differ less in ideology and style from their male and white colleagues than do their Democratic counterparts—may actually be linked. Thomsen (2015), for example, argues that the decision to run for office is influenced by one's level of ideological conformity with the party. Because Republicans in Congress have displayed less ideological variation than Democrats (see also Bonica 2013), fewer women select in to running for office, and those who do are more likely to be similar to their male peers stylistically.

We conclude, therefore, that while race and gender are not themselves often significant predictors of where legislators start out stylistically, there are differences in the distributions of style across groups. These differences resonate with our understanding of descriptive and collective representation, and of the role women and minorities play in Congress.

Majority Status and Freshman Style

The final factor to explore in more detail is the relationship between partisan majority versus minority status and freshman style. Earlier, we hypothesized that whether an MC entered Congress as a member of the ruling party or the opposition could affect style, as majority status shapes party strategy and the enticements that the leadership has to distribute. However, in the aggregate analyses, we found no effect of such status—membership in the majority was not a significant predictor of being a district advocate or policy specialist versus a party soldier.

Majority status is important enough, though, that it warrants further investigation. One possibility is that there are different patterns for majority and minority status for Democrats versus Republicans, linked, perhaps, to differences in party structure and centralization (i.e., the conventional wisdom that Democrats are more of a big umbrella, while the Republican leadership, particularly when the party is in the majority, holds tighter on the reins). However, when we test for an interaction with party by splitting the sample by Democrats/Republicans and rerunning the analyses from table 4.2, we once again find no effect of majority status. Indeed, this null finding is robust to a variety of specifications of the model.

Another possibility to consider is that status itself does not matter for freshman style, but that *changes* in majority control do. For example, new MCs swept into office as part of a majority change where the party is front and center may be more likely to be party soldiers. This could be due both to a selection effect (potential candidates with a propensity toward the soldier style are more likely to run and win in those contexts) and to an opportunity structure that rewards new members who commit to being part of the party team. Recall, for example, freshman David McIntosh (R-IN), whose party-centered approach in the 104th Congress won him the respect of his Republican peers and the attention of the leadership. In contrast, MCs elected to office in a year when their party loses the majority may hunker down as district advocates, attending to their district but otherwise staying below the radar. To assess these hypotheses, we split the sample by party and calculated the distribution of styles for freshman Democrats and Republicans in each of the 101st–110th Congresses. These are presented in figure 4.5.

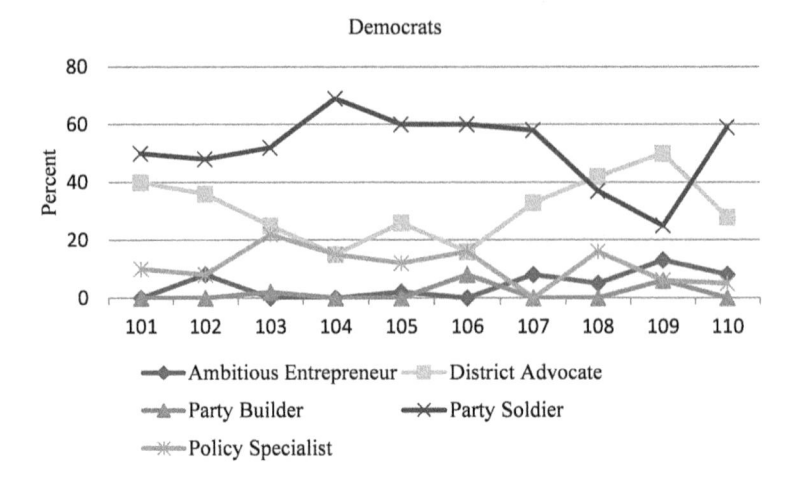

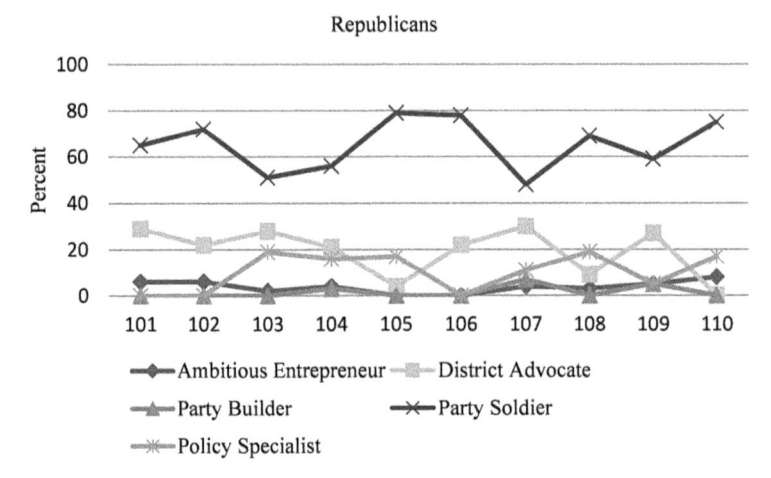

FIGURE 4.5 Distribution of freshman styles by congress
Note: Proportion of new MCs from each party who adopted each of the five styles in each congress.

The most important result to come from these figures is the lack of one—there is no clear pattern to be discerned. We do see considerable up and down movement in the proportion of styles from congress to congress, but some of this is due to a relatively low N (i.e., for eight of the twenty party-congress observations, there are fewer than twenty new freshmen included in the calculations). If we compare the distribution of styles in the 104th Congress (when the Republicans won the majority for the first time since the 83rd Congress) to the 103rd, there is a relatively steady proportion of party soldiers and district advocates for the newly-in-power Republicans. The predicted spike in soldiers and concomitant drop-off in district advocates does occur, but it is delayed, not happening until the 105th Congress. For Democrats, we see the same pattern, but their changes happen in the 104th. Thus, contrary to expectations, the shift to Republican control brought a (brief) surge in soldiers and decline in advocates, but for both parties. A similar pattern holds in the 110th Congress, when Democrats took back the majority. For both Democrats and Republicans, there were more party soldiers and fewer district advocates than in the congress before.

What might explain this pattern? Again, as was the case with careers and race and gender, it is important to underscore that there is not an *independent* effect of majority status on style. This holds even with tinkering with the model (for instance, replacing the congress dummies in table 4.2 with an indicator for "new majority," or removing the control for the number of copartisans). Nonetheless, there is some evidence in the raw data that majority shifts bring about more freshman party soldiers and fewer district advocates from both the winning and losing parties. This may be due to an increase in the salience of the party team during times of transition, as the newcomers to the victorious party set about governing, and as the freshmen in the losing party fill in the gaps left by their recently departed colleagues.

Conclusions

The patterns for precongressional careers, race and gender, and majority status reflect the broader story to emerge from the analyses in this chapter. Our theory of the origins of style suggested that they should be predictable, and indeed they are. Whether an MC starts out his or her congressional career as a party soldier, district advocate, policy specialist, or, more rarely, party builder or ambitious entrepreneur is affected by his or her political experience, personal characteristics, district composition, and by the political context of his or her freshman term. Importantly, though, none of these is deterministic. For example, it is not the case that all members of a particular demographic group adopt the same style, that MCs given an exclusive committee assignment always become party soldiers, or that majority and minority party MCs differ greatly in their styles. Even ideology, perhaps the most important covariate in explaining style, accounts for just about one-quarter of the variation in freshman styles.

Therefore, styles reflect individual choices. Even similar individuals facing similar contexts may sometimes make different decisions about how to proceed with their jobs as legislators. As we have seen, the initial set of decisions MCs make about how to behave manifest themselves in their freshman styles—what "kind" of legislator they are. Although we expect these styles to be relatively sticky, it is also the case that as legislators' careers progress, they face new choices and changing contexts, and these may lead to shifts in style. In the next chapter, we move beyond the freshman term to explore the dynamics of these transitions.

CHAPTER FIVE

Transitions in Style

The thing that will keep me in the job until I get defeated is that I cannot conceive of any place on earth where you can learn more about more different things. To me, it is the most fascinating educational institution on all subjects, with, curiously enough, a fair amount of opportunity for the individual to decide what he is going to specialize in next in terms of learning. — An MC explaining to Charles Clapp the appeal of a long career in the House (1963, 490)

West Virginia representatives Alan Mollohan and Nick Rahall had a lot in common. Both were Democrats, born within a few years of each other, and each arrived in Congress in the late 1970s or early 1980s to embark on what would be long careers in the House of Representatives. By the time our data collection begins (in 1989, the 101st Congress), both were well ensconced in their jobs, with Mollohan pursuing local issues through his seat on the Appropriations Committee and Rahall doing the same through his seat on Interior and Public Works[1] (Barone and Ujifusa 1989). Given these similarities, it is not surprising that they demonstrate some similar stylistic tendencies, both serving for long stretches as district advocates. However, while Mollohan maintained a consistent approach across the twenty years in which we follow MCs, never veering from that style, Rahall displayed more variability, appearing as a party soldier in the 101st Congress, switching to the district advocate style for the next six terms, and then, in the 108th–110th Congresses, oscillating between the policy specialist and district advocate styles.

These transitions in legislative style (or lack thereof) are important to understand, both for the insights they offer into the origins of style and for setting the groundwork for assessing its effects on MCs' career paths. Throughout this book, we have argued that legislative styles are characterized by competing forces of stability and change. On one hand, we expect them to be rather sticky. Once MCs have established patterns of behavior and a style, it is likely that habit and the factors that led them to adopt the style initially will produce high levels of consistency across time. On the other hand, legislative life is not static. The electoral and legislative context in which MCs find themselves may change, particularly over a long period of service, and we anticipate that MCs adapt to these changing circumstances, learn from their successes and mistakes, and evolve in their outlook as their careers progress. These shifts in perspective may, in turn, induce transitions in style.

To better grasp the dual dynamics of stability and change, in this chapter we address a variety of interrelated questions about stylistic shifts and patterns in style across legislators' service in the House of Representatives. For example, when in MCs' careers are changes most likely? Does where MCs start out explain their stylistic trajectory across their careers? What are the characteristics of MCs who are the most and least likely to adapt their styles across time? What sorts of shifts in context bring about transitions (i.e., Majority status, changes in electoral security, new responsibilities in the chamber, or a natural progression across time)? Do transitions from one style to another tend to be gradual or abrupt?

Together, the answers to these questions offer a richer depiction of legislative styles, enable us to further test the implications of our theory of style, and provide the basis for our explorations in the chapters to come of the electoral, legislative, and career effects of legislators' stylistic choices. We begin by establishing in more detail the extent of stability versus change in MCs' styles across their time in the House of Representatives.

Stability and Change

This is not the first time we have addressed consistency in style. In chapter 3, where our focus was more aggregate in nature, we demonstrated that similar proportions of MCs adopted each style across congresses (i.e., to show that styles were not time-bound), and that, at the individual level, the amount of stability from one congress to the next varied by style. District advocates, for example, almost always remain district advocates in the next congress, whereas party soldiers and ambitious entrepreneurs are the most prone to change.

TRANSITIONS IN STYLE 93

Here, we offer some additional investigations of stability, focusing less on the relative consistency of the five legislative styles, and more on patterns across MCs. Overall, we find that over three-quarters of MCs (77%) maintain their styles in successive congresses (i.e., from congress t to congress $t + 1$). In any given congress, most MCs behave as they had done in the recent past, and, as a result, they tend to display the same styles. As shown in figure 5.1, which targets the proportion of MCs who change styles by congress (i.e., the 101st to the 102nd, 102nd to 103rd, and so on), this pattern is fairly constant across the congresses we study. These patterns also indicate that majority shifts in control (following the 103rd and 109th Congresses) do not appear to have a consistent effect on changes in styles. We see a relatively low proportion of shifts when the Republicans took control in the 104th (the relevant bar is the one for the 103rd Congress, as it reflects shifts going into the 104th), but a relatively high percentage of transitions when the Democrats took back control in the 110th Congress. Given the importance of majority shifts and partisan changes, we explore their effects in more detail later in this chapter.

Next, we examine whether consistency in style varies across the stages of MCs' careers. For example, we might expect more transitions in style

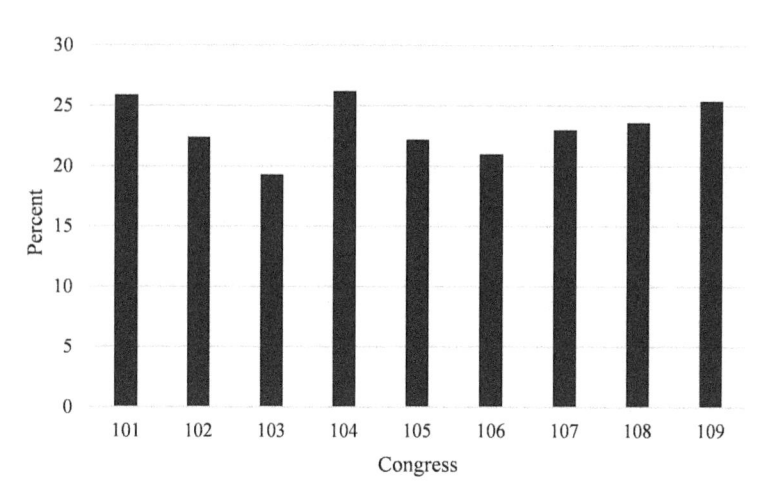

FIGURE 5.1 Transitions in style by congress
Note: Proportion of MCs in each congress who shifted to a different style in the next congress. Analyses are necessarily limited to MCs who served in at least two consecutive congresses.

in legislators' early years in Congress as they learn the ropes and settle in. In figure 5.2, which presents the proportion of shifts in style by seniority cohorts (i.e., from the first to second term, second to third term, etc.), we see that indeed the highest proportion of changes in style occurs between the freshman and sophomore terms, where close to one-third of MCs experience a transition. This is not surprising, given how many freshmen begin as party soldiers and then move on to another style. After that initial transition, shifts in style are relatively stable, at about 20% of MCs per congress. For the most senior legislators (the 10% of observations with service greater than twenty years), transitions are again more common, at close to 30%. We speculate that this may be due to changes in patterns of behavior as MCs gear up for a run for higher office or begin thinking seriously about retirement. Regardless, style appears the most unstable for very junior and very senior members.[2]

For our final assessment of overall stability, we investigate the consistency in individual MCs' styles across their careers. Specifically, for each MC, we consider the number of congresses served (out of the ten possible in our data set), the number of congress-to-congress transitions in style that occur, and the total number of styles displayed by the MC.[3] Figure 5.3 presents these patterns. For both, we limit our analyses to

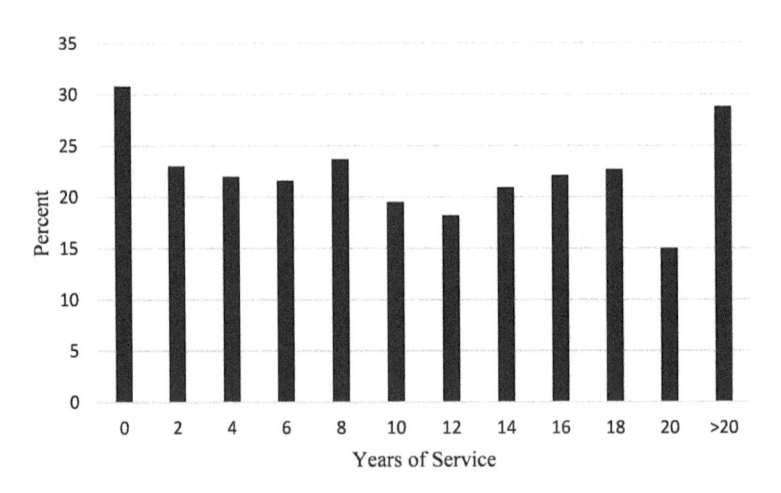

FIGURE 5.2 Transitions in style by seniority
Note: Proportion of MCs by years of service (0 = first term, 2 = second term, etc.) who shifted to a different style in the next congress.

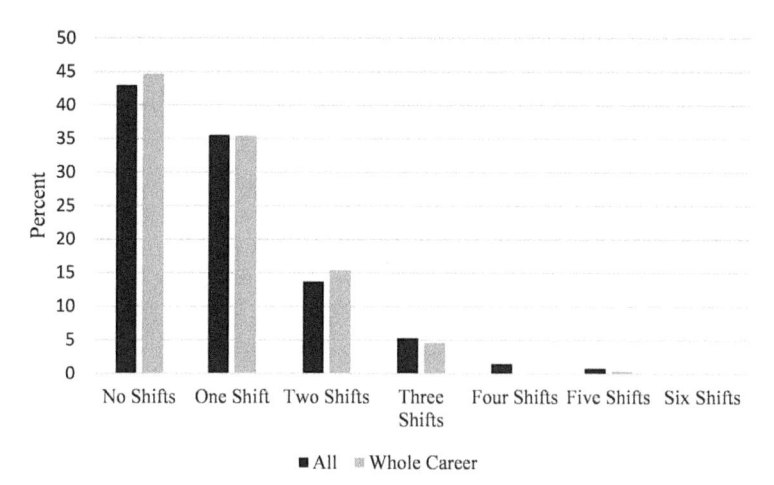

FIGURE 5.3 Styles across MCs' careers
Note: This figure presents, for MCs who served more than one term, the total number of shifts in style that occurred for that MC and the total number of different styles he or she displayed. $N = 847$ for "all" MCs and 240 for "whole career" MCs.

MCs who served more than one congress during the period of study because, otherwise, no transitions are possible. We also calculate these values separately for two groups of MCs. The first is the entire sample—the 847 legislators who served more than one term (out of 1,011 total MCs). The second is an important subgroup—those for whom we capture the entire career of House service. In other words, these are MCs who began their careers in the House no earlier than the 101st Congress and who ended their service before the beginning of the 111th Congress. Out of the 302 MCs who meet these criteria, 240 served more than one term. We include the comparisons between this subgroup and all MCs in our data set to assess the extent to which our sample, which is necessarily both left-censored (some MCs entered Congress before our data collection begins) and right-censored (some MCs continued their careers after our efforts cease), adequately approximates the important dynamics of MCs' careers.[4]

These patterns are revealing. They demonstrate that the congress-to-congress stability in style we discussed earlier also applies when looking over the longer term—about 43% of MCs who serve more than one term never change style, and this is true whether we look at all MCs in our sample or just those for whom we capture the entirety of their careers. But also as expected, styles are not completely static over the long term. Most MCs experience at least one shift and, hence, more than one style. However, the majority of "shifters" will have just one transition, and only 5–7% will experience more than two.[5] The results also provide some evidence that MCs who do shift a lot tend to be switching back and forth between a small set of styles (e.g., a la Nick Rahall from the opening example), as the range for total number of styles is less than that for total number of shifts. Overall, we find that about 85% of MCs display just one or two styles across their careers in the House.

All of the patterns, then, are in line with the expectations of our theory of style. Styles are generally quite stable, no matter how we measure them. Nonetheless, for most MCs, changes do occur over the long run, and understanding how and why these transitions in style happen is a central piece of the puzzle. In what follows, we explore this phenomenon from a variety of different angles, beginning with the first potential transition, and the most common phase of MCs' careers for a shift in style to occur, from the freshman to the sophomore term.

Transitions from the Freshman Term

In moving from their first to second terms, legislators face an important choice: Will they continue along the course they had set for themselves as freshmen, or will they steer a new one? Their own predilections, a sense that their stylistic choices have worked for them electorally and legislatively, and sheer force of habit lead many to maintain their styles going forward. For others, perhaps especially the large contingent who begin as party soldiers, the shift to the sophomore term creates an opportunity for change.

The potential impetuses behind such shifts are varied. Some MCs who began as gung-ho team players may become disillusioned with their party leadership and, moving to the sophomore term, choose to devote their efforts beyond the party, even if they remain reliable partisans in their roll call voting. Others, having had an introduction to party life, may decide to invest further, becoming party builders. Still others, having bidden their time as freshmen, may receive the committee assignment they really want and settle in for the long term as policy specialists. And others, having learned more about their districts and constituencies, may come to believe that their key to a long career in the House is to adopt a district advocate style.

In addition, changes in style may not be entirely a function of conscious decisions made by representatives, and may be due as well to the natural evolution that comes with seniority. With the passage of time, some of the MCs we observe as freshmen may become more legislatively active because they know how the system works (and may have bills from the previous congress ready to place in the hopper). Others may become more selective in these efforts, understanding better what is and is not likely to be successful. Experienced MCs may have the capacity to give more campaign funds to copartisans because being a known quantity makes their fund-raising efforts more effective, or because they have a better sense of their own levels of security and what they need to spend to retain their seats. They may also gain positions of power that affect the opportunities open to them and their colleagues' interactions with them. These factors could all affect their behavior, and, hence, the styles MCs display.

As a first step in investigating the freshman-to-sophomore transition, we calculate, for freshmen in each style, the proportion of MCs with that style who adopt it and each of the others in their sophomore terms. These results are presented in table 5.1. Over 90% of the new MCs in our sample returned for a second term,[6] though our N is lower than that because these analyses also exclude MCs who were freshmen in the 110th (since that is the final congress of our data collection and we do not have data on their styles in the next term).

Some interesting patterns emerge. First, the district advocate and policy specialist styles are very stable. MCs who begin their careers in those styles overwhelmingly maintain them into the sophomore term. The other styles are less so. A substantial proportion (29%) of freshman party

TABLE 5.1 **Freshman to sophomore styles**

	Party soldier	District advocate	Policy specialist	Party builder	Ambitious entrepreneur
Party soldier ($N = 262$)	57.6	3.4	29.0	9.1	.8
District advocate ($N = 115$)	2.6	90.4	1.8	2.6	2.6
Policy specialist ($N = 60$)	0	8.3	90.0	1.7	0
Party builder ($N = 9$)	11.1	0	33.3	55.6	0
Ambitious entrepreneur ($N = 13$)	15.4	30.8	0	23.1	30.8

Note: This table presents the proportion of freshman MCs from each style who adopted each of the five styles in their sophomore terms. $N = 459$.

soldiers become policy specialists in the next congress (though, interestingly, it is a one way street, as NO freshman policy specialists become sophomore party soldiers), and about one in ten soldiers will become a party builder. We also see substantial movement for the freshman party builders and ambitious entrepreneurs. The majority of party builders remain so, though others become either policy specialists or party soldiers (and none become district advocates or ambitious entrepreneurs). In contrast, freshman ambitious entrepreneurs are spread across four styles (all but policy specialists) as sophomores, and, in fact, only a minority of them remain as ambitious entrepreneurs.

To ascertain what becomes of freshmen stylistically, it is useful to track them over the longer term. There are two potential dynamics going on—the propensity for MCs who start in a particular style to stay in the House or exit (voluntarily or involuntarily), and the stylistic paths of those who remain. We (mostly) bracket the first dynamic for the time being, as the relationship between styles, electoral success, and progressive ambition is the subject of chapters to come. For now, we focus on patterns in MCs' styles, highlighting the first five terms (ten years) of their careers.[7]

We begin, once again, with a comparative assessment of stability. As illustrated in Figure 5.4, by the fifth term in office, about one-third of those who began as district advocates will still be in the House of Representatives, and 71% of those will still be district advocates.[8] Fifty-four percent of freshman policy specialists will remain, and 82% of them will still be policy specialists. Forty-three percent of freshman party soldiers remain, but just 17% of them will be party soldiers. Among the two rarest styles for freshmen, four of the nine builders will remain in the House, two of them builders and two of them policy specialists. Four of the thirteen ambitious entrepreneurs remain as well, with one party builder, one ambitious entrepreneur, one party soldier, and one policy specialist each.

Perhaps the most obvious pattern to jump out here is the desertion of party soldiers from that style. Ten years in, the vast majority of freshman district advocates and policy specialists maintain those styles, but fewer than one in five soldiers do. In the short term, many freshman soldiers will become policy specialists. As discussed above, 29% will make that leap in their sophomore terms, and they will be joined by an additional 15% in the third term. By the fifth term, over half (52%) of those

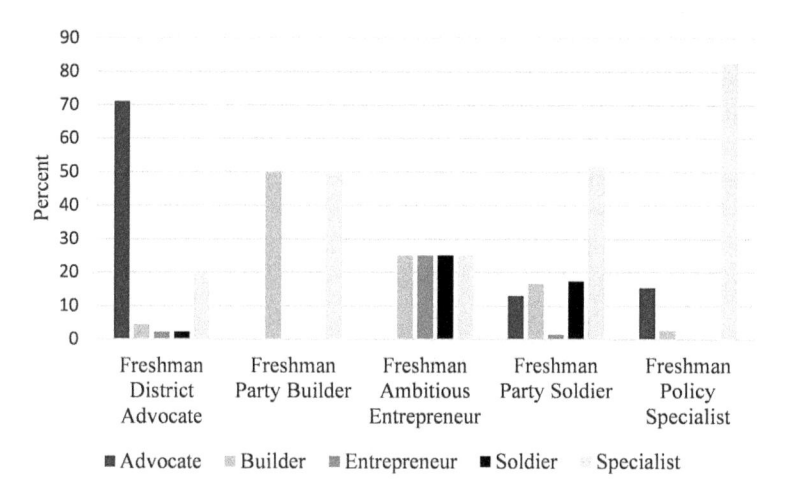

FIGURE 5.4 The distribution of (former) freshmen's styles in their fifth terms
Note: The figure presents, for the group of MCs who had each style as freshmen and were still in office in the fifth term, the distribution of their styles in that term. $N = 231$

who started as party soldiers will be policy specialists, a proportion that holds across the next several terms.

At the same time, and perhaps less obviously, soldiers are also becoming party builders. By the fifth term, 17% of party soldiers have become builders—the movers and shakers in their parties.[9] In comparison, only 3% of those who began as policy specialists are party builders by year ten, as are just 4% of those who began as district advocates. Put another way, 89 of the 567 freshman MCs in our sample will demonstrate the party builder style in at least one congress (of the ten we observe). Over two-thirds of those eventual party builders began as party soldiers.

These patterns provide strong evidence that where MCs start out matters. Freshman styles enable us to predict styles down the road. In particular, the decision to begin as a policy specialist or district advocate often indicates both a short-term commitment to that particular style as well as a longer term indicator of the stylistic path an MC's career will take. The party soldier style, on the other hand, is clearly a way station, but an informative one. Freshmen who begin there generally take one of two routes—they either settle down in the policy specialist style, or they begin the path to becoming a party builder. Thus, far from being a dumping ground for unclassifiable freshmen, the party soldier style is an incubator for future styles.

From Freshman Soldiers to . . .

To explore more rigorously soldiers' styles going into the sophomore term, we examine a variety of characteristics of MCs and the political context that might explain the choice to remain a soldier or to transition to another style. Thus, our question is what variables are associated with the tendency of freshman soldiers to remain so, or to shift to the party builder, policy specialist, or district advocate style in the sophomore term. We estimate our model, presented in table 5.2, using multinomial logit, where the sample is limited to freshman soldiers and the dependent variable is their style in the sophomore term, with remaining a soldier the baseline. We omit soldiers-turned-ambitious-entrepreneurs from these analyses, as only two freshmen made that shift.

In this and our models of transitions in style to follow, we target four categories of variables. The first is the level of fit an MC had with his or her style in congress t. Recall from our discussion in chapters 2 and 3 that, based on an MC's patterns of behavior in a particular congress (i.e., his or her scores on the indices of legislative activity), our clustering algorithm calculates for each MC the probability that he or she falls into each cluster. MCs are then assigned to the cluster (aka style) for which their probability was highest. We concluded that MCs' fit into their clusters is generally quite good. Across all observations in the sample, the mean "maximum soft probability" is .87.

However, there is variation in fit across individuals (maximum soft probabilities ranging from .33 to 1), and this variation may affect the probability of a transition in style in the next term, with lower levels of fit producing higher likelihood of a shift. Take, for example, Arizonans J. D. Hayworth and John Shadegg, both freshmen in the 104th Congress. Based on his activity in the 104th, the clustering algorithm assigned Hayworth to the party soldiers cluster with a probability of 1.0. Shadegg, while also a party soldier, fit into that cluster with a .72 probability, and had a .27 probability of being a policy specialist. In the 105th Congress, Hayworth remained a party soldier, but Shadegg became a policy specialist.[10]

Thus, some transitions in style may be the result of MCs moving away from a style for which they were not a solid fit (i.e., those MCs who demonstrated hybrid styles, with relatively high soft probabilities for more than one stylistic category).[11] Indeed, there is a significant difference in the maximum soft probability scores for MCs who maintain their styles from one congress to the next and those who change (.90 vs. .78; $t = 19.1$, $p < .05$). To give a more concrete example, among the nine freshman party builders, all returned to Congress for a sophomore term, and five of those remained builders. If we rank those nine by their soft probabilities in the freshman term (i.e., their relative level of fit within the party builder style), those who remained so in the sophomore term—Mike Rogers (R-MI), Debbie Wasserman Schultz (D-FL), Tom Price (R-GA), and Jerry Weller (R-IL)—occupy four of the top five slots, with freshman builder probabilities of .96–.99. Thus, MCs who were "strong" party builders as freshmen remained so as sophomores, while those with lower soft probabilities were more likely to transition to new styles.

The second category of predictors of shifts from the freshman soldier style consists of characteristics of MCs themselves. We include their ideological extremity, partisan identification, political experience, age, race, and gender. We expect that the covariates that explained initial styles for new MCs might also explain their choices going into the sophomore term. For example, in chapter 4 we saw that ideologues were less likely to be district advocates. Does the same pattern hold for transitions? Among freshman soldiers, does ideological extremity (negatively) affect the probability of transitioning to the district advocate style?

Third, we consider the context in which MCs find themselves at congress t (in this case, the freshman term)—their vote share going into that term, whether they held a leadership position or had a seat on an exclusive committee, and whether their party was in the majority or minority. This enables us to take into account the fact that, in general, security and status may affect the probability of shifting between clusters.

Fourth, and finally, we include indicators of *change* in context from congress t to congress $t + 1$. For example, did an MC gain or lose vote share (relative to the previous election),[12] gain a leadership position[13] or exclusive committee assignment,[14] change committees,[15] did his or her party gain or lose the majority, and was his or her district the subject of substantial redistricting?[16] Our general expectation is that such changes in context may comprise significant enough "shocks" to break at least some MCs from their habitual patterns of activity and induce changes in style.

Accounting for Second-Term Shifts

The results in table 5.2 provide support for these predictions. Beginning with characteristics of individuals, we see that, among freshman soldiers, ideological extremity decreases the probability that an MC will become a district advocate in the next term. This suggests that the sophomore term may bring some "corrections," as, for example, when ideological moderates move to the more copacetic district advocate style.

We also observe that, among soldiers, young age (under thirty-five

TABLE 5.2 **Explaining freshman soldiers' sophomore styles**

	Party builders	Policy specialists	District advocates
MC characteristics			
Ideological extremity	−.41 (2.88)	1.05 (1.64)	−14.11 (7.26)**
Democrat	.61 (.76)	.92 (.46)**	−3.43 (1.91)*
Under 35	1.35 (.78)*	−.12 (.70)	1.22 (1.68)
Over 55	.36 (.76)	.16 (.50)	.37 (1.41)
Woman	.61 (.61)	.02 (.43)	1.80 (1.22)
Ethnic/racial minority	−.07 (.91)	−.62 (.61)	.49 (1.70)
Freshman context			
Leadership position	1.61 (1.49)	1.76 (1.07)	−11.14 (2127.83)
Exclusive committee	−.33 (.61)	−.13 (.38)	−1.53 (1.30)
Vote share	.06 (.03)*	.06 (.02)**	.04 (.08)
In majority	.21 (.67)	−.10 (.42)	2.55 (1.89)
Sophomore context			
Gained leadership	1.61 (.82)*	−.35 (.61)	1.69 (1.12)
Gained exclusive	.38 (.72)	.81 (.49)*	−.35 (1.35)
Changed committee	.13 (.54)	−.56 (.37)	−.032 (1.11)
Gained vote share	1.52 (.63)**	.44 (.38)	3.57 (1.94)*
Lost vote share	1.11 (1.10)	.36 (.55)	1.86 (2.37)
Gained majority	−.033 (.98)	−.58 (.71)	−13.47 (665.73)
Lost majority	−2.32 (1.39)*	−1.23 (.66)	.43 (1.62)
Redistricted	−.05 (.68)	−.14 (.43)	.20 (1.32)
Freshman style fit	−1.71 (2.13)	−2.12 (1.34)	−11.34 (3.96)*
Constant	−5.83 (2.80)	−3.14 (1.76)	5.11 (6.29)
N		260	
Pseudo R^2		.18	

Note: The table presents multinomial logit coefficients with standard errors in parentheses. The dependent variable is each freshman soldier's style in the sophomore term, and party soldiers are the baseline category. We omit those who became ambitious entrepreneurs from the analyses due to the very low N.
** = $p < .05$; * = $p < .10$

years at first election) is associated with a quick transition to the party builders style. This may be because these young party soldiers are ambitious about their future in the party and act accordingly, and/or because senior party leaders identify promising new legislators as future party leaders (formal or informal) and provide them with opportunities that shape their behavior, bringing them in line with the party builders style.

Democratic soldiers are also more likely than Republicans to transition to the policy specialist style and are less prone to becoming district advocates. This mirrors the (small) overall partisan differences in styles discussed in chapters 2 and 3. We see no overall effect of race or gender on freshman soldiers' transitions to the sophomore term.

The results for context are perhaps the most interesting and instructive. As expected, changes in MCs' status are associated with shifts in style. Freshman soldiers who attain leadership positions as sophomores are more likely to become party builders, and those who gain exclusive committee assignments are more likely to become policy specialists. Among the former in our sample (i.e., soldiers turned builders who gained their first leadership position in the sophomore term) are future House leaders John Boehner (R-OH) and Eric Cantor (R-VA). Among the latter are Hilda Solis (D-CA), who won a coveted seat on Energy and Commerce in her sophomore term, and after three terms as a policy specialist, parlayed those interests to a cabinet position (Secretary of Labor under Obama); and John Culberson (R-TX), who earned a seat on Appropriations in his second term, and as of this writing, serves as Chair of the Subcommittee on Military Construction, Veterans Affairs, and Related Agencies.

In chapters to come, we explore the direction of causality—does, for example, becoming a leader change one's behavior, making one a builder, and/or are those MCs with builder-like tendencies more likely to attain leadership positions? For now, it is sufficient to note that the propensity of freshman soldiers to shift styles is, at least in part, a function of changing context. Indeed, one reason that transitions in style are common at the beginning of MCs' careers may be that gaining such positions tends to happen early, after which legislators settle into their committee assignments. For example, 14.3% of freshmen (and 8.9% of sophomores) will gain exclusive committee assignments going into their next terms, compared to just 1.3% of more senior MCs. The same pattern holds for leadership positions, though with a smaller gap (6.6% of freshmen and 8.7% of sophomores vs. 5.6% of more senior MCs).

We also observe some effects of electoral and majority status. Already-secure soldiers, those who further gain in vote share, and those do not lose the majority are more likely to become builders; secure soldiers (regardless of whether they gain in vote share) are more likely to become specialists; and those who see an uptick in their fortunes are more likely to become advocates. The last of these is less immediately explicable (i.e., because we might expect a loss in votes to push soldiers to move toward a district advocate style), but, overall, the pattern suggests that electoral security often leads MCs to be more likely to transition in style, perhaps because it gives more freedom to explore new patterns of behavior.

Explaining Shifts in Style

Of course, transitions from freshman to sophomore styles (and from the party soldier style to the others) are not the only shifts of interest. More broadly, we want to explain what types of MCs are the most likely to change and to explore what accounts for particular shifts. To do so, we build on the foundation set above, beginning with the most basic question—who changes?

To investigate this question, our dependent variable is simply whether, for each observation in the sample (i.e., an MC-congress), there was a change in style from one congress to the next. Again, we expect that shifts in style are a function of characteristics of individuals, as well as changes in context. Thus, we include the variables from our discussion of transitions in freshman style, as well as indicators for seniority and whether the MC is new. We also control for the style the MC has at time t, as we know the probability of maintaining or shifting style at time $t + 1$ varies depending on one's initial style. And, in a second model, we include whether an MC had maintained the time t style from time $t - 1$. Doing so requires that we omit freshmen from the analysis, but enables us to ascertain whether longevity in a style affects the likelihood of a shift. These results are presented in table 5.3.

The findings are in line with our expectations and our previous findings. The better an MC fits into his or her style in one congress, the less likely he or she is to change that style in the next, and, as shown in Model 2, if he or she has held a style for more than one consecutive term, the probability of a transition in style in the next term is even lower. The dummy variables for style at time t capture the aggregate differences

TABLE 5.3 **Who changes?**

	Model 1	Model 2
MC characteristics		
Ideological extremity	−.66 (.25)**	−.86 (.33)**
Democrat	−.15 (.06)**	−.19 (.09)**
New	.16 (.09)*	—
Seniority	.01 (.00)**	.01 (.01)**
Under 35	.11 (.21)	.75 (.36)**
Over 55	−.08 (.07)	−.09 (.08)
Woman	.16 (.08)**	.10 (.11)
Ethnic/racial minority	.01 (.09)	.04 (.11)
Context at time t		
Leadership position	−.01 (.08)	−.02 (.08)
Exclusive committee	−.09 (.06)	−.11 (.07)
Vote share	.00 (.00)	−.00 (.00)
In majority	.00 (.07)	.05 (.10)
Change in context at time t + 1		
Gained leadership	.14 (.10)	.14 (.12)
Gained exclusive	.31 (.12)**	.28 (.16)*
Changed committee	−.02 (.07)	−.01 (.08)
Gained vote share	.02 (.07)	−.01 (.08)
Lost vote share	.06 (.07)	.04 (.08)
Gained majority	.00 (.10)	.02 (.12)
Lost majority	−.01 (.10)	.02 (.11)
Redistricted	.02 (.07)	.05 (.08)
Style at time t		
District advocate	−1.24 (.09)**	−1.15 (.12)**
Party builder	−.62 (.10)**	−.48 (.12)**
Ambitious entrepreneur	.28 (.15)*	.50 (.22)**
Policy specialist	−.87 (.07)	−.68 (.08)**
Fit of style at time *t*	−2.81 (.15)**	−3.45 (.20)**
Maintained style from *t* − 1	—	−.40 (.09)**
Constant	2.36 (.23)	3.03 (.30)
N	3623	2410
Pseudo R^2	.20	.22

Note: The table presents probit coefficients with standard errors in parentheses. The dependent variable is whether an MC changed style from one congress to the next. The analyses are limited to cases where we have observations for an MC in two consecutive terms. Standard errors are clustered on the MC. ** = $p < .05$; * = $p < .10$

in the stability of styles—relative to soldiers (the baseline group), advocates, builders, and specialists are less likely to shift style in the next term, and entrepreneurs are more likely to do so.

Characteristics of individual MCs also affect the probability of a transition in style. Ideologues are less likely than their moderate colleagues to shift styles, perhaps because they are more set in their ways, or because their ideological inclinations limit their stylistic options. Democrats are less prone than Republicans to changes in style, and women shift more often than do men. The seniority results accord with the patterns we uncovered for stability in styles across careers—new MCs are significantly more likely to shift their styles, and change is also positively associated with seniority (i.e., it is MCs in the middle of the seniority spectrum who are the most stable stylistically).

We see less effect of contextual variables and changes therein. In fact, only one of these variables (gaining an exclusive committee assignment) is significantly associated with changes in style. However, this lack of findings is not particularly surprising, as we should expect the effects of these contextual changes to be conditional based on one's style at time t, and may also affect the probability of a shift to certain styles but not others. For example, if one is already a party builder, then gaining a leadership position is unlikely to result in a change in style. However, if that legislator is, say, a party soldier or policy specialist, a transition to the builder style may be more likely.

The Conditional Effects of Contextual Shocks on Stylistic Transitions

Accordingly, to understand shifts in style in a more nuanced way, we need to model the effects of these contextual variables on the likelihood of MCs from each style transitioning to each of the other four styles in their next terms. To do so, we estimate five multinomial logit models (one for MCs in each style) with independent variables identical to those in table 5.3. The dependent variable in each of these models is MCs' style in the next congress, with the baseline being their current style. For ease of presentation, we do not present all five models, and instead, in table 5.4, provide a summary of the significant ($p < .10$) effects.

This table indicates, for each of the eight "shocks," whether that shock has a significant effect on the likelihood (positive or negative) that an MC in one style shifts to each of the other styles in the next term (with the baseline being maintaining the current style). There is a lot to sort through in these results. A useful way to approach them is to consider what happens to MCs with a particular style when something good happens to them (e.g., gaining a leadership position or exclusive committee

TABLE 5.4 **Effects of contextual "shocks" on transitions in style**

	Gained leader	Gained exclusive	Gained majority	Gained vote share	Changed committee	Redistricted	Lost majority	Lost vote share
Advocate to builder					+		−	
Advocate to entrepreneur		+			−	+	−	
Advocate to soldier								
Advocate to specialist		+	+					
Builder to advocate			−					
Builder to entrepreneur	−						+	+
Builder to soldier	−	−						
Builder to specialist		−					+	
Entrepreneur to advocate	−		+	−				
Entrepreneur to builder		+	−			+	−	
Entrepreneur to soldier				+				
Entrepreneur to specialist		+	−			+	+	
Soldier to advocate								
Soldier to builder	+							
Soldier to entrepreneur	−						−	
Soldier to specialist		−						
Specialist to advocate			−					
Specialist to builder	+		+					
Specialist to entrepreneur								
Specialist to soldier			+					

Note: This table presents a summary of a series of multinomial logit models where the dependent variable is, for MCs in each style, their style in the next term (with maintaining the current style the baseline) and the independent variables are the characteristics of MCs, the context at time t, and contextual changes at $t + 1$. The + and − signs indicate whether there is a significant ($p < .10$) effect of a particular change in context, and, if so, the direction of that effect.

assignment, doing better at the polls, or having their party gain the majority), something bad occurs (losing vote share or losing the majority), and something that could be either good or bad transpires (changing committees, serving in a district that underwent substantial redistricting). Viewed this way, the story that emerges is clear.

Starting with builders, we see that good outcomes make MCs more likely to remain builders and less likely to transition to other styles. For example, builders who gain a leadership position are less likely to become soldiers and specialists, those who gain an exclusive committee position are less likely to become soldiers, specialists, and entrepreneurs, and those who gain the majority are less likely to become advocates. However, when bad things happen, this can induce a shift. A drop in vote share makes a builder more likely to transition to the entrepreneur style (perhaps because this is a style that combines the visibility of the party builder style but requires less public support of the party), and builders who are newly in the minority party are more likely to become specialists and entrepreneurs.

Thus, for builders, already among the movers and shakers in their parties, positive changes reinforce their current stylistic choices. For MCs from other styles, these same good changes make them more likely to shift styles. For example, gaining a leadership position leads MCs who were previously soldiers and specialists to be more likely to become builders. These positive shocks also seem to keep, or to bring, MCs into the party fold. Soldiers who gain a leadership position or exclusive committee seat are less likely to become entrepreneurs (who, recall, tend to vote against the party more often, though they do give to copartisans and the party organization at high rates). Entrepreneurs who get a plum committee assignment are more likely to become builders and soldiers, and a gain in vote share raises the probability they become soldiers.

For MCs in other styles, a boost in status serves to bring them out from under the radar. Advocates, for example, who gain an exclusive committee position are more likely to become entrepreneurs or policy specialists, and when their party gains the majority, are more likely to become policy specialists.

Bad shocks, though, seem have just the opposite effect. Losing vote share makes builders more likely to shift to the entrepreneur style, perhaps in the hope that distancing themselves from the party a bit will yield electoral rewards. Similarly, losing the majority increases builders' likelihood of a shift to the entrepreneur or specialist style. A loss of majority status also makes advocates, soldiers, and entrepreneurs less likely to become builders by, in essence, reducing the flow of minority party MCs to the movers and shakers style.

The "indifferent" or indeterminate changes seem to affect advocates and entrepreneurs the most. A shift in committee assignments leads advocates to be more likely to become builders (perhaps because changes are most often actually good ones, reflecting the party leadership rewarding the requests of an MC) and less likely to become entrepreneurs. Redistricting, in turn, makes advocates more likely to become entrepreneurs and entrepreneurs more likely to become builders.

Thus, despite the overall stability we observe in style, major electoral, majority, and status shocks do appear to have the power to induce shifts in style, and those changes in style follow a meaningful pattern. In particular, positive shifts tend to make the builder style more likely (either in maintaining it, if one is already a builder, or in shifting to it, if one is not), and negative changes work in the opposite direction. And, of course, we see the most evidence of context-induced changes in style for MCs who belong to styles that, in the aggregate, display less stability across time. However, even for advocates and specialists, the most stable of the styles, changes in status can produce systematic shifts.

Equally important, these shifts can be substantial in magnitude. For example, if we take a builder who is in the minority party, lacks a leadership position, and does not have a seat on an exclusive committee (and hold all other variables from the analyses in table 5.4 at their means or modes),[17] if nothing changes for that MC in the next term, he has a .51 probability[18] of remaining a party builder (and a .37 probability of becoming an ambitious entrepreneur, a .08 probability of becoming a policy specialist, and a .04 probability of becoming a district advocate). However, if his party gains the majority and he attains both a leadership position and a seat on an exclusive committee, the probability of remaining a builder rises to .99. And, even if we take a more common scenario, assuming the MC is in the majority already, there are still major differences when status changes. If a builder gains a leadership position and an exclusive committee seat, the probability of remaining a builder jumps from .66 to .98.[19]

Compare this to a policy specialist (again, in the majority party, with the control variables set at their means or modes) who, at time t, lacks both a leadership position and an exclusive committee assignment. If that context remains constant into the next term, she has a .87 probability of remaining a policy specialist, a .07 probability of becoming a soldier, a .05 chance of becoming a builder, and a .01 chance of becoming a district advocate. If she gains both a leadership position and an exclusive committee assignment, the probability of remaining a specialist plummets to .54 and the probability of becoming a party builder rises to .32.

In sum, then, relatively major shocks can move MCs from their habitual patterns of activity and induce shifts in style. Moreover, the directions of these shifts align with our intuitions about how positive or negative circumstances might affect particular styles differently. Importantly, these effects are more than just statistical regularities; they also have a substantively meaningful impact on the likelihood of MCs transitioning to particular styles.

Majority Shifts and Partisanship

Given the potential importance of majority shifts and leadership acquisition to understanding stylistic changes, we turn now to explore them in more detail. We begin with a further investigation of the effects of changes in majority control, especially the potentially differential effects for Democrats and Republicans. We are cautious about what we can conclude, as there are just two instances of shifts in majority control across our time period—in the 104th, where control shifted from the Democrats to the Republicans, and in the 110th, where control shifted back to the Democrats. And, of course, the context of these shifts differed greatly. The Republicans' win in the 104th marked the first Republican control of the House in four decades, while the 110th reflected a return to Democratic control after just fourteen years in the minority. Nonetheless, examining the changes that do and do not occur with these shifts in majority status offers further insight into the nature of transitions in style.

First, as discussed earlier in this chapter, the mere presence of a shift in control does not affect the overall propensity for MCs to transition in style. About 26.5% of MCs changed style in the 104th and 110th Congresses versus 22.9% in others ($t = 1.49$). This finding holds when we split out shifts in majority control to gaining control (22.5% shift when their party gains vs. 23.4% otherwise, $t = .37$) or losing it (21.9% shift vs. 23.5%, $t = .65$).

These findings confirm, once again, that styles are sticky—they are not driven entirely by outside forces, and most legislators do not drastically alter their patterns of behavior in response to changing circumstances, even those as dramatic as a change in majority status. On the other hand, as we have seen throughout this chapter and chapter 4, MCs' responses to context (and changes therein) are not uniform, and instead are conditioned by their styles. When we combine that with the small differences in the overall distribution of style for Democrats and Republicans, there is reason to believe that it is at this level that we may see the clearest evidence of the effects of changes in majority status.

To investigate this possibility, we examine shifts in style for MCs from each party and each style, comparing pairs of congresses where they had the majority and lost versus maintained it, or did not have the majority and won it versus remained in the minority. Given the low Ns of some of the comparisons, we opt for t-tests, where the quantity of interest is the proportion of MCs who shifted style. Some interesting patterns emerge from these analyses. First, as shown in table 5.5, neither party's entrepreneurs are sensitive to majority shifts, perhaps because this pattern of behavior attracts MCs whose style is less defined by a relationship to the party. For the three largest styles (district advocates, party soldiers, and policy specialists), Democrats are more likely than Republicans to respond to a change in majority status with a shift in style. Among Democratic advocates previously in the minority party, gaining the majority results in a higher rate of transitions, and we see the same pattern for Democratic specialists. What is producing these transitions for Democrats? The differences are relatively small in magnitude, but gaining the majority does appear to move more Democratic advocates to the policy specialists style (10% vs. 2.7%) and move policy specialists to builders (8% vs. 4%).

TABLE 5.5 **Effects of shifts in majority status by party and style (%)**

	Dem gain	Dem loss	GOP gain	GOP loss
District advocates	20 / 8.4**	4.1 / 8.9	9.1 / 5.2	4.5 / 9.7
Party builders	19.4 / 19.2	24.1 / 11.4	40 / 7.1**	42.9 / 18.0**
Ambitious entrepreneurs	66.7 / 73.3	20 / 26.1	50 / 64.7	57.1 / 52.8
Party soldiers	33.3 / 49.3	25.4 / 41.3**	26 / 38.4	43.2 / 44.6
Policy specialists	20.5 / 10.1**	8.7 / 20.2*	21.6 / 21.0	28.1 / 19.5

Note: This table presents the proportion of Democrats and Republicans in each style who shifted style in the next congress, comparing congresses where they gained the majority (vs. remaining in the minority) and lost the majority (vs. remaining there). Means for these groups are compared using t-tests. ** = $p < .05$; * = $p < .10$

Democratic specialists who *lose* the majority are also less likely than their stylistic peers who remain in the majority to change their styles in the next term (9% shift vs. 20%, $t = 1.7$), a pattern also displayed by Democratic soldiers (25% of those who lose the majority shift vs. 41% of those who maintain it, $t = 2.0$). These effects are both driven by the fact that losing the majority effectively stops the normal flow of soldiers and specialists to the builder style. For example, in a situation where the majority Democratic Party maintains this status (as in the 101st to 102nd or 102nd to 103rd), 11% of soldiers become builders. However, when the Democratic majority loses control (from the 103rd to the 104th), less than 2% of soldiers make this move. There is a similar pattern (though smaller in magnitude) for specialists, where about 6% of those in congresses where the Democrats maintain the majority shift to the builders style, compared to just 2% when they lose it.

In contrast, winning or losing the majority does not affect the relative propensity of Republican advocates, soldiers, and specialists (or entrepreneurs) to maintain or change their styles. However, Republican *builders* seem the most attuned to changes in majority status. Neither gaining nor losing the majority affects the relative probability that Democratic builders will shift styles, but, interestingly, both gaining and losing the majority increase Republicans' propensity to shift away from the builder style. This seems to be driven by movement among Republican elites from the builder to the entrepreneur and specialist styles. When the Republicans gained the majority in 1994, several prominent members who had been party builders in the 103rd Congress—including Newt Gingrich, Tom DeLay, and Dick Armey—transitioned to the ambitious entrepreneur style. If we look at their careers longitudinally, these are MCs who move between these two styles across time, likely in response to changing circumstances. With the exception of Gingrich, these legislators all shifted back to the party builder style in the 105th Congress, perhaps having settled into the new normal of being in the majority.

Other former Republican Party builders, who found themselves out of step with Gingrich and the leadership, transitioned to the policy specialist style. Take, for example, Henry Hyde (R-IL), described by the *Almanac of American Politics* as viewed by some fellow Republicans as "insufficiently partisan" (Barone and Ujifusa 1993, 403) and "out of sync with some of the policies of Newt Gingrich's Contract with America" (Barone and Ujifusa 1995, 433). As they described the context in which Hyde found himself:

> When Republicans won the majority, Hyde had several choices. He could keep a position in the leadership, possibly remaining as Republican Policy Committee chair.... But in choosing to chair the Judiciary Committee, Hyde won the opportunity to make changes he has voted for unavailingly for as long as 20 years and benefited from the reputation for fairness and competence to withstand purely partisan attack. (433)

This choice, and the patterns of activity that accompanied it, resulted in Hyde being classified as a policy specialist in the 104th Congress.[20]

We see a similar dynamic for Republican elites fourteen years later when, in the 110th Congress, the Democrats retake the majority. Prominent Republican builders in the 109th Congress, such as John Boehner (House Majority Leader in the 109th), Deborah Pryce (Chair of the Republican Conference), and Tom Reynolds (Chair of the NRCC), formerly part of the leadership establishment, find themselves plunged into the minority, and respond with shifts in behavior that make them ambitious entrepreneurs. Other former builders, such as Bob Goodlatte, Paul Ryan, and C. W. "Bill" Young, turn to focus more on policy, becoming policy specialists. In all cases, these are MCs who had histories as policy specialists before becoming party builders, and so the loss of the majority seems to bring them back to those roots.[21]

Leadership

These findings about majority and minority status also highlight the potential importance of leadership positions in inducing changes in style. Accordingly, we now turn to a more detailed examination of the effects of leadership positions. In our overall analyses above of transitions in style, we included a single dummy variable for whether an MC had obtained a leadership position of any type. We did so because the relatively low Ns for particular styles coupled with the large number of control variables meant that a more finely tuned measure of leadership status would not be particularly meaningful. Here, though, we supplement these analyses with a more in-depth look at the relationship between gaining leadership positions and transitions in style. Not all leadership positions are the same—some, for example, focus more on policy and others are explicitly political or electorally oriented—and certain moves may have differential effects depending on MCs' styles before gaining the position.

In undertaking these analyses, we also examine the effects of *losing* a position. Earlier, we justified not including such a measure in the aggregate analyses, as it is rarer (compared to gaining positions) to lose positions in the absence of a majority shift, and because the parties' consistent "fiddling" with the leadership structure means that it is not clear that an apparent loss of a position is truly a loss.[22] (To give just one example, in some congresses, the DCCC and NRCC give most members of the committees official titles, but in other congresses there are fewer official titles and more at-large members.) Nonetheless, it is useful to test for the effects of losing a position to ascertain whether or not these assumptions are correct.

We break leadership positions into four categories. "Major" leadership positions include Speaker of the House, Majority Leader, Minority Leader, and Whip. "Party" leadership positions include Deputy Whips, chairs and vice chairs of the parties' caucus/conference, and steering and policy committee chairs. "Campaign" leadership positions include named positions (i.e., not just membership) in the DCCC or NRCC.[23] "Committee" leadership positions include serving as the chair or ranking member of a (full) committee.[24]

We expect, of course, that the causal arrows between style and leadership may go both ways. For example, styles may affect the likelihood that MCs are tapped for leadership positions, a question we explore in chapter 8. For present purposes, our focus is on whether change in leadership status precipitates a transition in style. We begin with gaining positions. Our general expectation is that attaining leadership status should move MCs toward the party builder style, but the likelihood of such a transition depends upon one's initial style and upon the type of leadership position one gains. For example, we hypothesize that party and campaign leadership positions will serve to bring legislators into the party fold. Committee leadership positions, in contrast, may have less effect on transitions, as they are more policy focused. And, even with the erosion of seniority norms, they are still driven largely by seniority and, as such, are more automatic.

To determine whether differences exist, we conducted t-tests, calculating the proportion of MCs in each style at time t who became builders in the next term, and comparing these rates for those who did and did not gain a specific type of leadership position in that term. These results are summarized in figure 5.5. In these graphs, an asterisk next to the name of the style indicates that there is a significant ($p < .10$) difference in the proportion of builders for those who did and did not gain a particular category of leadership position.

As shown, all types of leadership positions tend to elevate soldiers to the builder style—those who gain party, campaign, or committee leadership positions are all more likely than their peers to become party builders in the next congress. In line with our hypothesis, though, the magnitude of the effect is smallest for the committee leadership position comparison (a difference of 20% for party leadership positions, 12% for campaign leadership positions, and 10% for committee leadership positions). There is a similar pattern for policy specialists. For them, gaining either a party or committee leadership position increases the likelihood of being a specialist in the next term, but whereas 26% of specialists who get a party leadership position become builders, only 15% of those who gain a committee leadership position do. Interestingly, gaining a campaign leadership position has no effect for specialists, likely because they are not as motivated by the rewards those types of positions offer, or because they engage in campaign fund-raising to achieve their policy goals. Henry Waxman, for example, noted that:

> The luxury of a safe seat meant that I didn't need to raise much money for my own reelection. Instead, from the time I arrived in Congress, I donated to those whom I considered allies. Though it displeased some traditionalists, this practice has had positive results. Year after year, many of the members I supported have cast key votes on important legislation. (Waxman and Green 2009, 33)

We also see that, once again, the advocate style is fairly immovable—very little leads a district advocate to change his or her style. However, there is evidence that gaining a *committee* leadership position induces a shift to the builder style. About 10% of advocates who gain such a position become builders, compared to just 1% of those who do not. This may be because committee leadership provides some district advocates, who for constituency reasons are generally wary of being a visible member of the party team, a way to both please the district (if the committee position is in an area of policy interest to constituents) and contribute to party-building efforts.

Finally, entrepreneurs can also be induced to become builders, but only a campaign leadership position has this effect. We know that entrepreneurs, in general, redistribute campaign funds to the party at high

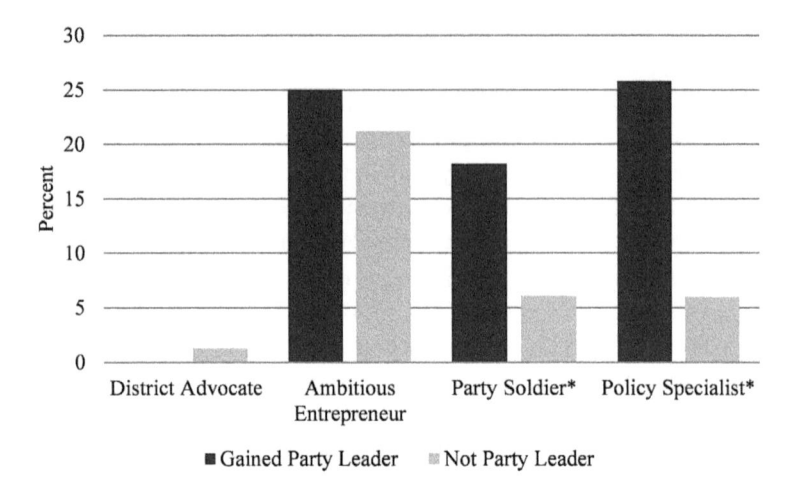

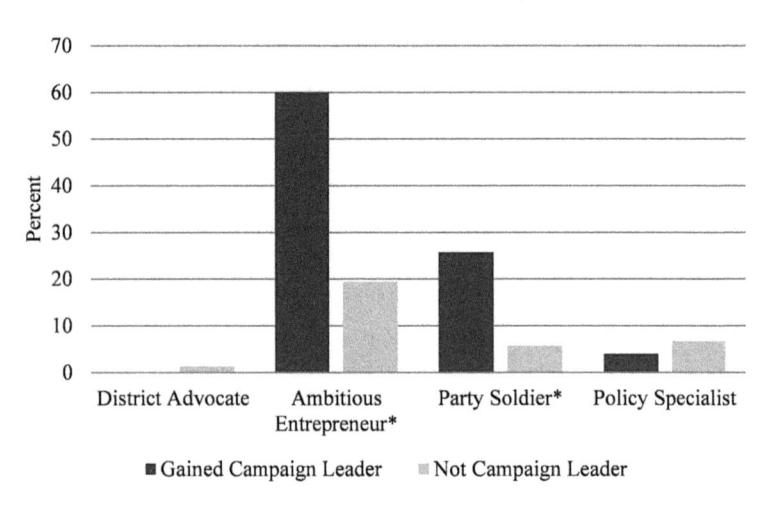

FIGURE 5.5 Gaining leadership and transitioning to the builder style
Note: This figure presents the proportion of MCs in each style who transitioned to the builder style in the next term and compares the propensity to do so for those who gained a leadership position in that term and those who did not. * = $p < .10$.

TRANSITIONS IN STYLE 117

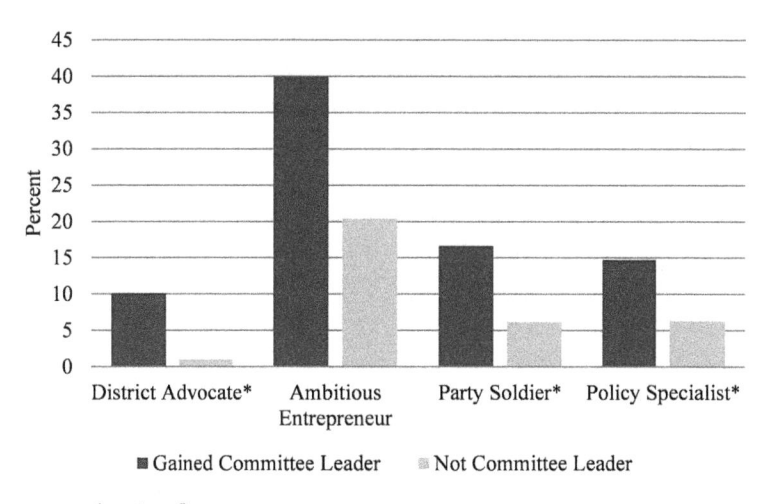

FIGURE 5.5 (*continued*)

rates, but being recognized for these efforts with a formal position in the campaign fund-raising infrastructure serves to bring their styles more in line with those of builders. Given the low *N* here, however (only five entrepreneurs gain campaign leadership positions), we should be cautious in drawing conclusions.

Thus, gaining a leadership position is related to transitions in style, though once again, the precise effects vary depending on MCs' styles before attaining leadership. Does *losing* a position have the same effect? To answer this question, we replicate the analyses in table 5.5, this time comparing the likelihood of shifts in style for MCs who had a particular type of position at time t and held on to it at $t + 1$ and those who had a position, but then lost it in the next congress. As predicted, we find much less evidence of systematic effects. In fact, for just one comparison do we find a significant association. Party builders who lose party leadership positions are less likely to be builders in the next congress than those who maintain them (63.6% vs. 85.5%; $t = 2.57$, $p < .05$). Resonating with the findings above about the effects of majority loss, a substantial proportion of these former party builders become ambitious entrepreneurs.

We conclude, therefore, that gaining leadership matters for changes in style, but losing it does not (likely due in large part to the ways in which leadership structures change from congress to congress). And, while the magnitude of the effects is sometimes small, we should note that our analyses only target the immediate effects of gaining leadership—whether the position induces a change in style during the congress in which he or she receives it. For some MCs, the effect might lag if there is a slow shift from one behavioral pattern to another. For example, a district advocate who rises to a committee chair might begin to invest more legislatively or to vote more with the party, but those changes might take some time to build before they manifest themselves in a full-blown shift in style.[25]

The Speed of Change

This brings us to our final question about transitions in style, which is how quickly they occur. In other words, when we observe a shift in style, is this relatively abrupt, or are the roots of such changes observable earlier on? These patterns shed light on the nature of change in behavior and styles and help to further establish how shifts in context affect transitions in style.

Earlier in this chapter, we demonstrated that the "maximum soft probability" scores for MCs who maintain their styles from one congress to the next are higher than those of legislators who change styles (a mean of .90 vs. .78; $t = 19.1, p < .05$). Thus, the more solidly one falls into his or her style at time t, the less likely he or she is to be categorized in a different style at time $t + 1$. This pattern holds across four of the five styles—the more "advocate-y" a district advocates is, the more likely he or she is to maintain that style, and the same is true for party builders, party soldiers, and policy specialists. Only for ambitious entrepreneurs do we see no difference in maximum soft probability for those who change and those who continue on as entrepreneurs.

As a next step, we turn this question around to focus only on those MCs who *did* change styles from one congress to the next to investigate, based on their maximum soft probability scores, how many of those changes were abrupt versus "expected." Recall that most MCs fit quite well into their styles at any point in time, which, in turn, explains in part why transitions are relatively rare. Across all observations, the mean maximum soft probability score is .87 and the median is .95; indeed, for only about a quarter of observations is the maximum probability score less than .75. Nonetheless, there is variation across MCs, and we leverage this variation to explore the nature of transitions.

For these analyses, we define "abrupt" changes as those where an MC had a maximum soft probability of his or her time t style of at least .75 but transitioned to a different style in the next term. In other words, these are cases where we might expect, based on the soft probability scores, that an MC was solidly within his or her current style and, hence, would be less likely to change. Contrast this with an "expected" change, where an MC had a hybrid style, with soft probabilities split fairly evenly between two or more styles. By this definition, most changes (57%) are abrupt, but this is because most MCs have very high maximum soft probabilities. However, a much higher proportion of shifts in style occur among those with maximum soft probabilities below .75 (45% of those MCs change styles in their next term) than among those with maximum probabilities above .75 (for whom just 16% change styles).[26]

What, then, explains whether a transition is abrupt or expected? In the models in table 5.6, we include dummy variable indicators of MCs' time t and time $t + 1$ styles (to take into account that MCs in some styles may make more abrupt changes, or that changes to particular styles tend to be more abrupt than others) and the indicators of MC-level characteristics and changes in context from previous analyses. In the second model, we also include a control for whether the MC maintained his or her style from time $t - 1$ to time t, which allows us to ascertain whether abrupt shifts are less common among MCs who have displayed a particular style for a longer period of time. This also means, however, that the N is lower for this model, as we cannot include first-term MCs.

We find that changes to the builder, entrepreneur, and specialist styles tend to be more abrupt (soldiers are the baseline group), as are changes from the entrepreneur style. Changes from the specialist style tend to be more expected. Perhaps unsurprisingly given that many new freshmen adopt the party soldier style and fit well into it, new MCs make more abrupt changes than do their senior peers. We also see evidence that many of the "shocks" we study bring about abrupt rather than gradual changes. In particular, among MCs who had a transition in style, gaining a leadership position, seeing a rise in vote share, and changing committees are all associated with an abrupt change.

The overall pattern of results is a bit different when we include a control for whether an MC had been in his or her previous style for more

TABLE 5.6 **Explaining abrupt and expected transitions in style**

	Model 1	Model 2
MC characteristics		
Ideological extremity	−.05 (.44)	.53 (.55)
Democrat	.08 (.11)	.03 (.15)
New	.52 (.15)**	—
Seniority	−.00 (.08)	−.00 (.01)
Context at time t		
Leadership position	−.02 (.13)	.07 (.15)
Exclusive committee	.01 (.11)	.16 (.12)
Vote share	.00 (.00)	.01 (.00)
In majority	−.11 (.13)	
Change in context at time t + 1		
Gained leadership	.30 (.17)*	.20 (.21)
Gained exclusive	.07 (.19)	.43 (.27)
Changed committee	.20 (.12)*	.26 (.15)*
Gained vote share	.21 (.13)*	.16 (.16)
Lost vote share	.08 (.13)	−.07 (.16)
Gained majority	−.20 (.19)	−.27 (.23)
Lost majority	.14 (.18)	.12 (.21)
Redistricted	−.03 (.12)	.05 (.14)
Style at time t		
District advocate	−.27 (.21)	.03 (.24)
Party builder	−.09 (.19)	.38 (.22)*
Ambitious entrepreneur	1.00 (.25)**	1.75 (.35)**
Policy specialist	−.36 (.17)**	.03 (.21)
Change in style at time t + 1		
To district advocate	.05 (.20)	.15 (.22)
To party builder	.35 (.19)*	.24 (.21)
To ambitious entrepreneur	1.03 (.28)**	1.04 (.29)**
To policy specialist	.54 (.21)**	.46 (.23)**
Maintained style from $t - 1$	—	.99 (.17)**
Constant	−.56 (.39)	−.98 (.48)
N	751	509
Pseudo R^2	.12	.15

Note: The table presents probit coefficients with standard errors in parentheses. The dependent variable is whether, for MCs who experienced a transition in style, that transition was "abrupt" (for MCs whose probability of fitting into their style at time t was .75 or greater) or "expected" (for MCs with lower levels of fit). Standard errors are clustered on the MC. ** = $p < .05$; * = $p < .10$

than one term. That variable is strongly negatively related to abruptness, indicating that when MCs who have held a style for more than one term have a transition, they are less likely to experience an abrupt change to a new style. Here, the dummy variables for coming from or going to a particular style remain significant, but there is no independent effect of the shocks. Importantly, though, this is due not to the inclusion of the lagged style variable, but to the fact that these analyses do not include freshmen. Indeed, if we rerun Model 1 but limit it to nonfreshmen, only a change in committees is associated with abrupt shifts. In all, this suggests that these shocks bring about quick transitions for freshmen to their sophomore term, but across all MCs, whether or not a transition is abrupt or expected is more a function of their most recent styles and their past stylistic history.

Conclusions

In this chapter, we have covered a lot of ground in explaining transitions in style. Our analyses have revealed that, in line with our theory of legislative styles, MCs generally display consistent styles, but when they do experience transitions in style, those changes are predictable. In particular, the propensity to change style is a function of characteristics of individual members and of shifts in the context in which they find themselves. Also as expected, the effects of these contextual changes are contingent on MCs' styles. For example, gaining a leadership position generally affects party soldiers differently than district advocates or ambitious entrepreneurs.

To illustrate these dynamics, it is useful to draw on an example. For this, we return to the 110th Iowa delegation discussed in previous chapters. Democrats Bruce Braley and David Loebsack were new members in the 110th Congress, and so we do not have observations across multiple congresses for them. However, for their senior copartisan Leonard Boswell, we can observe his trajectory from the 105th through 110th Congresses. Boswell entered Congress in 1996 as a district advocate, and not much changed for him over the next ten years. He gained neither a leadership position nor an exclusive committee seat, and while he experienced some fluctuations in vote share, none were particularly dramatic. Thus, it is unsurprising that he maintained his style across these congresses, particularly since he started out as an advocate, the most stable of styles.

Nonetheless, we do see some evidence of attentiveness to changes in context for him. The biggest contextual shift that occurred during Boswell's service was the Democrats' gaining of the majority in the 110th, and although he maintains the advocate style in that congress, we do see a drop in his fit into that style (from a probability of .98 to 1 in the previous four congresses to a probability of .78 in the 110th).

The story for Republican Steve King, who came to Congress in 2004 as a party soldier, is similar. King also gained neither a leadership position nor an exclusive committee seat during the congresses in which we observe him, and while electorally more secure than Boswell (with vote shares in the 60s rather than 50s), experienced even less fluctuation in his margins. King too maintains a consistent style. Unlike many of his freshman soldier peers, he continues that style into his second and third terms, though, like them, he does display some movement toward the policy specialist style over time. Specifically, in his freshman term, his pattern of behavior yields him a .86 probability of being in the soldier cluster and a .14 probability of being a specialist, but the former drops to .63 in his sophomore term and the probability of the latter increases to .37.

Tom Latham experienced the most transitions of the delegation. He entered Congress in the 104th Congress as a party soldier, transitioned to the policy specialist style in the 105th (maintaining that style in the 106th and 107th), and then transitioned again to the district advocate style in the 108th, where he remained in the 109th and 110th Congresses. When we examine what happened to him across his service in the House, these changes are understandable. Like many freshman soldiers, he became a specialist as a sophomore, a transition that may have been precipitated by gaining an exclusive committee position—a seat on Appropriations.[27] His shift to the district advocate style in the 108th might have been influenced by two changes from the 107th—a substantial redistricting and a concomitant decrease in vote share (from 70% in the 2000 election to 56% in 2002). Moreover, by our categorizations, this shift was not abrupt, as his probability of the specialist style in the 107th was .63, a decrease from a high of .92 in earlier congresses.

That transitions are rare but explicable is a crucial piece of the puzzle in explaining legislative style. It reinforces our assertion that the halls of Congress are occupied by several distinct types of legislators and that their stylistic patterns tend to be enduring. However, legislators, as goal-oriented actors, are also sensitive to context, and major changes therein can result in shifts in style. The effect of these shocks is probabilistic rather than deterministic, shaped by characteristics of individual MCs, their preexisting patterns of behavior, and, likely, the relationships between the two.

Having established the foundational dynamics of legislative style—where MCs start out and how they change over time—we turn our attention in the remainder of the book to a different type of question, focusing on the consequences of styles. In particular, how do styles impact MCs' electoral fortunes, their legislative success, and their career trajectories? We begin in the next chapter with an exploration of the relationships between style and electoral security.

CHAPTER SIX

The Electoral Consequences of Legislative Style

Are, then, congressmen in a position to do anything about being reelected? If an answer is sought in their ability to affect national partisan percentages, the answer is no. But if an answer is sought in their ability to affect the percentages in their own primary and general elections, the answer is yes.... It will be argued that they think they can affect their own percentages, that in fact they can affect their own percentages, and furthermore that there is reason for them to try to do so. — Mayhew (1974, 32–33)

It is a fact of congressional life that (most legislators, most of the time) want to be reelected. It is this reality that led David Mayhew to "conjure up a vision of United States congressmen as single-minded seekers of reelection" (1974, 5) and to determine how much of legislative behavior and organization such a vision might explain. His answer, famously, was "quite a lot."

In the four decades since Mayhew wrote those words, the idea of the electoral imperative has become fundamental to our conceptions of legislative behavior and representation. Indeed, it is now the central organizing idea when congressional scholars hypothesize about why MCs do what they do. What is sometimes overlooked in discussions of electoral incentives, however, is that Mayhew meant his argument as a simplification, and it is.[1] For most MCs, reelection is *not* the only aim, although it is often the most proximate one. As highlighted in chapter 1, our theory of legislative style holds that legislators harbor multiple goals and want to be reelected while also pursuing other ends of value to them—making policy, supporting their party, promoting their careers, and so on. Thus, they choose patterns of activity that they believe will enable them to achieve these multiple goals. As a result, MCs do not move in lockstep, and we see variation in legislative styles. In the spirit of Mayhew, though, we assume that these styles are chosen because legislators believe they will help them to accomplish their electoral goals, or, at the least, to not interfere with them.

The logical next question is whether we expect these stylistic choices to manifest themselves in legislators' *future* electoral success. A common corollary of electoral connection theories is that legislators' behavior in office will affect their electoral prospects—that "good" (i.e., electorally focused) behavior will be rewarded at the polls and bad behavior punished. However, as we discuss in more detail below, evidence for such effects is mixed, perhaps because the fact that all legislators are reelection oriented actually makes it more difficult to uncover electoral consequences for their behavior.

The goal of this chapter is to undertake a nuanced investigation into how legislative styles are (or are not) related to electoral success. In what follows, we assess the links between the styles MCs adopt and a variety of indicators of such success, including their vote shares and the presence and quality of competition in primary and general elections. We also explore patterns in styles within congressional districts across time to address how the context by which MCs come to office shapes whether they converge or diverge from the styles of their predecessors. Such patterns help us to further understand the role of styles in congressional behavior and elections. We begin, however, with some background—a discussion of the literature on legislative behavior and electoral success.

The Electoral Effects of Legislative Behavior

Legislators themselves clearly believe that their choices in office are consequential for their electoral futures. This is a theme that emerges from nearly every study that draws on interviews with MCs or their staffers (see, for example, Kingdon 1989; Koger 2003; Matthews and Stimson 1975). In fact, even ostensibly very secure legislators report worry about the electoral impact of their governing behavior, perhaps because most MCs, even those who are currently safe, have faced at least one close election in their careers, and all have seen seemingly "safe" colleagues lose their bids for reelection (Arnold 1990; Jacobson 2001; Mann 1978). As Fiorina (1974) explained:

> Granted, the overwhelming bulk of Congressmen are reelected. But, by the same token, never does a congressional election pass without leaving one or more Representatives and/or Senators consigned to political oblivion. There is always an example or two of a misstep that wiped out a political career. The costs of defeat are so enormous that the probability of defeat pales by comparison. Choosing discretion over valor, the representative votes as if the probability of his action becoming a campaign issue is unity. (124)

Interestingly, however, firm evidence that legislators' behavior actually translates to electoral reward or punishment has been harder to come by. For example, the claim that volume of activity (e.g., introductions, cosponsorships, and other entrepreneurial behaviors) helps MCs at the ballot box receives, at best, mixed support (see Box-Steffensmeier et al. 2003; Johannes and McAdams 1981; Ragsdale and Cook 1987; Wawro 2001). The same holds true for assessments of constituency service and district attention. In reviewing the findings from this literature, Fiorina (1981) observed that one might reasonably conclude that incumbents could "spend less money, go home less often, abolish their district offices, fire their staffs, and cut down on constituency service activities" without harming their electoral prospects (546).

There have been a variety of reasons offered for the apparent lack of strong electoral effects of in-office behavior. One is that savvy MCs work to anticipate potentially thorny situations—those that may come back to haunt them on Election Day—and avoid them. In fact, scholars such as Arnold (1990) argue that such anticipatory representation is a central mechanism driving responsiveness to constituency concerns. Importantly, the hallmark of success in these efforts is a *lack* of a constituency response to an MC's behavior. We do not observe the counterfactual of what would happen if an MC chose to ignore the electoral implications of his or her behavior (or, more notably, actively tried to lower his or her own approval ratings) because, as Mayhew put it, "there is no congressman willing to make the experiment" (1974, 37). In the aggregate, then, widespread rational anticipation of constituency reaction will produce a situation wherein we observe little or no relationship between MC behavior and subsequent vote shares.

Another possible contributor to the lack of strong connections between legislators' activities and their electoral fortunes is that they may develop representational or policy reputations that exist apart from the actual amount of time and effort spent in any particular term (Bianco 1994; Rivers and Fiorina 1992), or, as our theory of style might suggest, that are a function of a combination of activities rather than a single behavior. Thus, while their patterns of activity may produce electoral security over the long run, we may not observe strong relationships between behavior in a specific congress and performance in the next election.

This is not to say that there is *no* evidence of the electoral effects of legislative behavior. Work on roll call voting has shown that MCs who are "out of step" with their districts (typically by voting at high rates with their parties and opting to prioritize party over constituency) tend to perform worse at the polls (Ansolabehere, Snyder, and Stewart 2001; Canes-Wrone, Brady, and Cogan 2002; Carson, Koger, et al. 2010), and that, under certain conditions, even a single "wrong" vote might matter (Nyhan et al. 2012; Theriault 2005).

And, while the sheer *volume* of activity undertaken by MCs might not affect electoral prospects, the content of that activity can. Sulkin (2005, 2011), for instance, finds that legislators who take up their previous challengers' issue critiques and who follow through on their own campaign appeals at high rates do better in the next election than their colleagues who engage in fewer of these behaviors. Sulkin, Testa, and Usry (2015) demonstrate that when an MC is active on the issues a constituent views as "most important," that constituent is more likely to approve of the job the MC is doing (though, importantly, the effect is limited to copartisans). And there is evidence that legislative effectiveness may yield electoral dividends, with success in the legislative realm begetting success in elections (Miquel and Snyder 2006; Volden and Wiseman 2014).

Overall, then, while MCs are not wrong in assuming that their actions can yield electoral dividends or punishments, actually uncovering such effects is made difficult by the very fact that legislators care about reelection so much. As one of the staffers interviewed by Kingdon (1989) remarked:

> It is not enough to observe that because congressmen win in general elections by large margins and because they rarely face primary opposition, they therefore need not be concerned about constituency reaction to their behavior. Such an argument neglects the possibility that they may be so seemingly secure partly because they were careful about catering to their constituen-

cies. . . . I asked a staffer why a politician from a safe district should be worried about how his constituents react. His answer was as simple as it was profound: "They're safe *because* they vote that way." (62)

Nonetheless, careful analyses can often identify subtle electoral effects, especially at the margins. And, given that most legislators are reelected, we argue that the margins are precisely where one needs to look for such effects.

Style and Electoral Success

For all of these reasons, we expect that the relationship between legislative style and success will be subtle and potentially complicated. We anticipate that MCs will attempt to calibrate their styles to their reelection calculations, adopting patterns of behavior that map on to the context in which they find themselves. This calibration, if done correctly, will dampen the observed relationships between an MC's style in a particular term and his or her subsequent electoral success. Thus, in line with the "rational anticipation" arguments, the effect of a well-chosen style, particularly over the long term, will be to produce a lack of electoral response. However, the effects may not be erased entirely. Choosing the "correct" style for one's constituency and context can help electorally, but may only go so far. For example, MCs who face electoral disadvantages due to the partisanship of their districts may not be able to compensate completely, even with careful strategizing about their activity. Legislators may also sometimes make miscalculations in their electoral math, or they may choose to sacrifice some electoral security in favor of another goal. If these tendencies are widespread, and/or if they vary by style, this will manifest itself in aggregate patterns of electoral success.

This argument underscores the basic supposition underlying our approach in this chapter: electoral success is not so much a function of style itself (i.e., that, for example, being a district advocate or policy specialist or ambitious entrepreneur is, in general, a better reelection strategy for all legislators), but of the "fit" between an MC's constituency and the style he or she adopts. If one is a poor fit for the district (ideological or otherwise), then to stay in office, he or she needs to adopt a style that ameliorates this mismatch. Most obviously, being a district advocate and devoting time and resources to the district might help MCs to build electoral coalitions that enable them to maintain their seats, even in the absence of strong policy agreement with their constituents.

Aggregate patterns in styles provide evidence of such calibration. For example, although only about 25% of MCs (both Democrats and Republicans) are district advocates, these rates are much higher for Democrats in the "Solid South" and for New England Republicans.[2] Indeed, 45% of Southern Democrats are advocates (jumping to 55% for white Democrats from that region), as are 79% of New England Republicans. This includes such well-known legislators as Gene Taylor (MS), Sanford Bishop (GA), and Bud Cramer (AL) on the Democratic side, and Charles Bass (NH), Olympia Snowe (ME), and Nancy Johnson (CT) for the Republicans. These MCs are able to hold on to their districts, and even do quite well, because they adopt a style that is appropriate to their situation. If, instead, they'd opted to be party soldiers or policy specialists, they would probably have lost their seats early on.

On the flip side, an MC who is a good fit with the district stands little to gain from a district advocate style and might even do better with another style. These MCs have the freedom to pursue a more activist, visible, party-centered style, and in fact, that may be what their constituents want from them.[3] In this sense, fit is like capital, and MCs with this capital can and should spend it. Along these lines, we see that Republicans from the Solid South adopt the district advocate style much less often (13%) than the overall average, and the effect is even clearer for New England Democrats (where only 6.5% are advocates). Perhaps unsurprisingly, the party builder style is overrepresented among Southern Republicans and New England Democrats. Seventeen percent of Republicans and 20% of Democrats have this style, compared to just 12% in the sample as a whole. Among the Republicans, this includes prominent members and leaders such as Tom DeLay (TX), Eric Cantor (VA), and Dick Armey (TX), and, among the Democrats, MCs such as Joseph P. and Patrick Kennedy (MA and RI, respectively) and Barney Frank (MA).

As another illustration, consider the cases of Phil Sharp and David McIntosh, the two representatives who served Indiana's 2nd district in the 1980s and 1990s. The district, as described by Fenno (2007), was generally racially homogenous and politically conservative. Sharp, "a vintage 'Watergate baby,' a surprise Democratic victor in 1974[4] . . . had established himself in a typically Republican district" (2007, 206) and held that district until his retirement in 1994. He had done so, Fenno recounts, via a careful cultivation of important subconstituencies, balancing the interests of the business community with those of his base. This description seems to correspond well with the district advocate style. And, in fact, Sharp emerges as a district advocate in all three of the congresses for which we have data for him (the 101st–103rd).

David McIntosh, who succeeded Sharp in office after the latter's retirement, took a decidedly different approach to the job. As we described in chapter 4, he began his career as the archetypal party soldier, with a party-focused style and desire to attain a position of leadership among his fellow freshman Republicans in the 104th Congress. As Fenno described him:

> It is important to recognize that *he had adopted a philosophy before he had adopted a home constituency*. He was neither born, nor raised, nor educated in the district he came to represent. He moved to the district as an adult with a fully formed, strongly held conservative socioeconomic philosophy.... He brought them *to* the constituency; he did not take them *from* the constituency. (2007, 198, italics in original)

McIntosh maintained this party soldier style into his sophomore term before transitioning to the ambitious entrepreneur style in his third, and final, term.[5]

These accounts suggest that Sharp was able to maintain his seat *because* of his style. This was in large part due to his efforts to attend to the district, not because of his positions or philosophy. It seems unlikely that a Democrat with another style would have been able to win majorities in Indiana's 2nd district. McIntosh, in contrast, benefited from his fit with the district, which enabled him to adopt, and be successful with, another style. In fact, it is possible that, had he decided to maintain Sharp's district advocate style, he would have gotten criticized by (and even faced a primary challenge from) segments of his constituency that expected more or different governing behavior from him.

Overall, we do not see large differences in Sharp's and McIntosh's vote shares, though McIntosh does slightly better. In the elections to the congresses for which we have data, McIntosh attains between 55–62% of the vote, compared with 53–59% for Sharp. These patterns are consistent with our expectations about fit, style, and electoral effects. Sharp does worse than McIntosh, but it is not because being a district advocate is not an electorally wise choice for him. Instead, that advocate style is likely what kept him in office, though it could not make up entirely for the disadvantages he faced as a Democrat in a predominately Republican district.

This underscores the crucial point that electoral concerns are not something that go away after an MC secures a solid vote share. If Sharp had misread his reasonably comfortable victory margins as a sign that he could now safely shift his behavior away from the advocate style, he would have been wrong. Mayhew (1974) offered a similar appraisal of the relationship between legislators' behavior in office and their electoral security:

> When we say "Congressman Smith is 'unbeatable,'" we do not mean that there is nothing he could do that would lose him his seat. Rather, we mean "Congressman Smith is unbeatable as long as he continues to do the things he is doing." ... What characterizes "safe" congressmen is not that they are beyond electoral reach, but that their efforts are very likely to bring them uninterrupted electoral success. (37)

This calibration between style and the district may also contribute to the consistency we observe in styles across time. Because MCs' constituencies are relatively unchanging, once a legislator thinks he or she has hit upon a style that works, there is incentive to keep with it.

Our basic expectation, then, is that any electoral effects of style will be conditional on fit. More precisely, we hypothesize that MCs who come from districts for which they are relatively poor fits should benefit from a district advocate style, whereas MCs who are good fits for the district will get more bang for their buck with another style. To test this hypothesis, we need to develop a measure of MCs' level of fit with their districts and then assess the relationship between style and electoral success after taking fit into account. Before doing so, however, we first step back to discuss in more detail how we intend to approach the dependent variable — electoral success.

Indicators of Electoral Success

In our analyses of the electoral implications of style, we choose to target a variety of indicators of electoral success, beginning with what is perhaps the most fundamental: whether an MC who runs for reelection wins and returns to Congress in the next term.[6] In our sample, 95% of MCs who stand for reelection are successful in their attempts. Overall, this measure would appear to offer little variation to explain. However, with our large sample size (4,276 MC-congress observations), there are a substantial number of MCs (199) who are unsuccessful in their bids to return to Congress, and given the centrality of the reelection imperative, it is useful to explore relationships between style and loss, even as a rare event.

A more commonly used measure of electoral success is an MC's vote share in an election, particularly the "two-party vote"—the proportion of the vote he or she receives relative to his or her major party opponent (i.e., omitting any minor party candidates or write-ins). Although our theory of style does not presume that MCs necessarily try to maximize their vote shares (because they may balance goals), the tendency of incumbents to "run scared" means that, for most, the higher the vote share, the better. On this measure, there is considerably more variation to explain. MCs in our sample received between 34.8 and 100% of the two-party vote in their districts. Among MCs who won their elections, the mean vote share was about 71%. Table 6.1 presents descriptive statistics on these two-party vote shares as well as our other measures of electoral success.

That vote shares range up to 100% highlights another potential indicator of electoral success, which is the ability of incumbents to ward off challengers. After all, the easiest way to guarantee victory in a race is to run unopposed. Theoretical and empirical research on political ambition demonstrates that challengers are more likely to enter a race when they feel that the circumstances are favorable to them and that they have an opening for effectively criticizing an incumbent (Carson 2005; Jacobson and Kernell 1983; Lazarus 2008; Schlesinger 1966). Legislators actively try to fend off strong challengers in a variety of ways—for example, by amassing a "war chest" of campaign funds to demonstrate their

TABLE 6.1 **Measures of electoral success**

	Range	Count of MCs	Mean
Lost	0–1	199	4.7%
Vote share—winners	50–100	—	71.2%
General election unopposed	0–1	504	13.4%
General election quality challenge	0–1	461	16.6%
Primary election challenge	0–1	765	23.2%

Note: The table presents descriptive statistics on the electoral performance of MCs in our sample in their next election.

strength (Box-Steffensmeier 1996; Goodliffe 2001), by engaging in uptake of their previous challengers' campaign themes (Sulkin 2005), and by keeping their own campaign promises (Sulkin 2011). While they are not always successful in such efforts, these examples highlight the potential for linkages between legislative styles and the presence or absence of competition.

We examine three types of competition. The first is whether an MC faced a general election challenger. Most, of course, do—87% of incumbents running for reelection in our sample were challenged by a member of the other party. However, this leaves a total of 504 instances in which an incumbent faced no opposition.

Our second indicator of competition is whether MCs faced a "quality" challenger. Scholars of congressional elections have demonstrated that such challengers—generally operationalized as those who have held previous elected office—are more formidable foes to incumbents. Having successfully run for public office in the past, and then held that office, positively affects the ability of experienced challengers to gain name recognition, raise money, and receive organizational support from their party. Not surprisingly, these experienced challengers do better on Election Day than their politically inexperienced peers (see Carson, Engstrom, and Roberts 2007; Jacobson 1978; Squire 1989), winning four times as often (Jacobson 1990).

Furthermore, many scholars argue that compared to amateurs, quality challengers' entry decisions are more strongly affected by their perceptions of the likelihood of victory. It is risky to engage in behavior that would offer these potential challengers an opening, and so incumbents should do all they can to avoid such a possibility. Our data suggests that incumbents are generally successful at this—among those with a major party challenger, just about 17% (461) faced a "quality" opponent with prior elected experience.

The third and final type of competition is whether an MC faced a primary challenger. We expect that a primary challenge from a copartisan may be driven by different dynamics than general election challenges. Most notably, it seems likely that such challenges should be most common in districts where the MC is a good fit for the district because the real competition in such districts is within the party rather than between the Democrats and Republicans. Primary challenges are relatively rare across the time period we study, though they do occur for nearly one-quarter of incumbents (765 instances).

Styles, Success, and Fit

Our goal in the analyses to follow is to explore the relationships between styles, electoral victory/loss, vote margins, and the presence and quality of competition. As discussed above, we expect that these relationships will be conditioned by the level of fit between an MC and his or her district. Given the centrality of the idea of fit to our expectations, it is critical that we develop a valid measure of it. This is easier said than done, as fit is a multidimensional concept. Most often, though, when one considers whether a representative "fits" her district, one is thinking about the extent of the ideological match between them—for example, a very liberal MC is an excellent fit with a liberal district, but is less so for a moderate or conservative district.

It is important to acknowledge up front that these fit relationships are, by their very nature, endogenous to behavior and subject to selection. Candidates who are good fits for their districts are more likely to be elected in the first place than those who are not, MCs' voting records (the source of our measures of their ideology) are affected by their perceptions of their constituents' preferences, and so on. There is no getting around this. Thus, for the purposes of assessing the electoral implications of style, we take these as a given and focus on establishing whether effects of style emerge above and beyond fit, and on examining whether we observe different relationships between style and success depending upon fit.

To calculate our measure, we rely on Kernell's district ideology scores (see Kernell 2009) and individual MCs' NOMINATE scores. Because these are measured on different scales, we cannot compare them directly. Instead, we rank districts (or, more accurately, district-congresses) by ideology from liberal to conservative, and assign each observation to the appropriate decile. We do the same for MCs' NOMINATE scores, such that each observation is assigned a decile, from liberal to conservative. We then subtract the latter from the former and take the absolute value. This provides us with a (rough) measure of the relative ideological distance between the MC and his or her district.[7] For example, a legislator who scored in the 30th percentile (or 3rd decile) on NOMINATE (indicating a solidly liberal voting record) and came from a district that scored the same on Kernell's measure would have a distance score of zero, indicating a very good ideological fit. If that same MC came from

THE ELECTORAL CONSEQUENCES OF LEGISLATIVE STYLE

a district in the first or fifth decile (indicating extreme liberalism or middle-of-the-road moderation, respectively), he or she would have a distance score of two. And, if he or she represented a conservative district, in, say, the eighth decile, the distance score would be five, indicating a poor fit.

Figure 6.1 demonstrates the distribution of these fit scores. Not surprisingly, most MCs are good ideological fits for their districts, with about a quarter falling within the same decile, 60% falling within one decile, and less than one-fifth falling outside of two deciles. A quick glance at these scores suggests that the measure validly captures variation in MCs' ideological distance from their districts. For example, Phil Sharp (D-IN) has a distance score of four (as a moderate in a conservative district), whereas David McIntosh has a distance score of two (as a strong conservative in a conservative district). Moreover, the mean distance score for Southern Democrats exceeds that of Democrats from other regions (1.61 vs. 1.18; $t = 7.3$, $p < .01$), and the same holds true for New England Republicans compared to other Republicans (2.07 vs. 1.58; $t = 3.0$; $p < .01$).

Equally important, fit is significantly associated with electoral success. For example, distance scores are negatively correlated with vote

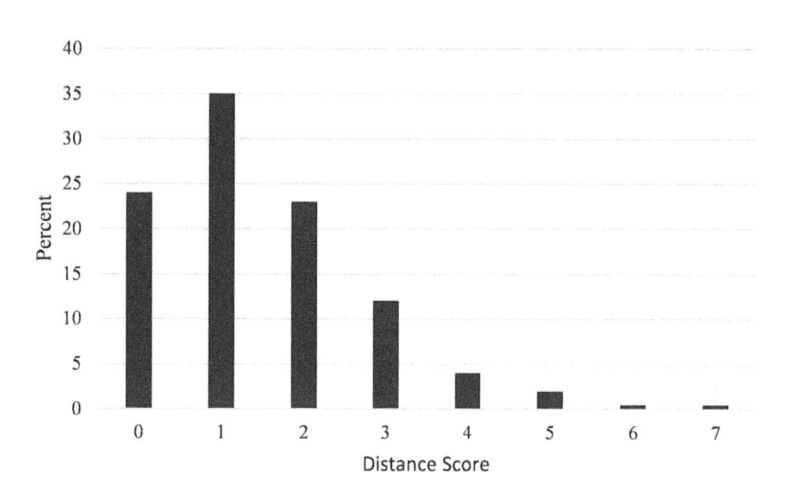

FIGURE 6.1 Distribution of distance scores
Note: Distribution of distance scores across MCs, with a range of zero (i.e., the MC's ideology falls within the same decile as the district's) to seven.

shares ($r = -.25$, $p < .01$), and if we compare the MCs who are reasonably good fits (distance scores ≤ 2) with those who are poor fits (distance scores > 2), we find that the former lose less often (3.8% of the time vs. 11.3, $t = 8.1$, $p < .01$), are more likely to run without opposition in the general election (14.2% vs. 9.3%, $t = 3.4$, $p < .01$), and, when they are opposed, are less likely to face an experienced challenger (14.7% vs. 25.7%, $t = 6.0$, $p < .01$). Those with good fits are, however, more likely to face a primary challenge (24.1% vs. 18.3%, $t = 3.0$, $p < .01$). This is not surprising, because, as mentioned above, in districts that are ideological matches with the incumbent, the real competition is more likely to be at the primary rather than the general election level.

These results bear on our expectations about the nature and magnitude of the relationships between style and success. Specifically, although there are significant differences in the success of MCs who are good and poor fits with their districts, the vast majority of poor fits still win, and with comfortable vote margins. Accordingly, we expect that styles may explain some variation within these overall results, but given these ranges, it is simply not possible for these effects to be very large. Thus, we are looking for subtle differences.

As a first take in testing our hypotheses about fit, style, and electoral security, we examine how style is associated with the two most fundamental measures of electoral success—the probability of winning or losing the next race and MCs' vote shares in that race. Our independent variables in these models include the dummy variables for legislative style (with party soldiers again the baseline category) and the "usual suspects" variables in studies of electoral success—the MC's seniority, his or her vote share in the previous election, whether he or she holds a leadership position (of any variety) or is in the majority, and, to account for partisan trends, the proportion of the vote his or her party netted nationally that year in congressional elections. We split the sample by fit, with one group consisting of those with good fits (distance scores of two or less) and those who are poorer fits (distance scores of more than two).[8] All models are limited to incumbents who ran in the next election, and the models for vote share are limited to incumbents who won.[9] We estimate the models for win/loss using probit and vote shares using OLS regression, and cluster our standard errors on the MC. Results are presented in table 6.2.

The results from these models demonstrate that styles appear to be related to success, and that the relationships between style and electoral security vary depending on fit. Specifically, the coefficients indicate that

TABLE 6.2 **Style, fit, and electoral success: Losing versus winning and vote margins**

	Lost next Fit = 1	Lost next Fit = 0	Next vote Fit = 1	Next vote Fit = 0
District advocate	.14 (.11)	−.10 (.16)	−2.15 (.68)**	2.40 (1.02)**
Party builder	−.58 (.23)**	−.31 (.28)	.54 (.89)	3.26 (1.84)*
Ambitious entrepreneur	.09 (.23)	−.04 (.44)	−1.62 (1.32)	6.75 (1.95)**
Policy specialist	−.12 (.11)	.28 (.20)	.62 (.59)	2.14 (1.13)*
Seniority	.01 (.01)	.02 (.01)*	−.07 (.03)**	−.05 (.08)
Previous vote share	−.02 (.00)**	−.07 (.02)**	.41 (.02)**	.50 (.06)**
Leader	−.43 (.16)**	−.06 (.19)	.20 (.64)	.22 (1.36)
In majority	.22 (.13)*	.40 (.20)*	−3.91 (.82)**	−3.05 (1.73)*
Party national percentage	.00 (.03)	−.01 (.04)	.25 (.15)*	.10 (.31)
Constant	−.73 (1.24)	3.62 (2.24)	33.57 (7.09)	28.35 (13.66)
N	3280	684	3135	597
Pseudo R^2/R^2	.08	.15	.19	.30

Note: This table presents probit (for lost/won) and OLS (for next vote share) coefficients for models that assess the relationship between the set of independent variables and legislators' success in their next election. Analyses for both dependent variables are limited to MCs who ran for office for the next term, and the vote share models are limited to MCs who won. ** = $p < .05$; * = $p < .10$

for MCs who are good fits, builders are less likely than soldiers to lose, but among MCs who are poor fits, no relationships emerge between style and victory or loss. Clearer effects emerge for vote shares. Here, we see that relative to the baseline, advocates perform worse when they are good fits for the district and better when they are poor fits.[10] This latter finding provides initial support for our hypotheses that the payoffs of style are conditional on fit, and that, in particular, the district advocate style is helpful in assisting MCs who are poor fits to maintain their seats, but may actually hurt legislators who are good fits. The findings for other variables are in line with research on electoral success—for example, MCs in the majority are more likely to lose and, even if they win, obtain lower vote shares than minority party incumbents, and past electoral performance is a good predictor of future success in the electoral realm.

To gain further insight into how MCs from each of the styles do relative to each other (i.e., not just compared to the baseline), we estimated the predicted vote share and confidence interval around it for MCs in each of the styles when the other variables are held at their means. These are presented in figure 6.2. As shown, among the group of MCs who are good fits with their districts, advocates have the lowest predicted vote shares and indeed fall significantly below party builders, party soldiers, and policy specialists. However, among MCs who are poor fits, advocates' predicted vote shares are in the middle of the pack, and there are

**NEXT VOTE SHARE
FIT = 1**

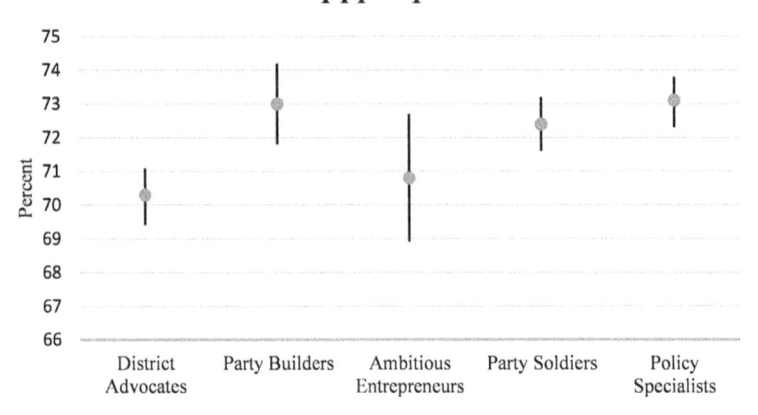

**NEXT VOTE SHARE
FIT = 0**

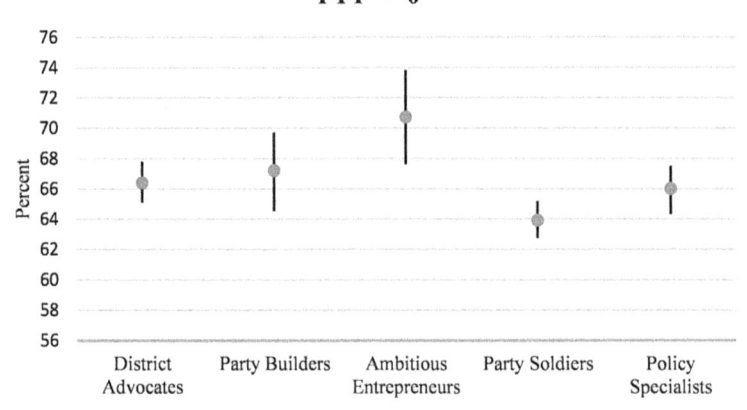

FIGURE 6.2 Style and vote shares by fit
Note: Mean vote shares (indicated by circles) and 90% confidence intervals for each style for MCs who are good fits (distance scores ≤ 2) and poor fits (distance scores > 2) for their districts.

no significant differences in the performance of advocates versus the other groups.[11]

These patterns are consistent with a story in which being a district advocate offers no advantage if one is a good fit with the district, and may even disadvantage incumbents, whereas MCs who are poor fits may be able to use the style to inoculate themselves against electoral punishment. Of course, the strongest evidence for this would be if advocates from poorly matched districts actually achieved significantly *higher* vote shares than MCs from other styles. We do not see that in the results, but this may be due to the fact that our measure of fit is a reasonable, but still noisy, proxy for the amount of leeway that legislators have. Even among the "poor fits," those who adopt other styles may do so because they sense (correctly) that they can—that they need not adopt a mostly district-focused style to hold the seat. For example, the poor fits include a number of high profile party builders such as Tom Coburn (R-OK) and John Dingell (D-MI). These MCs both come from districts in the 5th decile on ideology (conservative or liberal), but their own NOMINATE scores place them on the extremes, producing relatively high distance scores.[12] However, Coburn and Dingell held on to their seats,[13] probably because their value to the district derives from something other than ideological closeness or district service—for example, from their stature in the chamber. It is not surprising, then, that at least some legislators with styles other than that of a district advocate do well, especially when we consider the selection effects at play (i.e., if being a party builder yielded substantial electoral harm for Dingell, he would have been pushed from Congress long before our data collection began).

And, as mentioned above, it may also be the case that given the high reelection rates of incumbents, even those who are poor fits, we really have to look at the margins to uncover effects. For example, being a district advocate may not yield a substantial benefit for moderately poor fits, but for the *truly* poor fits, it could. We do indeed find evidence of this, even for the bluntest measure of electoral success—winning or losing the next election. Among MCs with distance scores of greater than three (274 observations, or about 2.5%), advocates lose just 10% of the time, compared to 13% for party builders, 20% for party soldiers, and 24% for policy specialists.[14] Thus, at the extremes, style may have the potential to make the difference between returning to Congress or not.

Legislative Styles and Electoral Competition

The results thus far have demonstrated that the styles MCs adopt are related to their future electoral prospects, even after taking into account past performance. Furthermore, and as expected, these effects are conditional on fit between the MC and his or her district. What we cannot tell from the results to this point, however, is whether these effects are direct (i.e., MCs with certain styles do better among voters, regardless of the nature of opposition they face), or whether they are filtered through level and type of competition. If some styles elicit more or better opposition, that too qualifies as an electoral effect.

Our approach to testing for such effects is to replicate the approach we took in table 6.2, but to use as dependent variables the presence of competition and its quality.[15] Recall that 13% of the incumbents in our sample are unopposed in their next election and that about 17% face a quality (i.e., politically experienced) challenger. Thus, the modal situation is for an incumbent to have opposition, but for that opposition to be "low quality." And, importantly, this is true for both groups of MCs—those who are good fits and those who are poor fits for their districts. As shown above, legislators who are poor fits are less likely than their better-situated peers to have the luxury of running unopposed, and a higher proportion of their challengers have political experience. Nonetheless, about one in ten benefit from a complete lack of opposition, and nearly three-quarters of the others still face relatively weak challengers. Thus, the effects of style are, once again, likely to be subtle.

The results are presented in table 6.3. As was the case in the win/loss and vote shares analyses, we see that past levels of competition are generally good predictors of future competition. Beginning with the results for running unopposed, for MCs who are good fits with their districts, there is no effect of style (relative to the baseline) on the propensity to face a lack of opposition. For legislators whose fit is poorer, we once again see an advantage to being a district advocate—those legislators are more likely to be unopposed. Again, to compare the groups directly, we estimate probabilities and confidence intervals for each group, holding other variables at their means (with the exception of whether they were unopposed in the *previous* election, which we hold at zero). Figure 6.3 illustrates these patterns. The average probability of good-fitting MCs running unopposed is basically the same for advocates, builders, specialists, and soldiers (about 13.5–14%), and slightly higher for ambitious entrepreneurs (at 16.6%). None of these differences is significant, however. For MCs who are poor fits, rates of running unopposed are lower. They hover between 8.5–8.9% for advocates, builders and entrepreneurs, and lower for specialists (at 6.6%) and soldiers (at 3.5%), though, at least with the controls set as they are, this is not a significant difference.

We next turn to the quality of general election opposition. In these

TABLE 6.3 **Styles and electoral competition**

	Next unopposed Fit = 1	Next unopposed Fit = 0	Quality challenger Fit = 1	Quality challenger Fit = 0	Primary challenge Fit = 1	Primary challenge Fit = 0
District advocate	−.01 (.09)	.45 (.22)**	.15 (.10)	.03 (.16)	−.08 (.08)	.24 (.18)
Party builder	−.03 (.12)	.43 (.30)	−.08 (.15)	−.02 (.24)	−.15 (.11)	.45 (.27)*
Ambitious entrepreneur	.11 (.16)	.46 (.29)	.43 (.22)**	−.28 (.45)	−.59 (.22)**	.05 (.39)
Policy specialist	−.01 (.07)	.32 (.20)	−.11 (.09)	.17 (.21)	.04 (.07)	.28 (.21)
Seniority	.01 (.00)	−.01 (.02)	.00 (.01)	−.01 (.01)	.02 (.00)**	.01 (.01)
Previous vote share	.03 (.00)**	.05 (.01)**	−.03 (.00)**	−.03 (.01)**	.00 (.00)	.01 (.01)
Previous unopposed	−.20 (.13)	−.52 (.45)	—	—	—	—
Previous quality challenger	—	—	.52 (.09)**	.35 (.18)**	—	—
Previous primary challenger	—	—	—	—	.68 (.06)**	.88 (.15)**
Leader	−.04 (.08)	.10 (.24)	.09 (.10)	.20 (.18)	.02 (.08)	−.15 (.19)
In majority	.01 (.11)	−.20 (.32)	−.17 (.12)	−.29 (.23)	−.07 (.09)	−.42 (.23)*
Party national percentage	−.02 (.02)	.01 (.06)	.04 (.02)	.05 (.05)	.04 (.02)**	.06 (.05)
Constant	−1.74 (.92)	−5.60 (2.69)	−.81 (1.12)	−.98 (2.27)	−3.09 (.83)	−4.63 (2.21)
N	3205	655	2064	464	2814	553
Pseudo R²	.05	.21	.11	.07	.06	.09

Note: The table presents probit coefficients for models that assess the relationship between the set of independent variables and the presence of competition in the next election. Analyses for all models are limited to MC's who ran for office for the next term, and the quality challenger models are limited to MC's who faced opposition in the general election. N for the primary election model is lower due to incomplete data on primary challenges. ** = $p < .05$; * = $p < .10$

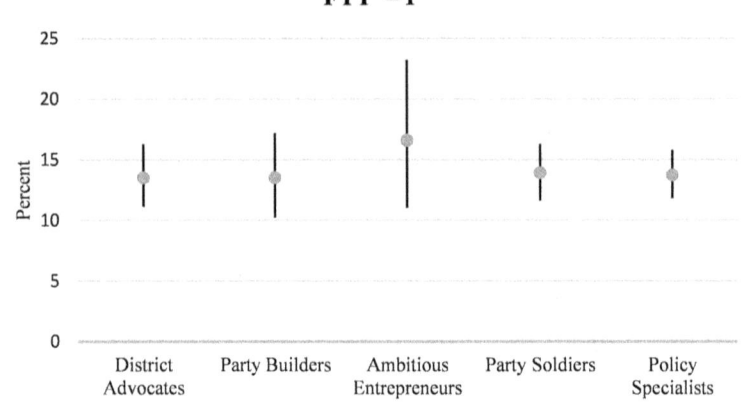

UNOPPOSED FIT = 1

UNOPPOSED FIT = 0

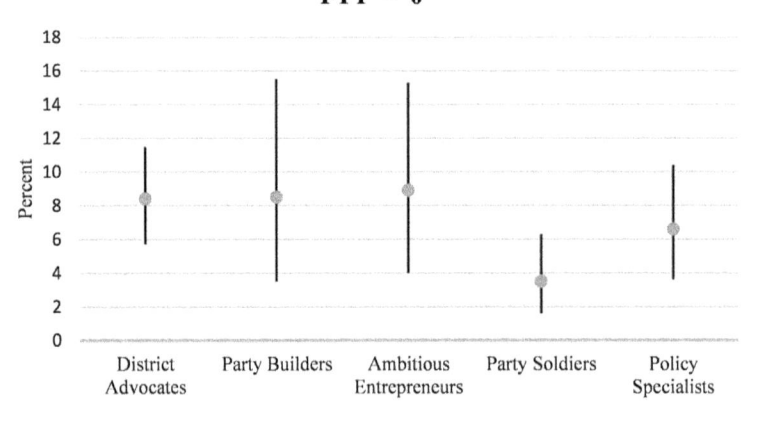

FIGURE 6.3 Styles and electoral competition
Note: Mean rates of unopposed, quality general election challenger, and primary challenger (indicated by circles) and 90% confidence intervals for each style for MCs who are good fits (distance scores ≤ 2) and poor fits (distance scores > 2) for their districts.

QUALITY CHALLENGER
FIT = 1

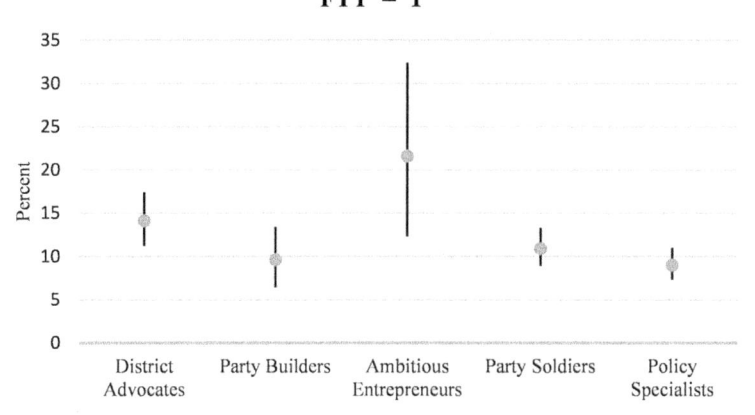

[Plot showing Percent on y-axis (0-35) with point estimates and confidence intervals for: District Advocates (~14), Party Builders (~10), Ambitious Entrepreneurs (~22), Party Soldiers (~11), Policy Specialists (~9)]

QUALITY CHALLENGER
FIT = 0

[Plot showing Percent on y-axis (0-40) with point estimates and confidence intervals for: District Advocates (~22), Party Builders (~21), Ambitious Entrepreneurs (~16), Party Soldiers (~21), Policy Specialists (~26)]

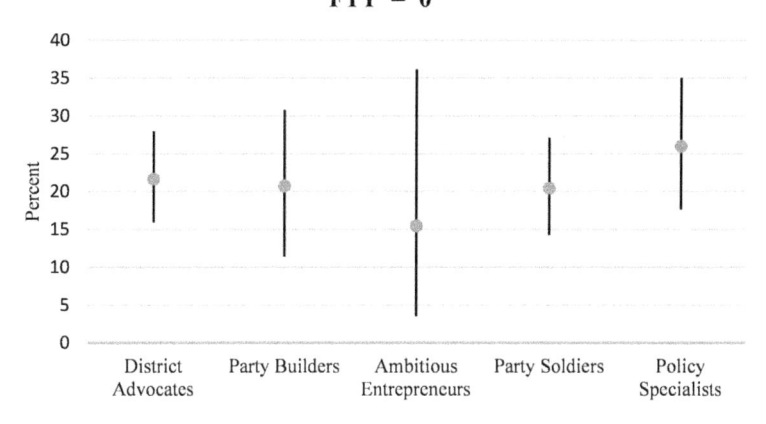

FIGURE 6.3 *(continued)*

models, the dependent variable is whether the MC faced a quality challenger, and we limit the analyses to MCs who faced opposition. These results indicate that (again relative to the baseline) ambitious entrepreneurs who are good fits are more likely to attract an experienced challenger. This may be because their visibility and idiosyncratic relationship

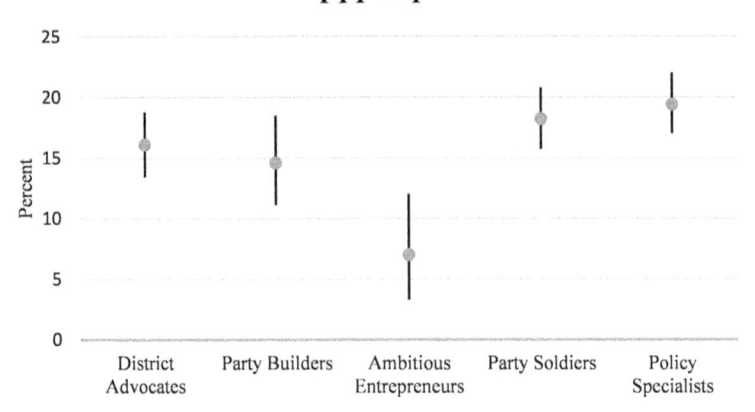

PRIMARY CHALLENGE
FIT = 1

PRIMARY CHALLENGE
FIT = 0

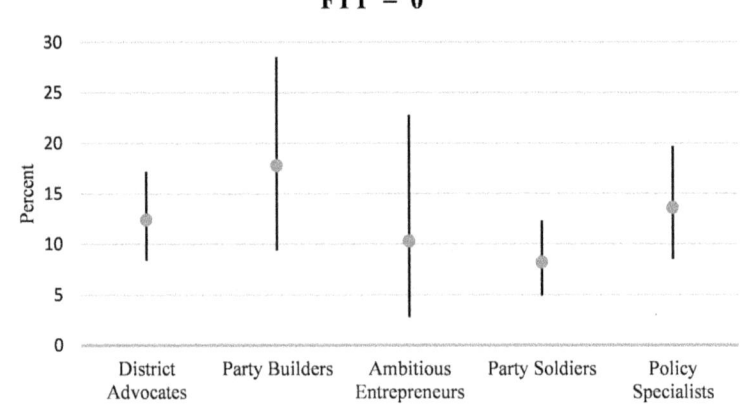

FIGURE 6.3 (*continued*)

with their party makes them a target. As shown in the second column, for the group of MCs who are not good fits, there are no significant differences.

For further insight, we once again estimate probabilities and confidence intervals, and these are presented in figure 6.3. These results approximate the patterns we have seen throughout these analyses. As expected, MCs who are good fits are, on average, less likely to face quality challengers. But, differences in the relative rankings of the styles vary by fit. For good fits, the mean probabilities for ambitious entrepreneurs and district advocates are higher than for party builders, party soldiers, and policy specialists. The differences between entrepreneurs and specialists and advocates and specialists are significant ($p < .10$). For MCs who are poor fits, the lowest raw probability is for ambitious entrepreneurs—remarkably, they face quality challengers at a lower rate when they are poor fits than when they are good fits. The highest raw probability of a quality challenger among good fits is for policy specialists, with district advocates, party builders, and party soldiers falling in the middle. None of these differences, however, is significant.

For our final indicator of competition, we examine opposition in *primary* elections. Here, we expect the relationships between fit, style, and competition to look different. Good fit should actually produce more competition rather than less, and indeed it does—about 25% of MCs who are good fits receive a primary challenge, compared to just 18% of poor fits. When we run the models, we find, as shown in table 6.3, that among MCs who are good fits (and relative to the party soldier baseline), ambitious entrepreneurs are less likely to face a same-party challenger, and among poor fits, party builders are more likely to do so. The latter is particularly interesting, as it suggests that their stature may not protect them in these contests. What we cannot tell from the data we have is whether such challenges are coming from the middle (i.e., a copartisan sees an opening to challenge a relatively extreme builder colleague in a moderate district) or even further out (if, for example, prominent MCs are good targets, perhaps with the criticism that they are not attentive enough to the district).

Figure 6.3 illustrates the mean probabilities and associated confidence intervals for each style. Among those who are good fits, policy specialists and party soldiers have the highest raw scores (i.e., are the most likely to face a primary challenge), entrepreneurs have the lowest (and are significantly behind soldiers, specialists, and party builders), and district advocates and party builders are in the middle. Among MCs who are poor fits, builders have the top raw probability and party soldiers and ambitious entrepreneurs the lowest, with district advocates and policy specialists falling in between. Again, though, the confidence intervals are broad and these differences are not statistically significant.

Putting It All Together

What, then, can we conclude about the relationships between MCs' styles and their subsequent electoral success? First, it is important to acknowledge that the effects we have uncovered are small in magnitude, and, in many cases, we do not see robust patterns of statistical significance. However, given the high success rates of incumbents—95% win again, three-quarters of them with a vote share over 60%—this is to be expected. And, we argue that there is much to be gleaned from the consistent patterns we see in the results across models. In short, there does appear to be a payoff to the district advocate style for MCs who are poor fits for their districts—in their vote shares, their probability of winning, and their likelihood of opposition. When MCs are good fits for their districts, though, being an advocate does not help and may even hurt.

For the other styles, there are less clear patterns, though soldiers do emerge as the foil for advocates. As illustrated by the example of Phil Sharp and David McIntosh, a soldier style works electorally when one is a good ideological fit for the district, but not otherwise. Party builders do not appear to enjoy any electoral advantages, perhaps because their stature is a double-edged sword, increasing support in some quarters, but decreasing it in others. Policy specialists also stay beneath the electoral radar; we find no evidence that this style is associated with electoral reward or punishment. Finally, we do see effects for ambitious entrepreneurs, and these are focused on the presence and quality of competition. When entrepreneurs are good fits, they are more likely to attract quality general election challengers, but are also well-suited to warding off primary challenges. Given that they do not generally toe the party line in voting makes the latter something of a surprise, but their combination of visibility and usefulness to the party in other ways (i.e., through the redistribution of campaign funds) may reduce their likelihood of being a target.

Style and Succession within Districts

For our final analysis of the electoral implications of legislative styles, we take a slightly different tack, exploring patterns in styles within a district (but across MCs) over time. This offers further insight into district "fit" and style and also enables us to assess how the context under which

THE ELECTORAL CONSEQUENCES OF LEGISLATIVE STYLE 147

an MC comes to office affects his or her style. In particular, do new MCs adopt the same style as their predecessors or diverge from these choices?

There are six basic scenarios that apply to such transitions. The previous MC can retire, run for higher office, or run and lose in a bid for reelection,[16] and in all of these cases, can be replaced by a copartisan or by an MC from the other party. Our sample includes 454 instances of transitions where we have data on the styles of successive MCs (i.e., we have to omit freshmen who started in the 101st Congress, the successors of MCs for whom the 110th Congress was their final term, and MCs whose service extended across the entire period). The reasons for departure from the House are split relatively evenly across the three scenarios—27% of MCs ran for higher office, 33% lost the next election, and 40% retired. Not unexpectedly, whether an MC is replaced by a copartisan or legislator from the other party is related to how he or she left office. Seventy-three percent of retirees and 64% of progressively ambitious MCs are succeeded by a copartisan, compared to just 17% of those who lose their reelection bids.[17]

Our expectations about succession are based on reasons for departure and whether the old and new MCs are copartisans, but they also depend upon the departing MC's style. For example, it seems unlikely that a builder will replace a builder, regardless of how the previous MC left office. Indeed, there are no cases in our sample of a builder succeeding a builder. And, given the low number of entrepreneurs, we observe just two cases of an entrepreneur replacing an entrepreneur. Accordingly, we focus on the three large stylistic categories—district advocates, party soldiers, and policy specialists.

Our expectations about the direct effects of party switches, reasons for leaving the House, and the departing MC's style are as follows. First, all else equal, we expect that copartisans will be more likely than outpartisans to continue their predecessor's style. Second, we expect that if an MC departs the House due to an electoral loss, the incoming legislator will be less likely to adopt his or her style than if that MC ran for higher office or retired. Third, we expect to see the highest levels of consistency in style when the previous MC was a party soldier. However, that is due less to the nature of the soldier style than to the fact that most new freshmen start out as soldiers.

The general patterns support these expectations, though evidence that they are systematic is mixed. Soldiers do have the highest levels of postelectoral transition consistency—61% of soldiers are replaced by an

MC with the same style, compared to 30% of district advocates ($t = 5.2$; $p < .01$) and just 14% of policy specialists ($t = 8.1$; $p < .01$). However, although the patterns are in the expected direction, copartisans are not significantly more likely to continue their predecessor's style (37% do, compared to 31% of outpartisans, $t = 1.3$), and MCs who lose are not less likely than those who run for higher office or retire to be replaced by a freshman with the same style. Thirty percent of losers do, compared to 38% of the progressively ambitious ($t = 1.4$) and 35% of retirees ($t = .9$).

Of course, we expect these effects to interact with one another, and so clearer patterns should emerge once we take that into account. Since we are positing three-way interactions that would not be easily interpretable within a regression framework, and, more importantly, that would lead to relatively low Ns for each of the comparisons, we opt for more descriptive explorations of the patterns in the data. In particular, we examine the distribution of styles among freshmen by various combinations of the style of their predecessors, the partisanship of the previous MCs, and their manner of leaving the chamber. These results are summarized in table 6.4.

These results are very telling. First, as also described above, we see (from the Ns) that most copartisans of a predecessor arrive due to that

TABLE 6.4 **Style and electoral succession (%)**

	Copartisans	Outpartisans
District advocates		
Overall	37 ($N = 76$)	24 ($N = 87$)
Predecessor lost	25 ($N = 8$)	24 ($N = 41$)
Predecessor ran higher	33 ($N = 27$)	26 ($N = 19$)
Predecessor retired	41 ($N = 41$)	22 ($N = 27$)
Party soldiers		
Overall	72 ($N = 46$)	53 ($N = 57$)
Predecessor lost	50 ($N = 6$)	48 ($N = 51$)
Predecessor ran higher	65 ($N = 20$)	78 ($N = 9$)
Predecessor retired	85 ($N = 20$)	43 ($N = 7$)
Policy specialists		
Overall	14 ($N = 70$)	13 ($N = 38$)
Predecessor lost	11 ($N = 9$)	9 ($N = 23$)
Predecessor ran higher	17 ($N = 18$)	17 ($N = 6$)
Predecessor retired	14 ($N = 43$)	22 ($N = 9$)

Note: The table presents the proportion of freshman MCs who adopted their predecessor's legislative style when the style, copartisanship between the freshman and predecessor, and reason the predecessor left the House are varied.

MC's retirement or decision to run for higher office, while the modal category for an outpartisan is to come to office due to the defeat of an incumbent. The findings for copartisans show that, for district advocates and party soldiers, MCs are least likely to continue their predecessor's style if he or she lost and are most likely to do so if he or she retired, with rates of consistency for progressively ambitious predecessors falling in the middle. This makes sense, as savvy MCs should be least prone to continuing a style that looks as though it may have led to a copartisan's failure. If, however, an MC chose to retire, there is more of a "passing of the torch" to the incoming freshman.

For outpartisan advocates and soldiers, the pattern looks different. We see little variation for advocates—about one-quarter of them continue the style, regardless of how the predecessor departed. Among soldiers, though, a higher proportion continue the style if their predecessor had run for higher office. Given the low N here, however, these results should be interpreted with caution.

The patterns for policy specialists, in turn, differ substantially from those of advocates and soldiers. Comparatively few MCs continue on the policy specialist style, and the rates are very similar across copartisans and outpartisans. However, an important difference not shown in the table is how these nonspecialist freshmen are distributed. Among copartisans, those who are replacing a specialist but do not adopt the specialist style themselves overwhelmingly are party soldiers (60–70% of them). Among outpartisans, though, these freshmen tend to gravitate to the district advocate style.

These results lead us to several conclusions. First, MCs do appear to respond to the electoral context in which they find themselves, more likely to continue their predecessor's style when that style appeared to pay off, and to diverge when strategic considerations dictate that would be wise. Second, and perhaps more importantly, these findings highlight that stylistic choices, while affected by district partisanship/ideology and MCs' fit with it, are not solely driven by them. If the latter were true, it would be rare to see any district advocates replacing a district advocate of another party, and yet that happens nearly one-quarter of the time. This could be because constituents come to expect a district-focused style, regardless of their representatives' partisanship, or it could be that some MCs just gravitate to that style and are able to make it work for them. Along these lines, it is not surprising that the policy specialist style, which, of the three big styles is perhaps the most driven by MCs' own preferences about how to approach their jobs, is the least likely to be "passed along," even by copartisans.

Of course, these patterns are no doubt shaped by the fact that most MCs start their careers as party soldiers, but few end them that way, so comparing the predecessor's last term to his or her successor's first will reflect this. Thus, as a follow-up we also examined the correspondence between styles in new MCs' *second* terms with their predecessors' last. Here, as expected, there are substantially fewer party soldiers and more policy specialists, but the same general patterns hold. Copartisan MCs are more likely to gravitate to the policy specialist style and less likely to hold on to the party soldier style if their predecessor had that style and lost in the previous election. Among outpartisans, we see no real differences across those whose predecessors had been advocates and soldiers, though for specialists, sophomores are more likely to take on that style if the predecessor had retired.

Thus, our results suggest that new MCs' choices to converge with or diverge from their predecessors' stylistic choices are a function both of strategic considerations and their own interests, motivations, and role orientations. While savvy MCs consider the electoral context and what became of the former holder of their seat, some new MCs will differ from their predecessor stylistically simply because they have different goals for their congressional service.

To give an example, consider the cases of Democrat Jack Flynt and Republican Mac Collins, who represented the same district in Georgia in the 1970s and 1990s and whose careers were followed by Fenno (2000) for his work on representational change in the South. Flynt, a conservative Democrat, sounded much like a district advocate:

> The main image they [his constituents] have [of me] is that if they come to me for help, I'll do anything I can to help them. Another part of the image I like to think I have is that they can talk to me, and that if they are talking, they feel that I am listening to them, listening to what they have to say. (20)

Fenno concluded that his initial assessment of Flynt's representational style as "person-intensive, personal accessibility" was strengthened by the fact that he had

> deliberately *rejected* the most prominent alternative strategy, a policy-intensive, policy advocacy representational style. . . . Neither outside nor in-

side of Congress was he a formulator or an articulator or a mobilizer or a leading decision maker in the realm of public policy. He never spoke of a bill, an amendment, or an initiative he was especially proud of. Flynt did not get into politics to make good public policy, and it was never a prominent goal of his. (31)

Flynt, first elected in 1964, was able to hold on to the increasingly Republican district by breaking from the Democratic party line and by assiduously cultivating his constituency. Toward the end of his career, though, he felt it slipping from his grasp, and he eventually chose to retire in 1978 after facing surprisingly strong challenges in 1974 and 1976 from an up and comer named Newt Gingrich (who would go on to win the seat in 1978).

Mac Collins came to Congress fifteen years after Flynt's departure, representing a district that had maintained its core, but had changed demographically, geographically, economically, and ideologically due to redistricting[18] and to the general shift toward Republicans throughout the South. In contrast to Flynt's district advocate style, Collins was described by Fenno as a "policy wonk" (105) who "came to 'make a difference' in public policy" (92). Not surprisingly, based on his patterns of activity, our clustering algorithm classifies him as a policy specialist.

To what can we attribute the stylistic differences between Flynt and Collins? One could argue that Collins (and Gingrich too) were closer matches with the district's ideology than was Flynt, giving them more leeway to pursue policy. However, as Fenno pointed out:

In terms of policy voting ... there is not much difference between Flynt's roll-call record and Collins's roll-call record. But in terms of policy development, policy influence, and policy activity, there is a large difference between the two representatives. (101)

Thus, Flynt's and Collins' differences seem more a function of who they were, how they viewed their jobs, and what motivated them. Whereas Flynt was mostly interested in knowing (and being known by) the district and providing the personal touch, Collins wanted to be a player in public policy. As a staffer noted, "The part of the job he [Collins] likes is the governing part, where he can deal with issues like budgets and taxes that he learned in the business world" (Fenno 2000, 105). Such individual-level differences, then, remain important in understanding how MCs, even those facing similar constituencies, navigate electoral constraints and pursue their careers.

Conclusions

In this chapter, we have explored a variety of electoral implications of legislative styles. As predicted, the observed relationships between style and electoral success are subtle. Importantly, though, this is not because style has little linkage with MCs' reelection prospects, but because it is so central that legislators are careful to calibrate their styles to their interpretation of their prospects, avoiding choices that will yield negative electoral consequences. Nonetheless, we do find evidence, particularly at the margins, that style can matter, especially for MCs who are relatively poor ideological fits for their districts. In these cases, the advocate style appears to offer some benefit, enabling legislators to piece together successful electoral coalitions built around something other than strong policy congruence.

These strategic considerations carry over to the decision to converge with or diverge from the stylistic choices of one's predecessor. Among new freshmen, for district advocates and party soldiers, the proportion of MCs who had a predecessor with that style and adopt the style themselves slightly outpaces the proportion of the sample as a whole with that style (30% vs. 26% for advocates and 61% vs. 58% for soldiers). Given the difficulty of comparisons and of ascertaining why they adopted that style, we cannot assert a causal link here (i.e., that the freshman took on the style *because* his or her predecessor had it). Nonetheless, we do observe evidence of strategic behavior when we assess the likelihood of carrying on a style as a function of copartisanship and the context under which the previous MC left office.

In sum, then, we conclude that styles do have the potential to affect MCs' electoral prospects. As such, they are a central part of the electoral connection, linking legislators to their constituents. Legislators cannot adopt a style willy-nilly and, indeed, would do so at their peril. Thus, successful MCs must balance their own preferences and goals with those of their constituents, choosing a style that resonates with the district while also enabling them to pursue their other aims.

CHAPTER SEVEN

Styles, Lawmaking, and Legislative Success

Here is the bottom line: With the possible exceptions of Ted Kennedy and John Dingell, no legislator in the past 50 years or more has had a broader impact on American society than (Henry) Waxman.... Little by little, bit by bit, Waxman expanded Medicaid to children and poor pregnant women, and found other ways to shape and strengthen the social safety net. Through a combination of political savvy, unmatched knowledge of the programs and their details, incredible patience, and great negotiating skills, Waxman got half a loaf here, a quarter loaf there. — Ornstein (2014), on the occasion of Waxman's retirement from the House

It is a fundamental fact of congressional life that success at lawmaking varies. Some MCs are better than others at pushing bills through the process, some committees process more legislation than do others, and some congresses produce more and higher-impact laws. Scholars have offered a host of explanations for this variation, and in this chapter, we add another possibility: that legislative styles are linked to individual and aggregate productivity.

Thus, while the previous chapter targeted the relationships between style and electoral success, here we examine style and legislative success. Styles shape how MCs approach their jobs, including their allocation of time and effort to lawmaking, and, further, how their colleagues react to their initiatives. Therefore, we expect that style will manifest itself in levels of success, such as the number of bills MCs are able to move through the legislative process and the relative productivity of committees and congresses.

Legislative Styles and MC Success

We begin at the level of individual legislators. The most recent work on individual legislative effectiveness,[1] by Volden and Wiseman (2014), argues that the most successful legislators are those who have the skills and status to pitch bills and build coalitions for them in committee and on the floor. Equally important from our perspective is that some legislators may just care more about legislating. In contrast to their less effective peers, they may be more focused on legislative success as a goal and/or view such success as more central in achieving their ultimate aims. For both of these reasons, we should observe variation in success across MCs. And indeed, the literature demonstrates convincingly that factors such as seniority, majority and leadership status, political ambition, and race and gender all shape levels of effectiveness at the individual level (see, for example, Anderson et al. 2003; Hasecke and Mycoff 2007; Volden and Wiseman 2014).

We discuss our specific expectations about style and success in more detail below, but we anticipate that policy specialists will be particularly effective lawmakers. Their interest in policy, their focused agendas, and their party loyalty should all combine to pay off for them in the legislative arena. As a result, we predict that they will score highly on indicators of individual success and that their relative prevalence within committees and congresses will be associated with aggregate productivity.

Our analyses utilize two general measures of individual legislative success. For the first, following Volden and Wiseman (2014) and others, we target the effectiveness of MCs at pushing their legislation through the stages of the legislative process. How many of their bills get committee action? How many move beyond committee? How many pass in the chamber? Become law? Second, we investigate the success MCs experience in building coalitions for their introduced legislation. This is measured as the mean number of cosponsors who sign on to an MC's bills, with greater numbers of cosponsors indicating higher levels of effectiveness in coalition-building.

Together, these measures offer insight into the relative legislative success of members. However, before moving on to develop our hypotheses about the relationship between style and success, it is useful to provide some general background on the legislative process as it pertains to bill progression, as well as some caveats about what bill success can and cannot tell us about the broader concept of legislative effectiveness.

Bill Progression in the US House

For an MC who wishes to see a bill passed into law, the first step is to introduce a measure by drafting it (or, more often, having it drafted by staffers or representatives of friendly interest groups) and then dropping it in the "hopper," a mahogany box at the front of the chamber where all introduced bills are placed. The primary sponsor of the bill can seek out cosponsors before or after introduction, typically via "Dear Colleague" letters and/or by working his or her personal connections. Many bills have no cosponsors at all, but others have dozens or even hundreds. Cosponsorship itself has no formal impact on a bill's progression, but it can have important indirect effects by signaling the overall level of support for the legislation or the ideological placement of the bill (Kessler and Krehbiel 1996; Koger 2003) and by effectively precommitting other members to vote in favor should it come up for a floor vote (Bernhard and Sulkin 2013).

After a bill is introduced, it is referred to one or more standing committees, which have considerable freedom to act (or not) on bills. Indeed, a major role of committees is to cull bills, and the vast majority of bills die there (see, for example, Krutz 2005 on "winnowing"). Accordingly, in Volden and Wiseman's formulation of legislative effectiveness, the first indicator of progression is whether a bill receives some action in committee/subcommittee, including markup, a hearing, or a vote. In our sample, the average MC will have two of his or her bills achieve this milestone, comprising about 16% of his or her total introductions.

The next stage of the process is for a bill to be reported out of committee[2] and to reach the floor of the House. A slightly smaller proportion of bills (about 13%) reach this stage. Once out of committee, a bill is placed on one of the House calendars.[3] Making it onto a calendar is no guarantee of further attention, as the Speaker then controls whether a bill gets floor action, and the powerful Rules Committee determines the context under which it will be amended and debated. To become law, bills that make it through these steps, reach a vote, and pass in the chamber (stage three of Volden and Wiseman's formulation) must also pass in the other chamber, have the conference committee proposal approved, and be signed by the President.

These are high hurdles to cross. Across the time period we study, only about 11% of introduced measures (bills and joint resolutions) pass in the House of Representatives, with a little over half of these bills eventually becoming law. For many MCs, then, failure is the modal category. In our sample, 46% of MCs had none of their bills pass in a particular congress. Very few legislators can introduce a bill expecting that it will pass, and indeed a desire to make a new law is only one of the motivations for introducing a piece of legislation. Legislators may also sponsor (and cosponsor) bills to signal their priorities and positions to constituents, to get a seat at the table in policy making on issues of importance to them, and perhaps to pave the way toward success in a policy area in the future (Kingdon 1984; Schiller 1995; Woon 2009).

The multiple motivations underlying introductions underscore an important point—that not all legislators are equally focused on the success of their bills. In addition, even for those who *are* primarily interested in lawmaking, a sole focus on bill progression misses the myriad other ways in which an introduced bill might achieve MCs' legislative goals. For example, legislators could reasonably claim victory if their bill blocked an undesired action or was incorporated into another, more successful, measure. Along these lines, Davidson et al. (2016) recount the story of retiring member of the House Robert Andrews (D-NJ), who declared that despite his lack of passed legislation—twenty-three years in office with no laws to his name[4]—he was actually quite successful because the ideas he raised found their way into other bills (210). As Andrews himself put it: "You should ask yourself how many of the ideas that were a seed planted in the bill that germinated in a larger bill. That's the way this really works" (Fahrenthold 2014). While this is clearly a defensive statement on Andrews' part, it also has an important element of truth to it. On the occasion of his retirement from the House of Representatives, President Barack Obama praised Andrews for his activity on workplace protections, education, and clean energy, and praised him as "an original author" of the Affordable Care Act, who "has been a vital partner in its passage and implementation" (Obama 2014).

For all of these reasons, bill progression alone cannot offer a full accounting of all of the ways in which MCs might influence lawmaking. Nonetheless, it is among the only readily observable and measurable indicators of individual legislative success, and so scholars necessarily rely on it. We follow suit, but with the caveat that this approach gives us just a glimpse into how styles might be associated with success.

Relationships between Style and Success

What are our predictions about the relationships between MCs' styles and their legislative success? As was the case with the electoral implications of style, we do not anticipate large differences in relative success to emerge, both because rates of success are low overall and because it is likely that legislators calibrate their introduction activity, sponsoring measures that resonate with their styles, and, potentially, their likelihood of success. For example, the average party builder might be more likely than the typical district advocate to have the status, skills, and connections to be able to push a bill through, but is also more likely to introduce high-profile and potentially controversial bills that have lower probabilities of success. In the aggregate, these competing effects may largely wash each other out.

Overall though, we expect that to the extent effects emerge, policy specialists will perform well, introducing policy-relevant measures at high rates and seeing those measures progress through the legislative process. Party builders should also excel in this realm due to their high profile and the infrastructural advantages that accrue to leaders. After all, senior members and leaders generally experience more success than junior rank-and-file members, and party builders are more likely to be senior leaders. On the other end of the scale, party soldiers are drawn disproportionately from the ranks of junior MCs, and so we should not be surprised to observe less legislative success for them.

In addition, because the focus and priorities of district advocates and ambitious entrepreneurs lie outside of the halls of Congress, we predict that they will be less legislatively successful than their specialist and builder peers. However, district advocates may benefit from norms of universalism (i.e., that encourage the distribution of benefits across districts), especially if their introductions focus on such matters. As such, we expect them to fall in the middle of the success spectrum.

Importantly, we do see some evidence that MCs of different styles tend to introduce different types of bills. In figure 7.1, we use Volden and Wiseman's tripartite categorization of bills as "commemorative" (dealing with symbolic measures such as naming post offices, minting coins, designating official days, and so on), "substantive" (dealing with matters

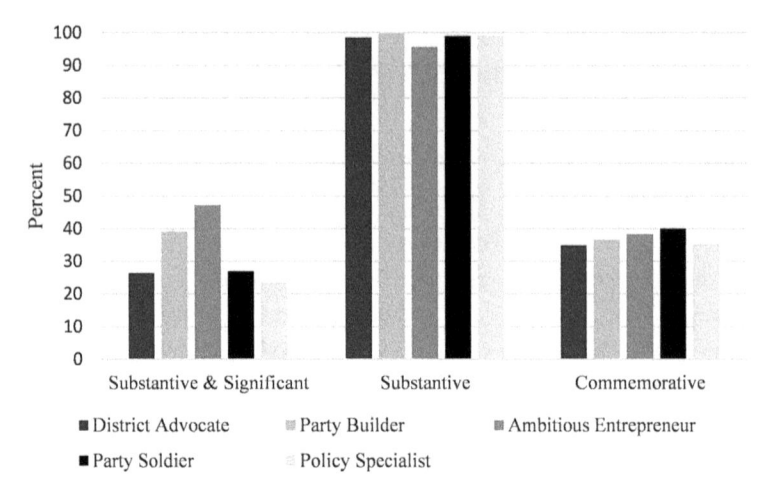

FIGURE 7.1 Bill introduction patterns by legislative style
Note: This figure presents, for each style, the proportion of MCs who introduced at least one commemorative, substantive, or substantive and significant bill.

of public policy), and "substantive and significant" (policy-focused bills of enough salience to warrant end-of-the-year write-ups in the *CQ Almanac*) (2014, 20–21), and calculate the proportion of MCs in each style who introduce at least one bill in that category.[5]

The differences are not large in magnitude, but the patterns are informative. First, nearly all MCs introduce at least one substantive bill, but only a minority of members introduces substantive and significant and commemorative bills. The least difference across styles occurs for substantive bills—the percentage of MCs that introduce at least one such measure ranges from 95.6% of entrepreneurs to 99.8% of builders. For the introduction of substantive and significant bills, the range is the largest, from 23.4% for specialists to 47.2% for entrepreneurs. Introduction rates for commemorative bills are in between, ranging from 34.9% for district advocates to 40% for party soldiers.

Some of the patterns in figure 7.1 are not surprising—for example, that party soldiers outpace party builders in the introduction of commemorative legislation, but that the opposite is true for more substantive bills. It is more unexpected that policy specialists are the least likely to introduce substantive and significant bills as, at least on first glance, it seems that these are the weighty bills that should be most likely to be associated with those with interests in policy. However, this is probably an artifact of coding "significant" bills as those that get attention in the *CQ Almanac*. The fact that these bills have progressed and seem on their way to passage may be what attracts that attention in the first place.[6] Indeed, those bills tagged by Volden and Wiseman as substantive and significant pass in the chamber at nearly ten times the rate of "regular" substantive bills (among bills introduced by members of our sample, 65.5% of substantive and significant bills pass in the House of Representatives versus 6.4% of substantive bills). Given this, it is perhaps not surprising that builders and entrepreneurs are more likely to be the sponsors of such measures.

Therefore, in what follows, we use as our locus of comparison a count of MCs' substantive bills that made it to each stage of bill progression. These comprise the vast majority of bills (for the median member, 95% of his or her introductions fall into this category) and avoid the potential problems of disentangling the endogenous relationship between salience and bill progression, or of including private bills in the analyses.[7] Figure 7.2 demonstrates, for substantive bills, how MCs from each style fare at each of the four stages of bill progression in Volden and Wiseman's

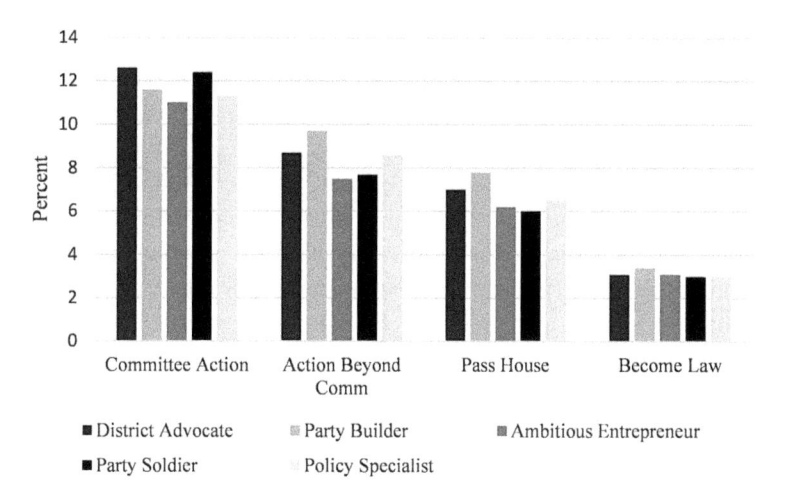

FIGURE 7.2 Bill progression by legislative style
Note: Proportion of MCs' substantive bills that reach each stage of bill progression, broken out by the style of the MC. Analyses are limited to MCs who introduced at least one substantive bill in a congress. $N = 4205$

formulation (action in committee, action beyond committee, passage in the House, and becoming law).

As shown, MCs from all styles appear to experience similar levels of success (or lack thereof) at all stages of the legislative process. For the final three stages of progression—moving beyond the committee, passing in the House, and becoming law, party builders edge out the other styles, with policy specialists and district advocates coming in second and ambitious entrepreneurs and party soldiers bringing up the rear. These differences, though admittedly slight, do accord with our general expectations about the relationships between style and success.

Ultimately, though, we want to isolate the effects of style itself, and for this, these raw comparisons are not sufficient. Instead, we need to assess the relationship between style and success taking into account other factors known to influence bill progression. For example, after considering seniority and leadership status, do party builders still outperform MCs from other styles? It is possible that they do—their style may be both a cause and consequence of being situated within the power structure in a way that enables them to push legislation forward (or, by virtue of this status, to be associated with legislation that is likely to pass), and they may be more focused on lawmaking success as a goal. On the other hand, we may see their advantage diminish once other characteristics are taken into account.

In this spirit, we are particularly interested in evaluating the relative success of policy specialists and district advocates. We know from chapter 3 that these two styles have the lowest scores on the lawmaking index, and so are not prolific sponsors or cosponsors of legislation. Thus, they are not likely to score highly on measures of success that reward *volume* of activity (i.e., the number of introductions made). However, there may be payoffs associated with these styles if, for example, other MCs respond positively to policy specialists' expertise, or if district advocates benefit from logrolling in their introduction of targeted legislation. If so, this should manifest itself in relative success in bill progression.

As an initial test of these hypotheses, we conduct a series of negative binomial regression analyses where the dependent variable is each MC's count of successful substantive bills[8] at each of Volden and Wiseman's four stages of bill progression—action in committee, action beyond committee, passage in the House, and becoming law, plus the mean cosponsorship coalition size for their introduced bills.[9] Our primary independent variables of interest are legislators' styles in a particular term, and as controls, we include a variety of other variables identified by Volden and Wiseman and others as potential contributors to legislative success: seniority, prior state legislative experience, majority status (we measure this both as whether one is in the majority and how many copartisans one has in the chamber, as these could exert independent influences on success), leadership status, size of the state delegation, ideological extremity, vote share, and demographic characteristics. We include additional controls for party and for the total number of bills introduced by MCs. These results are presented in table 7.1.

A few important points jump out from these findings. First, we see that the "usual suspects" in explaining bill progression are significant in our model as well. For example, majority party members and those with leadership positions are more likely to experience success at the various stages of the process, and junior MCs are less successful than their more seasoned colleagues. We also see a consistent negative relation-

TABLE 7.1 Success rates by legislative style

	Model 1 Action in committee	Model 2 Action beyond committee	Model 3 Pass in the House	Model 4 Become law	Model 5 Mean cosponsorship coalition
District advocate	−.20 (.08)**	.01 (.09)	.02 (.09)	−.12 (.12)	−2.84 (1.03)**
Party builder	−.16 (.09)*	.00 (.10)	.06 (.10)	.00 (.13)	.35 (1.28)
Ambitious entrepreneur	−.30 (.12)**	−.30 (.16)*	−.26 (.15)*	−.30 (.19)	3.24 (2.23)
Policy specialist	−.08 (.06)	.12 (.07)*	.13 (.07)*	.07 (.09)	−2.77 (.80)**
Democrat	−.03 (.09)	−.15 (.11)	−.11 (.13)	−.23 (.15)	1.92 (1.19)
Number of copartisans	−.00 (.00)**	−.01 (.00)**	−.01 (.00)**	−.01 (.00)**	.00 (.03)
In majority	1.18 (.12)**	1.57 (.16)**	1.67 (.18)**	1.52 (.21)**	2.08 (1.62)
New	−.22 (.07)**	−.03 (.08)	−.06 (.09)	−.25 (.14)*	−3.90 (.88)**
Seniority	.02 (.00)**	.02 (.00)**	.02 (.00)**	.02 (.01)**	.03 (.06)
Leader	.17 (.06)**	.27 (.07)**	.26 (.08)**	.40 (.10)**	3.02 (1.02)**
Exclusive committee	−.41 (.05)**	−.42 (.06)**	−.41 (.06)**	−.53 (.08)**	.50 (.73)
Ideological extremity	−.56 (.27)**	−.34 (.30)	−.38 (.32)	−.57 (.35)**	4.21 (3.58)
Woman	−.17 (.09)*	−.05 (.10)	−.08 (.11)	−.12 (.12)	2.87 (1.25)**
Racial/ethnic minority	−.08 (.09)	.08 (.11)	.14 (.11)	.16 (.15)	−1.34 (1.27)
Delegation size	.00 (.00)	.00 (.00)	.00 (.00)	−.00 (.00)	.08 (.03)**
Vote share	−.00 (.00)	−.00 (.00)	−.00 (.00)	−.00 (.00)	.02 (.02)
Number of bills introduced	.05 (.00)	.05 (.00)	.05 (.00)**	.04 (.00)**	−.25 (.03)
Constant	.32 (.48)	.23 (.59)	.53 (.66)	−.55 (.77)	17.70 (6.95)
N	4221	4221	4221	4221	4236
Pseudo R^2	.11	.12	.11	.11	.05

Note: The table presents negative binomial regression coefficients (for the bill progression models) and OLS coefficients (for the cosponsorship coalition size models) with standard errors in parentheses. The dependent variable for the bill progression models are a count of the MC's bills that made it to that stage. For the coalition model, it is the average number of cosponsors for an MC's introduced bills. Analyses are limited to MCs who introduced at least one bill. Standard errors are clustered on the MC. ** = $p < .05$; * = $p < .10$

ship between having a seat on an exclusive committee and bill progression. This may be because MCs on these prestigious committees face more competition in moving bills through, and because several of these committees do not consider individual members' bills in the same way as do more conventional committees. Another likely (and potentially related) contributor is that these committees push less legislation overall. On average, about 4% of bills introduced to exclusive committees make it beyond committee to receive action, compared to about 11% of bills introduced to other committees ($t = 4.4, p < .05$).

Second, we find that the advantages enjoyed by party builders that emerged in the raw data disappear with controls. This suggests that builders' greater success is due to their relative status in the chamber, not to their stylistic choices themselves. In contrast, the advantages that accrue to policy specialists hold up even after taking into account a variety of other factors that might explain success. Indeed, relative to the baseline, these MCs have a significantly larger number of introduced bills move beyond committee and pass in the House of Representatives. This does not hold true for district advocates, even though they did as well as specialists in the raw data. Their bills do not do significantly better beyond committee than those of their peers from other styles, and in fact fewer of their measures get action *in* committee. Finally, entrepreneurs appear to experience the least success, with significantly fewer of their bills receiving action in and beyond committee and passing in the House.

These patterns for bill progression in Models 1–4 are particularly interesting when paired with the results in Model 5, where the dependent variable is the average number of cosponsors an MC receives for his or her introduced bills. Admittedly, this is a noisy proxy for success, as the number of cosponsors a bill attracts is a function of a variety of factors. Nonetheless, the size of a cosponsorship coalition sends a signal about the MC's coalition-building prowess, and this can contribute to the likelihood of progression. Here we see that relative to the baseline, policy specialists and district advocates have *smaller* cosponsorship coalitions for their introduced bills and ambitious entrepreneurs larger. Put together, this means that policy specialists have less visible support for their substantive bills but are more likely to see them progress. This provides evidence in line with our supposition that specialists operate below the radar (and/or introduce the types of bills that attract fewer cosponsors), but that there are rewards that accrue for their specialization.

Another point to draw from these results, which is more of a caveat, is that the effect sizes for bill progression are generally small, amounting to less than one bill. This is due to the fact that the number of introduced bills is low—the average number of substantive bills introduced (among MCs who introduce at least one substantive bill) is eleven to twelve, and the maximum number of substantive bills that pass in the House is sixteen.[10] When we use CLARIFY (Tomz, Wittenberg, and King 2003) to compare the count of "bills beyond committee" for MCs where the style is varied but other variables are held at their means, we find that the predicted number of successful bills ranges from .49 for ambitious entrepreneurs to .73 for policy specialists (and .64–.66 for district advocates, party builders, and party soldiers), with a significant ($p < .05$) difference between specialists and entrepreneurs. Accordingly, the effects, though systematic, do not generally amount to large differences across individuals. This is not unique to the influence of styles—all studies of bill success deal in small numbers, and so most significant effects are nonetheless slight in magnitude. And, as with other studies of success, we find that the variables we identify do not explain most of the variation in success, again related in part to the small N.[11]

Nonetheless, we do see evidence of an association between styles and individual success, particularly for policy specialists. Before moving on to examine the aggregate relationships between styles and congressional lawmaking and productivity, we conduct one final analysis at the individual level, exploring whether there are differences in the factors explaining the relative success for MCs in each of the styles. For example, is majority status a stronger predictor of success for some styles than others? To explore such questions, we replicate the analyses from table 7.1,[12] but split the sample by style. Our dependent variable is the number of substantive bills that move beyond committee.[13] We also add an additional independent variable, which is whether an MC had maintained his or her style from the previous congress to the current congress. This enables us to test whether consistency in style is associated with success. For instance, if the rewards that accrue to policy specialists are a function of a reputation for expertise, then longer service as a specialist should be associated with higher levels of success. And, to further explore the relationships between leadership status and success, we replace the "any leadership position" variable from table 7.1 with the full set of leadership categories from previous chapters.[14] Our results are presented in table 7.2.

The findings indicate strong similarities across styles. Committee lead-

TABLE 7.2 **Explaining success of different styles**

	Model 1 District advocates	Model 2 Party builders	Model 3 Ambitious entrepreneurs	Model 4 Party soldiers	Model 5 Policy specialists
Lagged style same	.11 (.13)	.06 (.13)	.02 (.27)	−.13 (.13)	.16 (.09)*
Democrat	−.25 (.20)	−.02 (.25)	−.61 (.51)	−.13 (.27)	−.05 (.21)
Number of copartisans	−.00 (.01)	−.00 (.01)	.00 (.01)	−.01 (.01)	−.01 (.01)
In majority	.89 (.31)**	1.84 (.36)**	.11 (.77)	1.80 (.41)**	1.55 (.29)**
Seniority	.00 (.01)	.01 (.01)	.02 (.02)	.01 (.01)	.01 (.01)
Chamber/party leader	.25 (.26)	−.06 (.18)	−.22 (.33)	−.41 (.28)	.23 (.19)
Campaign leader	.28 (.28)	−.17 (.20)	−.56 (.36)	−.77 (.32)**	−.14 (.23)
Committee leader	.77 (.17)**	.38 (.19)**	1.06 (.46)**	.56 (.19)**	.58 (.16)**
Exclusive committee	−.21 (.13)*	−.44 (.18)**	.15 (.25)	−.48 (.13)**	−.50 (.10)**
Ideological extremity	.67 (.57)	.80 (.79)	−1.57 (.67)**	−1.27 (.48)**	−.36 (.50)
Woman	.11 (.18)	−.46 (.26)*	.52 (.40)	.13 (.20)	−.25 (.18)
Racial/ethnic minority	.04 (.31)	.19 (.24)	−.28 (.57)	.22 (.25)	−.02 (.17)
Delegation size	.01 (.01)	.01 (.01)	−.03 (.01)**	−.00 (.00)	.01 (.00)**
Vote share	.00 (.00)	.01 (.00)	.00 (.01)	−.00 (.00)	−.00 (.00)
Number of bills introduced	.06 (.01)**	.03 (.01)**	.04 (.01)**	.04 (.01)**	.05 (.01)**
Constant	−1.68 (1.12)	−1.49 (1.48)	−1.39 (2.64)	.88 (1.39)	.30 (1.12)
N	854	479	99	609	1178
Pseudo R^2	.13	.14	.22	.16	.14

Note: The table presents negative binomial regression coefficients with standard errors in parentheses. The dependent variable is the count of an MC's bills that made it past committee, with MCs from each style analyzed separately. Analyses are limited to MCs who introduced at least one bill, and, due to the inclusion of the lagged style variable, excludes freshmen. Standard errors are clustered on the MC. ** = $p < .05$; * = $p < .10$

ership is a predictor of success for MCs of all styles, and majority status is positively associated with it and exclusive committee status negatively related for all but ambitious entrepreneurs. This may be because entrepreneurs are less bound to, and less affected by, their institutional status. For entrepreneurs and policy specialists, MCs with campaign leadership positions are less successful in the legislative realm, perhaps because their priorities are elsewhere. We also see some differences in the effects of delegation size across styles—entrepreneurs do better legislatively when they hail from small states, while specialists are more successful when they come from large delegations, which may trace back to the importance (or lack thereof) of same-state networks in their lawmaking efforts. The effects are all small in magnitude, so not too much should be made of them, but they do suggest some subtle differences across styles, particularly between ambitious entrepreneurs and policy specialists.

Also as predicted, we see an effect of lagged style, but only for policy specialists. Specialists who had also been specialists in the previous term are more successful at pushing bills through committee than their peers who are new to the specialist style. Once again using CLARIFY to estimate the size of the effect, we find a difference of about one-third of a bill for returning specialists versus new ones. Though this effect is not substantively large in raw terms, given that the mean number of bills moved past committee by specialists is about two (and the median is zero) it reflects a comparatively large shift. To the extent that this effect is cumulative across time, we should expect even larger differences to emerge.

Styles and Aggregate Legislative Productivity

The results above indicate that individual MCs' styles can have implications for their own legislative success. As a corollary, we contend that styles may also affect the lawmaking process in Congress more generally. The clearest evidence of such an effect would be if the distribution of styles within a congress was related to the productivity of that congress—that is, the number of bills it passed. After all, if the policy specialist style is associated with more bill success at the individual level, then having more specialists in Congress may translate into more bills being passed. On the other hand, there are reasons why these individual-level dynamics might not play out on the aggregate level. For example, individual specialists may experience more success when they are low in numbers, and so an increase in the prevalence of their style might not lift productivity overall.

To assess these relationships, we calculate the number of substantive bills passed per congress across the ten congresses we study (this value ranges from 122 to 629), and the proportion of MCs in each style in each congress. District advocates range from 23 to 31%, party builders from 5 to 16%, ambitious entrepreneurs from 2 to 6%, party soldiers from 17 to 45%,[15] and specialists from 17 to 39%. This level of variation is sufficient to potentially explain levels of productivity, and we find that there are indeed relationships between the distribution of styles and the aggregate productivity of Congress. As shown in figure 7.3, the higher the proportion of builders and specialists in a congress, the greater the number of substantive bills passed ($r = .56$, $p = .09$ and $r = .69$, $p = .03$, respectively), and the more soldiers, the fewer bills are passed ($r = -.66$, $r = .04$). The correlations for district advocates and ambitious entrepreneurs are negatively signed but insignificant.

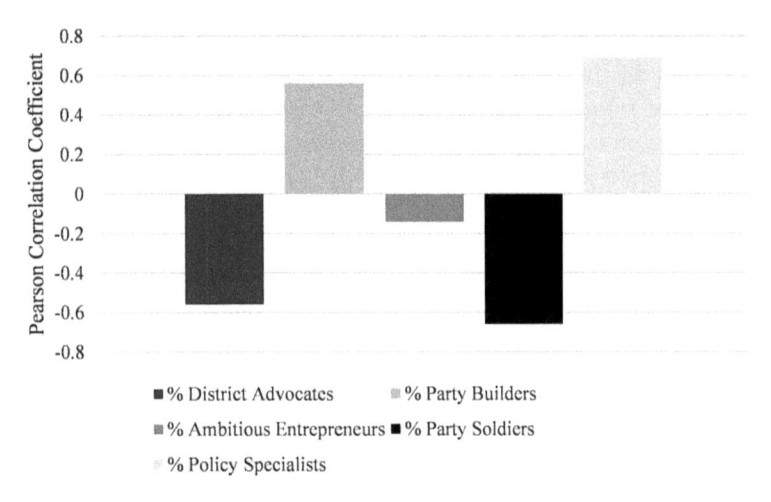

FIGURE 7.3 Styles and aggregate congressional productivity
Note: Correlations between the proportion of MCs from each style in each congress and the number of substantive bills that passed the chamber in that congress. Each bar represents a correlation coefficient. $N = 10$

Given the low N (just ten congresses), systematic analyses with multiple controls are not particularly appropriate. However, to assess the robustness of the correlations in figure 7.3, we specified some simple regression models, the results of which indicated that our findings hold with a control for the total number of substantive bills (i.e., so that variation in passing bills is not just an artifact of having more bills introduced), and are not driven by the number of new MCs in a congress. When we translate these proportions into counts of bills, we find that every additional specialist in a congress is associated with the passage of two to three additional substantive bills. Given the range of specialists per congress (from 74 in the 101st Congress to 167 in the 108th), this has the potential for a noticeable effect.

As throughout this chapter, we want to be careful about making causal claims, as there could be factors that explain both the distribution of styles and rates of congressional productivity. Nonetheless, in concert with the results for individual legislative success, these patterns suggest, once again, that styles matter for understanding variation in productivity. The distribution of style in the House as a whole has the potential to shape the volume of substantive legislation passed by the chamber.

Styles and Lawmaking in Committees

Having explored the effects of legislative style at the lowest and highest levels of aggregation, we now move to the middle to investigate style and lawmaking at the level of congressional committees. Committees are central to understanding policy making in the House, and so the composition of committees has long been a topic of interest to scholars of Congress. In the 1990s and early 2000s, heated and protracted scholarly debates about the nature of legislative organization centered in part around the role of committees, and, specifically, whether or not members of committees are "high demanders" in a policy area and/or ideological preference outliers relative to the chamber or party median (see, for example, Adler and Lipinski 1997; Krehbiel 1990; Shepsle and Weingast 1987).

We also argue that the composition of committees may vary, but we focus on a different dimension: the relative distribution of legislative styles. While we expect MCs from all styles to serve on all or most committees, it seems reasonable that, based on their policy content and the nature of the work they do, some committees may have greater representation from a particular style than others. For now, we are agnostic about whether this occurs due to variation in initial requests or in assignments,[16] and we recognize that the causal relationship between style and committees is likely complicated. Are MCs from particular styles drawn to certain committees, do committees "make" one a specific style, or is it a little bit of both? Instead, we focus on investigating differences in the distribution of styles across committees and the consequences of those differences for lawmaking.

The null hypothesis, of course, is that there will not be systematic variation in the distribution in styles across committees, except perhaps for those where assignments are a function of seniority and stature within the party. While we do not have a strong theory of assignments at the level of particular committees, we do expect that, for example, district advocates might be drawn to more particularized committees such as Agriculture and underrepresented on "inside baseball" committees such as House Administration, whereas the opposite will hold true for builders and perhaps specialists. It also seems likely that builders will be overrepresented on exclusive committees, and soldiers, given their relative youth as a group, will serve on more "entry level" nonexclusive committees.[17]

Table 7.3 presents our descriptive results on the distribution of styles across committees. The top row presents the proportion of each style in the sample overall, and the other rows present the distribution of styles for each committee (aggregated across all ten congresses). We indicate in bold when the proportion of MCs from a style on a committee is plus or minus at least one standard deviation from the overall percentage of MCs with that style.

These results confirm that the distribution of styles varies by committee. For example, we find that district advocates are overrepresented on Agriculture, Post Office, and Public Works—all committees that focus on local issues. As expected, they are also underrepresented on "internal" committees such as House Administration, Standards of Official Conduct, and District of Columbia,[18] as well as relatively prestigious committees dealing with national policy such as Judiciary and Homeland Security.

TABLE 7.3 **Legislative styles by committees**

	Advocate 26%	Builder 12%	Entrepreneur 4%	Soldier 27%	Specialist 31%
Agriculture	**+10**	−7	0	+2	−5
Appropriations	+5	+5	−2	**−13**	+5
Armed Services	+7	−3	−1	−2	0
Banking and Financial Services	+2	−2	−1	+7	−6
Budget	−4	−4	0	+2	+6
District of Columbia*	**−13**	+4	−4	**+18**	−5
Economic & Educ. Opportunities	−3	−3	−2	+6	+3
Commerce	−4	+2	−1	+1	+3
Foreign Affairs	−4	−4	+2	+8	−1
Government Operations	−1	−4	−1	+5	+1
House Administration	**−11**	**+14**	−4	−5	+6
Judiciary	**−19**	+2	−1	+5	**+13**
Merchant Marine*	+8	−9	+2	+10	−9
Interior/Resources	−3	−4	−1	+10	−2
Post Office*	**+11**	**−12**	+3	+9	−11
Public Works	**+11**	−7	−1	+2	−6
Rules	−7	**+13**	0	−5	−1
Science	+6	−6	0	+7	−6
Small Business	−1	−8	−2	**+17**	−7
Standards of Official Conduct	**−11**	−5	−4	−7	**+26**
Veterans Affairs	+1	−6	−1	+4	+2
Ways and Means	−7	**+10**	−2	−4	+4
Intelligence	+4	+3	+1	−7	−2
Homeland Security*	**−11**	**+23**	+1	−12	−2

Note: This table summarizes data on the proportion of MCs in each committee (across all congresses) who fall into each of the five styles, indicating how that proportion varies from the overall percentage of a style in the sample as a whole. Bold indicates that the difference is +/− at least one standard deviation from the mean.
* = Committee did not exist across entire ten congresses.

Ambitious entrepreneurs share some of the patterns with district advocates—they are underrepresented on House Administration and Standards of Official Conduct, which is not surprising given their more external focus. They are also underrepresented on DC and overrepresented on Post Office. However, perhaps due to their greater visibility, they do not suffer from underrepresentation on more prestigious committees.

Builders, in turn, tend to be the opposite of district advocates in terms of their committee patterns. They are overrepresented on House Administration and Homeland Security, as well as exclusive committees such as Rules and Ways and Means, but are underrepresented on the more particularized (and low prestige) Post Office committee. And, as shown, the "over/under representation" scores are oppositely signed from the district advocates on fifteen of the twenty-four committees.

Party soldiers and policy specialists also tend to display different patterns from one another, though there are fewer committees for which they are markedly overrepresented or underrepresented. Table 7.3 shows that soldiers are underrepresented on the Appropriations committee and overrepresented on District of Columbia and Small Business. Policy specialists, on the other hand, are overrepresented on Judiciary and Standards of Official Conduct (the opposite of district advocates), but there are no committees on which they are substantially underrepresented.

These patterns suggest that committees do have different "flavors" to them, and that these are not merely a function of the desirability of particular assignments, but of the types of members who serve on them. The question, of course, is whether this is related to their productivity. Does it matter, for example, that Agriculture has many district advocates and few policy specialists, while Judiciary has many policy specialists and few district advocates?

We are also interested in whether variation in the proportion of styles *within* a committee across time affects its productivity. For instance, if we assume that builders and specialists are particularly interested in acting on legislation, do we see higher rates of committee attention to issues in congresses when there is a larger proportion of builders or specialists on a particular committee?

To answer the first question, we pool our observations across committees, where the unit of analysis is the congress-committee. Our dependent variables are the proportion of bills referred to a committee that got action in committee, action beyond committee, and that passed into law. Our independent variables are the proportion of committee members in each of the five styles (with party soldiers again the baseline) and a control for the total number of bills referred to the committee in a congress. We cluster the standard errors on the committee. These results are presented in table 7.4.

How much does style matter for committee productivity? With this pooled cross-sectional approach, the answer is, not much. As shown, we see no effects for the distribution of styles on the proportion of introduced legislation that gets action beyond committee or is passed into law. Perhaps the most interesting and unexpected finding occurs for the first model, where the dependent variable is the proportion of bills that get at least some action within the committee or one of its subcommittees (e.g., a hearing or markup). Here, we see that relative to the baseline, committees with a lot of specialists and advocates attend to a lower proportion of the bills referred to them. Indeed, if we conduct analyses where we compare one style at a time to the sum of all of the others, we find that committees with high proportions of specialists address a significantly lower ($p < .10$) proportion of their bills, while committees with high proportions of soldiers process significantly more.

Why might this be? One possibility is that the relative youth and inexperience of soldiers makes them more reliant on their committee activity to make claims of legislative initiative, driving them to push for hearings and markup, perhaps indiscriminately (i.e., on bills that have no chance of passage). That the "soldier effect" does not persist beyond the committee stage offers some support for this hypothesis. In contrast, special-

TABLE 7.4 **Distribution of styles and committee productivity**

	Action in committee	Action beyond committee	Passed in the chamber
Percentage of advocates	−30.46 (12.21)**	−18.08 (11.59)	−.13 (.09)
Percentage of builders	−8.22 (30.05)	9.57 (28.21)	.16 (.27)
Percentage of entrepreneurs	−8.23 (42.12)	18.99 (34.59)	.28 (.31)
Percentage of specialists	−32.49 (12.96)**	−11.15 (11.01)	−.07 (.10)
Number of bills referred	−.00 (.00)	−.00 (.00)	−.00 (.00)
Constant	32.92 (7.44)	17.26 (6.27)	.11 (.05)
N	207	207	207
R^2	.10	.07	.10

Note: The table presents OLS coefficients with standard errors in parentheses. The dependent variable is the percentage of bills referred to a committee (pooled across committees) that received action in committee, action beyond committee, and that passed in the House of Representatives. ** = $p < .05$

ists may be more selective about the measures they pursue in committee and/or more devote more time and effort to individual bills.

Another possibility is that these results are an artifact of differences across committees. Committees are difficult to compare to one another on measures of success because of the variation in the amount and type of legislation they receive. For example, the number of bills referred in a congress ranges from zero (for the Budget committee in the 101st and 102nd Congresses and the Standards of Official Conduct committee in the 102nd, 105th, 106th, and 107th) to 2,318 (for the Ways and Means committee in the 110th). And, while the median committee attends to about one in ten of its referred bills, 10% attend to one-third or more of the bills they receive.

As a first take at exploring this, we split the sample by exclusive/nonexclusive committee and uncovered basically the same pattern of results.[19] However, this may still not be sufficient to capture committee-level differences. While we could control for these statistically, what we would really like to do is to drill down to the level of individual committees to explore how variation in the distribution of styles across congresses is related to committee success. For this, we calculate a series of correlations to assess, for each committee, the relationship between the proportion of MCs in a particular style and the productivity of that committee in terms of acting on legislation in committee, having legislation acted on beyond committee, and passing legislation in the chamber. Thus, these tests tell us whether the relative prevalence of each of the styles in each committee across time is associated with that committee's success at lawmaking. These results are summarized in table 7.5.

Here the effects of the specialist style, which also emerged in the individual- and congress-level analyses, are clear. For action beyond committee and passage in the House, for nine of the twenty committees, the proportion of specialists in the committee has a significant positive association with the volume of legislation referred there that gets action beyond committee and passes in the House. These committees run the gamut in terms of topic and exclusivity, and include Banking, Commerce, Government Operations, House Administration, Judiciary, Rules, Science, Standards of Official Conduct, and Ways and Means. Equally important, for *no* committees is the proportion of specialists negatively associated with success. In short, for these committees, the more specialists there are, the better the committee does at moving legislation. While confirming *why* these effects exist is beyond our scope here, we

TABLE 7.5 **Correlations between committee composition and success**

	Percentage with action in committee +	Percentage with action in committee −	Percentage with action beyond committee +	Percentage with action beyond committee −	Percentage passed in House +	Percentage passed in House −
Agriculture	—	—	—	—	—	—
Appropriations	—	Builder	Entrepreneur	—	Entrepreneur	—
Armed Services	—	—	Builder	Advocate	Builder	Advocate, soldier
Banking	—	—	**Specialist**	Soldier	**Specialist**	Soldier
Budget	Builder, **Specialist**	Advocate	—	—	—	—
Education	—	Builder	—	—	—	—
Commerce	Soldier	**Specialist**	**Specialist**	Advocate, soldier	**Specialist**	Advocate, soldier
Foreign Affairs	—	—	—	—	Builder	Advocate
Government Operations	**Specialist**	Advocate, entrepreneur	**Specialist**	—	**Specialist**	Advocate
House Admin.	Entrepreneur	Builder	**Specialist**	—	**Specialist**	—
Judiciary	Soldier	Builder	**Specialist**	Soldier	**Specialist**	—
Resources	Soldier	Entrepreneur	—	—	—	—
Public Works	Soldier	Advocate, builder	—	—	—	—
Rules	—	—	**Specialist**	—	**Specialist**	—
Science	—	—	**Specialist**	—	**Specialist**	Entrepreneur
Small Business	Builder, entrepreneur	—	Builder, entrepreneur	Advocate	Entrepreneur	Advocate
Standards	**Specialist**	Builder	**Specialist**	—	**Specialist**	Builder
Veterans	—	—	—	—	—	—
Ways & Means	Advocate	—	**Specialist**	Soldier	Builder, **specialist**	Soldier
Intelligence	Advocate	Specialist	Advocate	—	Advocate	—

Note: This table summarizes a series of correlations between the proportion of each style in each committee over time and the proportion of legislation referred to that committee that receives action in committee, action beyond committee, and that passes into law. The analyses are limited to committees that existed across all ten congresses. A style is listed in the table if it was significantly ($p < .10$) positively or negatively associated with success. Specialists are in bold to highlight their role at each of the stages.

hypothesize that this is most likely due to the focus these specialists have on issues of interest to them, resulting in "better"[20] legislation moving forward, and, relatedly, deference from colleagues in response to their expertise and skill.

In contrast, party builders do not seem to bring the same success to their committees. This may be because they are relatively few in number and/or because their comparative advantage is on the highest profile legislation, rather than the "regular" substantive bills that we study here. Thus, in general, party builders neither add to nor detract from committee productivity. The proportion of district advocates and party soldiers on a committee, however, is more often *negatively* associated with bill progression. There is only one committee (Intelligence) where more district advocates is associated with more success, and three to five committees (depending on whether we consider action beyond committee or passage in the House) where it is negatively related. There are also no committees where more party soldiers means more success beyond committee, and there are only a handful where they are associated with less success.

Interestingly, all of these patterns for what happens to bills after they leave committee (the second and third columns of the table) stand in marked contrast to the results we see for the proportion of referred bills that get attention *in* the committee (the first column). The findings for the latter are pretty muddled, but two conclusions can be drawn. First, no comparative advantage accrues to having more policy specialists. For three committees, they are associated with more action within committee and, for two, less. Second, whereas for action beyond committee and passage in the House, the proportion of party soldiers, when significant, was always negative, here the relationship is positive. There are four committees where more party soldiers equals more attention to referred bills, and no committees where their presence detracts from attention.

These results, although admittedly suggestive, offer support for our supposition above that soldiers are eager to work on legislation in their committees, but are, perhaps, indiscriminate about which measures they pursue. Specialists, in contrast, may address fewer bills in their committee work (which corresponds with our findings from the basic clustering results that they also introduce and cosponsor less than do soldiers), but appear to devote more time and effort to them and/or be better arbiters of quality, pushing stronger measures beyond their committees.

Conclusions

In this chapter, we have shown that legislative style has important relationships with individual and aggregate legislative success. On this dimension, policy specialists are the stars. They are able to navigate more of their own legislation through the process, and their relative presence across committees and congresses is related to aggregate productivity. By considering legislative styles, we therefore gain more nuanced insight into the dynamics driving lawmaking in Congress and to the role that policy specialists play in the House of Representatives.

More generally, these results suggest the value of disaggregating bill progression by type of bill and stage in the legislative process. We find that different dynamics drive action within committee and action beyond, including floor consideration and bill passage. Although our focus is on the effects of individual legislative styles and their distribution across committees, we expect these patterns may emerge with other predictors of success and productivity as well.

Taken together with the results about electoral success in the previous chapter, our findings here confirm that styles are related to MCs' potential for success in the chamber, and, perhaps, for their career advancement. In the next chapter, we focus explicitly on how styles correspond with MCs' broader career trajectories—whether they move up to positions of power within the House, whether they move on to higher office, and whether early styles can help us to predict the path that a new legislator's career will take.

CHAPTER EIGHT

Career Advancement and Legislative Styles

During the summer of 2011, a dinner was held in Kentucky marking the two hundredth anniversary of the great Henry Clay's inauguration as House Speaker. Three of the attendees were Boehner, Pelosi, and her predecessor as Speaker, Dennis Hastert. . . . Listening that night to both Pelosi and Boehner describe the elaborate plans they had made for the day when each of them ascended to the Speakership, Hastert thought to himself: "Wow. These two people have been thinking about all this for a long time." — Draper (2012, 43)

We began this book with the assertion that legislative styles are about MCs' careers. Legislators' styles reflect how they view their roles as members of the House of Representatives in the present, and also how they envision their careers progressing over the longer term. At any one point in time, some MCs are looking ahead to long tenures in the chamber, others are considering retirement, and still others harbor ambitions to move up to a Senate seat, to return to their home states as Governor, or even perhaps to one day become President. And, as we have seen throughout the previous chapters, among those who choose (or have it chosen for them by circumstances) to pursue long-term House careers, some aim for party leadership, some invest in policy entrepreneurship, and others are satisfied with their lots as back benchers.

Our contention throughout has been that MCs' stylistic choices are linked to their achievements in the chamber and beyond. Chapters 6 and 7 targeted the relationships between styles and legislators' electoral and legislative success. In this chapter, we highlight the effects of styles on other career variables, such as gaining leadership positions and preferred committee assignments.[1] We also examine the relationship between styles and how MCs end their House service, including whether they retire from public life or make a bid for higher office, and the conditions under which each decision occurs. We focus both on the immediate consequences of style (e.g., whether particular styles are associated with a run for higher office in the next election), as well as the predictive power of early styles on ultimate career achievements. Can we, for instance, predict who will eventually rise to positions of power in the chamber based on MCs' styles as sophomores?

In this chapter, we come full circle in our investigation of styles and career trajectories. Underlying our expectations about these relationships are theories of political ambition that have long been central to work on legislative politics. We begin, therefore, with a brief overview of ambition and career paths in Congress.

Styles, Political Ambition, and Career Decisions

The seminal work on the question of ambition is Schlesinger's *Ambition and Politics: Political Careers in the United States* (1966). At the root of Schlesinger's theory is the idea that all politicians are ambitious but that this ambition takes several different forms. "Discrete" ambition is where an elected official seeks to hold office "for its specified term" only and then to leave public office (10). Although rare among MCs, this type of ambition applies to some who promise to adhere to strict term limits and then do so, and some who serve a partial term to replace a departing representative, but who have no desire to themselves run for the seat in the next election.[2] "Static" ambition occurs when an elected official "desires to make a long career out of a particular office," which in the context of congressional careers has generally been viewed as the intention to stay in the House of Representatives until retirement from public life (10). "Progressive" ambition, the subject of a large literature in political science, applies when a politician who holds one office aspires to another that is thought of as more prestigious. In US legislative studies, this is typically operationalized as a representative running for a Senate seat or for the governorship of his or her state.

Although Schlesinger's tripartite classification remains the most commonly invoked in research on ambition, other scholars have rightly noted that it oversimplifies the opportunity structure in the House of Representatives by neglecting to capture what we might call "institutional ambition." Such institutional ambition reflects the desire to rise to positions of power and influence within the chamber, and it too varies across members (see Herrick and Moore 1993, Hibbing 1991). MCs with the goal to become, say, Speaker of the House are clearly ambitious in the colloquial sense of the term, but in Schlesinger's scheme, these members would be lumped together in the "static" category along with those who harbored no desire for leadership positions. As one of the party leaders interviewed by Loomis (1984) put it, there are differences between members who "want to sit on the heating and ventilating subcommittee" and those who want to become a whip (194). Thus, in what follows, we treat institutional and progressive ambition as topics of equal interest.

Among those MCs who serve out their careers in the House, whether as leaders or rank-and-file members, we are also interested in what drives their eventual decisions to retire or to run for an additional term. Some MCs are forced into retirement because of ailing health and an inability to do the job, but most have some control over the timing of their exits from the House. As we discuss in more detail below, scholars have shown that these choices are often strategic, a function of MCs' likelihoods of successfully retaining their seats in a reelection bid and of the value of their current positions to them (Groseclose and Krehbiel 1994; Hall and Van Houweling 1995; Moore and Hibbing 1998). Based on these calculations, most MCs will decide to throw their hats in the ring again, while others will bow out of public life, at least for the time being.

To delve further into the dynamics of these choices, we first establish the distribution of career decisions among members of our sample. Whereas in previous chapters, we focused mostly on the member-congress as the unit of observation, here we also consider the member across his or her career as that unit. Our sample includes 1,011 individuals for whom we have data on their style in at least one term.[3] Of these, 84% have completed their service in the House of Representatives at the time of this writing (late 2016, the 114th Congress), while 163 of the MCs are still in office. Among those who have left the House,[4] 30% lost,[5] 38% retired,[6] 22% ran for higher office, and 12% departed Congress in the middle of a term due to their death, resignation (often because of scandal), or, in a few cases, being appointed to an executive branch position.[7] Figure 8.1 presents some descriptive statistics on the career paths of our MCs.

The figure also illustrates the proportion of MCs in the sample who attained various leadership positions within the chamber between 1989 (the 101st Congress) and 2016 (the 114th Congress).[8] These calculations

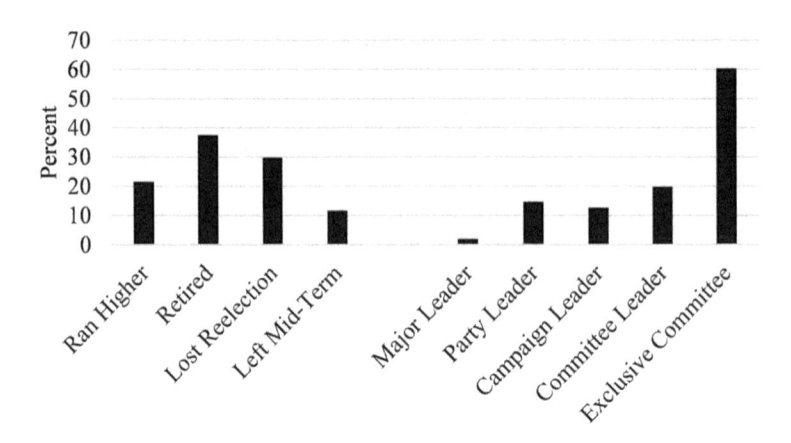

FIGURE 8.1 Career advancement and exit
Note: "House exit paths" of the 1,011 unique MCs in our sample, as well as the proportions who attained various types of leadership positions at least once in their careers.

include MCs who are still serving in the House as of the 114th Congress. As shown, over one-third of members have held a leadership position of some type, with 2% as a major leader (as discussed in chapter 5, this includes Speaker of the House, Majority or Minority Leader, and Majority or Minority Whip), 15% as a party leader (Deputy Whips, chairs and vice chairs of the parties' caucus/conference, and steering and policy committee chairs), 13% as a campaign leader (named positions in the DCCC or NRCC), and 20% as a full committee chair or ranking member. In all, 37% of the MCs in the sample have, at the time of this writing, held at least one leadership position,[9] and 60% have had an exclusive committee assignment.[10]

Explaining Advancement within the House of Representatives

Because MCs' careers in the chamber logically precede their exits from it, we begin our analyses there. We focus on two indicators of career advancement within the House—whether MCs attain leadership positions of various types and whether they get the committee assignments they request. We analyze first whether particular styles precipitate career success. In other words, is being a district advocate, party builder, ambitious entrepreneur, party soldier, or policy specialist in one term associated with obtaining a leadership position or preferred committee in the next? These analyses necessitate the member-congress as the unit of analysis. Then, later in this chapter, we consider the member across his or her career as that unit, investigating whether MCs' early styles help to explain their advancement within the House over the long term.

A central issue in studying all types of ambition—progressive or institutional—is that we cannot observe the ambition itself, only its expression—or, in some cases, only its fulfillment. As Herrick (2001) and LaForge (2012) have argued, ambition is nascent, a "psychological construct" (see also Fox and Lawless 2005). Although the literature tends to characterize all legislators as ambitious in the abstract—arguing, for example, that few would decline a prestigious committee, a leadership position, or a Senate seat or governorship if offered one with no strings attached—in reality the intensity of their preferences for such positions, and the lengths they will go to and the risks they will bear to get them, vary. However, we cannot measure directly which MCs most want a seat on a particular committee, to become a leader, or to move beyond the House. Instead, we must rely on behavioral measures. As we discuss in more detail below, for progressive ambition, we can observe who actually launches a bid for higher office. For institutional advancement, we can observe who requests particular committees, though that choice may itself be strategic—a function of whether the MC believes he or she will get the committee and the relative value of the alternative options to him or her (Frisch and Kelly 2006). For leadership positions, requests are generally unrecorded and/or are informal, so we can observe only whether MCs attain these roles.

Of course, the downside of our inability to measure ambition directly is that scholars' understanding of its nuances is necessarily limited. To the extent that there is an upside, it is that this reality makes it more difficult for us to uncover results, and so any differences we find in ambition and career advancement across styles are likely to reflect meaningful effects. For instance, if members who harbor a desire to attain an exclusive committee assignment behave differently and hence display different styles from those who do not, but those who have the goal of landing on an exclusive committee but have chosen not to make a request in a particular congress are combined with those who do not want an exclusive assignment, then this will dampen the differences we observe between the "expressers" and others.

Predictions about Style and Institutional Advancement

In chapter 5, we demonstrated that gaining leadership and exclusive committee positions can precipitate changes in style. In particular, rising to a leadership role often moves MCs from other styles to the builder style, and tends to keeps builders where they are (i.e., making it less likely they transition to a different style). Gaining a seat on an exclusive committee has more mixed effects for nonbuilders, but, as with gaining leadership, it appears to encourage builders to remain so.

A potential concern one might draw from such patterns is that styles are driven by positions—that MCs demonstrate the stylistic patterns they do solely as a function of the ways in which their place in the institution shapes their behavior. We argued against this interpretation there, and here we aim to provide direct evidence that, while positions may affect style, styles also precede positions, shaping who rises in stature in the House. In particular, we expect that the party builder style will pay off in terms of advancement within the institution. MCs who display builder tendencies will be on the radar screen of the existing leadership and will be more likely to be tapped for positions of influence. Importantly, this perception that builders are leaders in the making is not just a function of their loyalty to the party on roll calls, as party soldiers and policy specialists also vote with their parties and the leadership at high rates. Instead, we argue that their advantage accrues due to their displays of leadership-like behavior, and indeed we assume that MCs with aspirations for influence (and the leeway with the home constituency to pull it off) will behave differently from their peers.

As our first assessment of this hypothesis, we conduct some simple tests. In Model 1, our dependent variable is whether, in a particular congress, an MC gained a leadership position of any type (contingent on not having had one before). In Model 2, the dependent variable is whether an MC received an exclusive committee assignment. The primary independent variables of interest are dummies for MCs' legislative styles in the previous congress,[11] along with controls for seniority, majority status, and ideological extremity.[12] Table 8.1 presents these results. As shown, and as predicted, although members from all styles hold leadership positions and seats on exclusive committees, these prestigious positions flow disproportionately to party builders. Thus, it is not only the case that attaining such status serves to make builders. In addition, those who are builders already are more likely to be tapped for (or be successful candidates for) these positions.

Take, for example, the congressional career of J. C. Watts (R-OK), first elected to the House in 1994 as part of the Republican Revolution. A former college football player and one of only two African American Republicans in the House, his election attracted wide notice from journalists, constituents, and fellow MCs. Watts soon gained a reputation as a reliable conservative and a team player for the Republicans, and his party awarded him prominent speaking positions at the 1996 Republican National Convention and in delivering the Republican response to several of Bill Clinton's addresses, including the State of the Union (Barone and Ujifusa 1997, 1167). Perhaps unsurprisingly, after beginning as a party soldier, Watts had adopted the party builder style by his second term. In 1998, in his first bid for a leadership position, he ran against John Boehner for Republican Conference Chair, fourth in the leadership chain, and was successful, beating Boehner 121–93 (Barone, Cohen, and Ujifusa 2001, 1257). He would hold this position until his retirement at the end of the 107th Congress (2002).

TABLE 8.1 **Style, leadership positions, and committee assignments**

	Attained leadership	Attained exclusive committee	Received first choice committee
District advocate	−.21 (.12)*	−.29 (.32)	−.32 (.14)**
Party builder	.73 (.13)**	.78 (.40)**	.09 (.26)
Ambitious entrepreneur	.18 (.22)	.24 (.63)	−.13 (.29)
Policy specialist	−.05 (.09)	.07 (.25)	.33 (.12)**
Seniority	.01 (.01)	−.14 (.05)**	.01 (.01)
In majority	−.09 (.07)	−.54 (.20)**	.20 (.10)*
Ideological extremity	.23 (.32)	−.59 (.88)	−1.26 (.39)**
Previous exclusive committee	—	−.42 (.24)*	—
First choice exclusive	—	—	−.09 (.11)
Constant	−1.39 (.15)	−.35 (.42)	.00 (.20)
N	2640	385	686
Pseudo R^2	.04	.10	.03

Note: The table presents probit coefficients with standard errors in parentheses. The dependent variable in Model 1 is whether an MC attained a leadership position of any type in a particular congress; the dependent variable in Model 2 is whether an MC received an exclusive committee assignment (with the analyses limited to MCs who requested one); and the dependent variable in Model 3 is whether an MC received his or her first choice committee assignment (conditional on having made at least one committee request). Standard errors are clustered on the MC. ** = $p < .05$; * = $p < .10$

A builder-turned-leader with a somewhat less meteoric, but still instructive, rise is Nita Lowey (D-NY). Lowey was first elected in 1988, spending her first two terms as a party soldier before transitioning to the policy specialist style, and then, in the 104th Congress, to the party builder style. These styles reflect the descriptions provided of her service in the *Almanac of American Politics*—a party loyalist with a "fairly solid liberal record" who developed a focus on women's issues and the arts and evolved into an "avid fundraiser" (Barone, Cohen, and Ujifusa 2001, 1093). Although she held minor positions in the party in her early years in Congress, in the 105th Congress, her first after shifting to the party builder style in the 104th, she attained her first real leadership position as a Democratic Policy Committee cochair.[13] Lowey continues to serve in Congress, having held several leadership positions within the party and the DCCC, and is currently the ranking member of the Committee on Appropriations.

Watts and Lowey were not alone in seeing their builder style open the doors to leadership opportunities. In fact, the relative advantages that accrue to builders on this dimension of career advancement are substantial in magnitude. Among MCs who do not have a leadership position in a particular congress and who continue on to the next congress, 29% of builders will attain one then, compared to 6% of advocates, 9% of specialists, 10% of soldiers, and 13% of entrepreneurs. For gaining an exclusive committee, the difference is more modest—builders edge out the others by just a point or two. However, it is important to note that their greater rates of success are not due to differences in the tendency to request an exclusive assignment. When nonfreshman MCs make committee requests, these typically include at least one exclusive committee, and variation in the propensity to do so is small across styles, ranging from a low of 66% for policy specialists to a high of 69% for party soldiers.

We also see from the results in table 8.1 that, relative to their peers, district advocates face disadvantages in rising through the institutional hierarchy. In particular, they are significantly less likely to attain leadership positions. This is not surprising, as the advocate style is characterized by the general tendency to buck the party on roll call voting and to operate below the radar, focusing on constituency concerns. If we break out leadership positions by the types described in previous chapters (e.g., party, committee, and campaign), their greatest disadvantage is for rising to campaign leadership positions. Of course, this may not be a blow to advocates themselves, who may not aspire to such positions in the first place, and/or who are resigned to not receiving them.

Their reaction would likely be different, though, to the finding from Model 3 of table 8.1. Here, we extend beyond just exclusive committees to ask whether MCs' success at getting their "first choice" committee assignment varies across styles. This analysis focuses on the 686 returning MCs who made a request for a particular committee or committees going into the next congress, and the dependent variable is whether they were assigned to the committee they designated as their first choice. The specific policies and procedures for assigning committees varies by party and across time, but, in general, they are governed by the parties' Steering and Policy committees (with varying levels of intervention by the Speaker). Seniority is influential in assignments, but it is not the only factor. The credentials of MCs and their own efforts to secure a seat matter as well. As David Price (2004) described his campaign for a seat on a desired committee:

> I decided to run, and run hard. . . . Since the beginning of the 101st Congress, I had been casually visiting with Steering and Policy members. . . . Now I greatly accelerated that activity. My staff and I kept records of each contact. . . . I asked a number of colleagues to speak on my behalf to Steering and Policy members whom they knew well. (82–83)

In succeeding in these requests for preferred assignments, we see that advocates face difficulties—compared to the baseline, they are significantly less likely to have their requests met. Policy specialists, in turn, are significantly *more* likely to be granted their first choice committees. This suggests that for exclusive, prestigious committees, the party movers and shakers are advantaged, but that for lower profile committees, policy investment and expertise is rewarded.

In the short term, then, we observe some immediate consequences of style for career advancement. Builders are more likely than their peers to ascend to leadership positions in the next congress, and they and policy specialists appear to enjoy some advantages in the committee assignment process. District advocates, however, struggle on both of these dimensions—they are less likely to get leadership positions and less likely to receive their preferred committee assignments. Later in this chapter, we explore these dynamics across the course of MCs' careers, rather than just from one congress to the next. First, though, we investigate the relationships between styles and MCs' decisions about whether and how to continue their careers in public office.

Retire, Remain, or Run? Styles and MCs' Career Decisions

In addition to their choices about how to go about their business as legislators and representatives, MCs face another decision every congress: what to do next. Most will choose to run again, though others will retire from the House, and still others will launch a bid for higher office. Legislative scholars have devoted significant efforts to identifying the correlates of, and causal mechanisms underlying, these career decisions. The literatures on voluntary retirement from the House and progressive ambition have developed along largely separate lines (though see Kiewiet and Zeng 1993), but both with a focus on legislators as strategic actors, highlighting MCs' calculations of the expected utility of various options.

Studies of retirement are in general agreement that age is the most consistent predictor of the decision to leave office (Hibbing 1982; Livingston and Friedman 1993; Theriault 1998). Beyond that, however, they focus on legislators' strategic considerations. Some of these considerations are specific to particular periods of time. For instance, Jacobson and Dimock (1994) demonstrated that members affected by the 1992 House banking scandal were more likely than their peers to retire, and Groseclose and Krehbiel (1994) showed that the sunset of a campaign finance provision that allowed members to convert campaign funds to personal use led many to depart the House voluntarily in 1992 (see also Hall and Van Houweling 1995).

Other factors affecting the choice to retire are more general in nature and less time-bound. Most notable among these is MCs' assessment of their future electoral prospects. The argument here is that legislators who face concerns about being reelected often choose to retire rather than risk defeat at the polls. This may be to avoid the humiliation of being forced out after a long career in public life, because MCs think that their postcongressional opportunities in the private sector will be more lucrative if they leave without the taint of electoral loss, or because the conditions that produced their vulnerability lead them to believe that they can no longer pursue their goals within the chamber in a meaningful way. Evidence of strategic retirement in action has been somewhat mixed (see, for example, Brace 1985; Hall and Van Houweling 1995;

Moore and Hibbing 1998; Theriault 1998; Wolak 2007), although this may be in large part a function of differences in how incumbent prospects are operationalized and modeled (Stone et al. 2010).

Scholars argue that, in addition to taking into account their electoral prospects, MCs considering retirement will also evaluate the relative value of staying versus going by considering their place within the institution. Those with majority status and/or with attractive leadership or committee positions (or the belief that such positions will soon be within their grasp) may find continued congressional service to be more appealing and so will be more likely to remain in the chamber. Support for the "Congress is not fun anymore" retirement hypothesis is again mixed (Frantzich 1978; Cooper and West 1981; Kiewiet and Zeng 1993; Moore and Hibbing 1992), but Theriault (1998) demonstrates that it does apply to the group of MCs who have hit their "career ceiling" (i.e., long-serving members with relatively weak institutional positions), and Lawless and Theriault (2005) show that this holds particularly true for women legislators, who are more likely than men to opt out when their careers stall.[14]

How do styles map on to these expectations about retirement? Although any raw differences in the career decisions of MCs from different styles may be related to the variables described above (e.g., to the extent that vulnerability varies across style, those styles with a higher proportion of vulnerable legislators will demonstrate the highest rates of retirement), we anticipate that these differences may persist even after taking MCs' vulnerability and institutional status into account. This is because styles serve as indicators of the level of investment MCs have in their service in the House of Representatives. A priori, we might presume that party builders and policy specialists are the most invested and engaged. Builders are at the epicenter of legislative life, and as we saw above, even if they lack prestigious positions at a particular point in time, they are reasonable in assuming that they will come their way in the future. Policy specialists, in turn, derive satisfaction from pursuing their policy goals, something that House service is particularly well suited to allowing them to do.

Compare this to the situation faced by ambitious entrepreneurs. We have characterized such entrepreneurs as more instrumental in their decision making, ambitious and focused on their individual career goals, but without as much commitment to their party organizations, to potential policy priorities, or to the House of Representatives as an institution. Thus, all else equal, we predict that these MCs will be more likely to voluntarily opt out of congressional service to pursue other opportunities, even if those are outside of elected office.

We also predict that district advocates will be among the most likely styles to retire. Some legislators choose the advocate path voluntarily, viewing their role as a representative as district-oriented and not seeking the spotlight of leadership. Many others, however, probably feel compelled to adopt the advocate style due to fit (or lack thereof) with their district. Thus, while they may be committed to their constituents, they fail to reap many of the other rewards of life in the House, including, as we saw above, leadership positions and their preferred committee assignments. Compared to their peers, then, they will be more willing to walk away from a House seat.

For example, representative Butler Derrick (D-SC), Lindsey Graham's predecessor, watched his district became increasingly Republican-leaning over the two decades of his service in the House. As he described the situation to Fenno (2007):

> If I had wanted to, I could have stayed in Congress forever.... If you come up here [to Washington] and don't get too involved and go back home a lot and damn the government, you can get reelected forever.... But that doesn't fit with my values and I had no interest in doing it that way. (227)

Perhaps unsurprisingly, Derrick chose to retire from the House and from public life, returning to his precongressional career as an attorney.[15]

Party soldiers are more difficult to speculate about, in part because so many are freshmen who, having just started out, are less likely to retire. Nonetheless, their commitment to the party organization, and the fact that many soldiers eventually become builders (as shown in chapter 5), leads us to believe they will be more like party builders and policy specialists in their decision calculus about retirement and less like district advocates and ambitious entrepreneurs.

Retirements by Style

In the aggregate, we find that about 5% of party builders, party soldiers, and policy specialists retire in any given election year, compared to about 10% of district advocates and ambitious entrepreneurs. These patterns are in line with our predictions. To confirm that they are not just artifacts of differences in vulnerability and status across members, we conduct a probit analysis where the dependent variable is whether or not an MC chose to retire at the close of a particular congress. Our independent variables are MCs' styles in that congress, plus a host of controls designed to capture the characteristics of MCs and their situations that have been theorized to affect retirement decisions. These include legislator age, gender, and seniority in the chamber (along with a control for whether an MC is a freshman), vote share in the previous election, the constituency "distance score" (the measure of fit from chapter 6), whether or not the district was undergoing substantial redistricting prior to the next election, and whether the MC was in the majority party, held a leadership position, and sat on an exclusive committee. We also include controls for congress to pick up some of the dynamics discussed above regarding events in particular congresses, but in the interest of space, we do not present these coefficients. We limit the analyses to members who had chosen not to run for higher office in the next term (i.e., comparing just retirees to those who run for reelection to their House seats), though the substantive results are identical if the progressively ambitious are included as nonretirees. The results are presented in table 8.2.

These findings demonstrate that the high retirement rates of district

TABLE 8.2 **Styles and the choice to retire**

	Retire?
District advocate	.33 (.09)**
Party builder	−.08 (.14)
Ambitious entrepreneur	.35 (.19)*
Policy specialist	.14 (.10)
Age	.02 (.00)**
Woman	−.05 (.12)
Freshman	−.82 (.21)**
Seniority	.02 (.01)**
Vote share	−.01 (.00)**
Distance score	.06 (.03)**
Next redistricting	.21 (.20)
In majority	.03 (.07)
Any leader	−.08 (.09)
Exclusive committee	−.00 (.07)
Constant	−2.72 (.34)
N	42,874
Pseudo R^2	.14

Note: The table presents probit coefficients with standard errors in parentheses. The dependent variable is whether an MC ran for higher office at the end of a particular congress. The analysis is limited to MCs who had not chosen to run for higher office. ** = $p < .05$; * = $p < .10$

advocates and ambitious entrepreneurs hold with controls for a variety of other factors related to retirement. Thus, as predicted, age, electoral vulnerability, and ideological mismatch with the constituency all are positively related to the choice to retire, but even after taking these into account, advocates and entrepreneurs are more likely to voluntarily exit the House. To illustrate, if we limit our analyses to MCs who are over sixty years of age, who are poor fits for their districts, and who have vote shares less than 60%, we find that 17% of party builders and policy specialists matching this description retire before the next election, compared to 26% of district advocates. (Unfortunately, there are not enough ambitious entrepreneurs for comparison.) Accordingly, stylistic choices do appear to reflect MCs' levels of commitment to a career in the House, and/or perhaps their enjoyment of it, and thus help to explain decisions to retire or continue in office.

Progressive Ambition and Styles

We might reasonably think of the decision to retire from a career as an elected official as one end of the career spectrum (paralleling Schlesinger's discrete ambition), with the other side anchored by a decision to run for higher office. Compared to other types of ambition, progressive ambition has been the subject of the most interest from political scientists. As discussed above, the general assumption in the literature, following Schlesinger, is that all MCs harbor this type of ambition—that if a higher office were to fall into their laps, they would jump at it. Baker (1989) explained it in his analyses of differences between the House and Senate thusly: "In their heart of hearts . . . all House members hankered to be senators" (28).

Why is this the case? Put simply, the attractions of the Senate (or a governorship) are many. The Senate carries more prestige than the House, spares legislators from having to run for reelection every two years, and in the eyes of many members, allows an individual to have more impact. A governorship offers similar prestige, has the advantage of enabling its holder to be the single executive rather than one of many legislators, and is often seen as a launching pad for the presidency. Whether a particular House member views one position or the other as more attractive is likely a function of his or her own personal proclivities, as well as the nature of politics and party competition within his or her state.

But the fact that all members of the House might like to be a senator or governor (or both) does not mean that all take action toward this goal. As is the case with the decision to retire, the choice to make a run for higher office is strategic. In early work on progressive ambition, Rohde (1979) argued that MCs considering a bid for Senate or governor take into account the expected utility of doing so. This calculation is a function of the value of the current House seat to the member, the value of the higher office, and the probability of winning. Moreover, some MCs are by nature risk takers, while others are more risk averse, and so may weigh these considerations differently. Regardless, we should expect to see the highest probability of progressive ambition being expressed when the probability of winning a Senate seat or governorship is high and/or the cost of losing the House seat is low.

Accordingly, many of the factors that are associated with the decision to retire also shape progressive ambition. Age should matter, for example, though in a different way than for retirement. The youngest legislators realize that their lack of experience is likely to be a hindrance in a bid for higher office (and recognize that entering and losing a longshot race might negatively affect their future prospects), while those nearing retirement age and looking for an "out" might view retirement as a more attractive path out of the House (Brace 1984; Maestas et al. 2006; Schlesinger 1960).

MCs' status in the chamber should affect progressive ambition as well, though there may be competing dynamics. On one hand, high-profile MCs have more name recognition in their states and might therefore be seen as more viable candidates. On the other, those with satisfying careers in the House will be less likely to willingly give them up for a risky run for the Senate or a governorship. Prior research offers more evidence in favor of the latter prediction—leaders and minority party members, for example, have traditionally demonstrated higher rates of progressive ambition than their majority party peers (Copeland 1989; Gilmour and Rothstein 1993; Schansberg 1994).

The same competing logic holds for vote share. Electorally secure MCs might be stronger candidates (if their security is at all a referendum on their "quality"), but the risk of departing a safe seat is higher than that of leaving a seat where one was concerned about reelection. Similarly, changes to the district brought about by redistricting could make the MC safer, hence making the House seat more attractive, or could induce uncertainty about future prospects, increasing the chance that the MC views a run for higher office as a good bet.

In explaining progressive ambition, particularly the decision to run for a specific seat at a particular time, contextual factors matter as well. An MC pondering a run for the Senate or governorship will consider the level of competition he or she is likely to face. For example, is the seat open? If not and there is an incumbent, is that incumbent from the MC's party (meaning he or she would have to challenge the incumbent in a primary) or the opposite party? Savvy legislators will also consider how many other prospective candidates there are. MCs from large state delegations face more potential competition from their peers than MCs from states with just a few representatives. Overall, and in line with the findings of others, we expect that races for open seats, in small states, and where the other party is weak will elicit more progressive ambition (see also Brace 1984; Kiewiet and Zeng 1993; Rohde 1979).

To this list of factors explaining progressive ambition, we add legislative styles. Perhaps most obviously, we predict that ambitious entrepreneurs, despite being low in numbers, will run for higher office at high rates. As we have seen, entrepreneurs focus their energies on the types of activities—public visibility, fund-raising, and the like—that situate them well for a bid for higher office. In contrast, we anticipate that party builders will display lower levels of progressive ambition, because their ambition is focused on institutional advancement. In terms of the other styles, we expect that specialists' greater commitment to their policy work within the chamber should make House service attractive to them. Senators may have more individual impact, but the smaller size of the chamber necessitates more of a generalist approach to policy making. This should reduce relative rates of progressive ambition among specialists. District advocates, in turn, may be more prone to run for higher office. As we saw above for retirement, they, along with ambitious entrepreneurs, seem most willing to walk away from House service, suggesting that they may derive less utility from their careers there. A focus on "local" concerns may also translate well to statewide service, as does experience at successfully cultivating a heterogeneous constituency. Party soldiers are, once again, the most difficult to hypothesize about, though we anticipate that they will fall in the middle—not as committed to a career in the House as their builder and specialist colleagues, but also not as eager to look to greener pastures as entrepreneurs and advocates.

As our test of our predictions about progressive ambition, we begin with a model, presented in table 8.3, where the dependent variable is whether or not an MC ran for higher office during a particular congress. We limit our analyses to those cases where there was at least one opportunity for an MC to run for Senate or the governorship in the next election (i.e., where there was a race going on). This holds for about 80% of observations (i.e., MC-congresses) in our sample. Our independent variables are dummies for styles and measures that reflect the factors influencing ambition discussed above: the gender and age of the MC (as well as age squared, to take into account the non-monotonicity of the hypothesized relationship between age and progressive ambition); his or her seniority, leadership position, majority, and exclusive committee status in

TABLE 8.3 **Styles and progressive ambition**

	Run for higher office
District advocate	.21 (.12)*
Party builder	−.22 (.19)
Ambitious entrepreneur	.57 (.23)**
Policy specialist	−.23 (.13)*
Age	.04 (.05)
Age squared	−.01 (.00)
Woman	.06 (.15)
Freshman	−1.01 (.20)**
Seniority	−.01 (.09)
Vote share	−.01 (.00)**
Next redistricting	−.05 (.11)
In majority	−.18 (.09)**
Any leader	−.18 (.13)
Exclusive committee	.15 (.09)
Delegation size	−.02 (.01)**
Copartisan delegation percentage	.40 (.25)
Open seat	.56 (.09)**
Constant	−1.66 (1.23)
N	3356
Pseudo R^2	.15

Note: The table presents probit coefficients with standard errors in parentheses. The dependent variable is whether an MC ran for higher office at the end of a particular congress. The analysis is limited to MCs who had the opportunity to run for Senate or governor (i.e., at least one of those seats was being contested in an election) and had not chosen to retire. ** = $p < .05$; * = $p < .10$

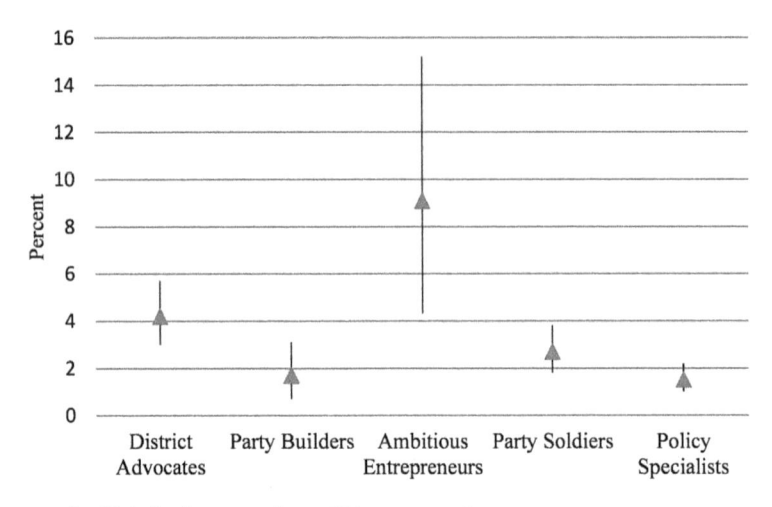

FIGURE 8.2 Variation in progressive ambition across styles
Note: Mean rates of progressive ambition (indicated by triangles) and 90% confidence intervals for each style.

the chamber; the vote share in the last election and whether the district is up for substantial redistricting before the next term; the size and partisanship of the state delegation; and whether at least one of the available opportunities to run was for an open seat.

Our results are largely in line with other studies of ambition. We find, for example, that MCs from larger states are less likely to run for higher office, that progressive ambition is increased when there are open seats, that minority party members run at higher rates than majority party members, and that electoral security is negatively related to the decision to launch a bid for Senate or governor, with legislators who are safe tending to stick around. Beyond that, the important effects are for style. As predicted, district advocates and ambitious entrepreneurs are more likely than their peers to display progressive ambition, and policy specialists are less so. The sign on the coefficient for builders is in the predicted negative direction, but relative to the baseline, is not significant.

Figure 8.2 demonstrates the magnitude of the differences across styles. As shown, ambitious entrepreneurs display the highest levels of ambition, running at significantly greater rates than party builders and policy specialists. District advocates are significantly more likely than policy specialists to run, and they come very close to edging out party builders as well (the confidence intervals overlap by less than one-tenth of a point). Indeed, the estimated mean levels of ambition for district advocates are over twice as high as those for party builders and policy specialists, and ambitious entrepreneurs run at rates nearly five times those of builders and specialists.

There is also interesting variation in the *nature* of the ambition expressed by MCs from different styles. Overall, about three-quarters (72%) of the MCs who were progressively ambitious ran for the Senate and the remainder ran for governor, but this division differs across styles. District advocates, for example, aim for the governor's mansion at a much higher rate than their progressively ambitious peers from other styles—39% of advocates who run do so for the governorship, compared to about 15–20% for MCs from other styles. This pattern corresponds to our understanding of advocates' interests and motivations—centered away from the beltway and focused more on subnational concerns. Their experiences cultivating (usually) heterogeneous constituencies on extrapolicy dimensions may also help them to build the coalitions necessary for a successful gubernatorial run. The choices of MCs from other styles to target the Senate rather than a governorship make sense as well, given their relative focus on national politics and policy making.

An additional question of interest about styles and ambition, going back to Rohde's (1979) work on risk bearing, is whether MCs from some styles are more risk acceptant about making a run for higher office. As discussed above, the least risky type of run is generally for an open seat, since winning such a seat does not require ousting an incumbent at either the primary or general election. When we do some simple t-tests[16] with the sample split by style to investigate whether MCs with at least one opportunity to run for an open seat race are more likely to launch a bid for higher office than those for whom all opportunities are for races contested by an incumbent, we find that for all styles *except* ambitious entrepreneurs, an open seat elicits significantly ($p < .05$) higher rates of ambition. For entrepreneurs, the difference is not significant, and moreover, as shown in figure 8.3, the direction of the relationship is flipped. Thus, whereas MCs from other styles are sensitive to context, expressing their ambition at the highest rates when the risk is lowest, entrepreneurs appear more risk acceptant, with their choices to run more heavily conditioned by other factors.

Finally, we also observe variation in success rates across styles. Nineteen percent of district advocates who run for higher office win, com-

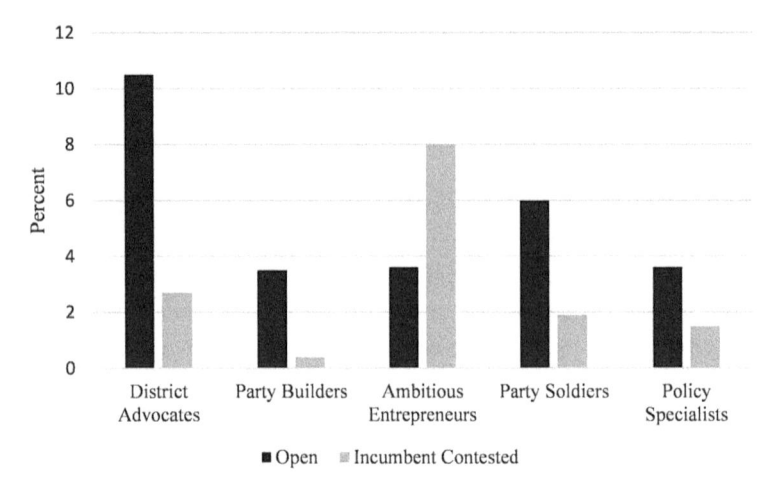

FIGURE 8.3 Progressive ambition by context and style
Note: Proportion of MCs from each style who run for higher office when there is at least one opportunity for an open seat versus when all of the opportunities are for seats contested by an incumbent.

pared to 38% of entrepreneurs and soldiers, 44% of specialists, and 67% of builders. This result holds with controls for type of race (Senate or governor) and whether the seat was open or contested by an incumbent. A few conclusions can be drawn from these patterns. First, party builders and policy specialists are, in general, more hesitant about running for higher office, probably because of the greater value and utility they attach to House service. When they *do* run, however, they succeed at relatively high rates. In comparison, ambitious entrepreneurs and district advocates display more progressive ambition, but are less likely to see their goals met. For entrepreneurs, our results suggest that the greater value they attach to higher office makes them more risk acceptant, willing to try even when conditions do not appear as favorable to them. For district advocates, the likely explanation, especially when coupled with the relatively high rates of voluntary retirement, is that continued House service is seen as an uncertain, or even less appealing, proposition compared to exiting, either by leaving public office or by trying for a different position.

Ambition and Advancement across Careers

The findings to this point have shown convincingly that MCs' styles in a particular term serve as useful signals about their intentions in the next election—whether they will run again, retire, or aim higher. In the remainder of this chapter, we step back to examine the arc of MCs' careers more broadly. In particular, we explore whether we can predict legislators' trajectories from their early styles. How long will their House careers last? Who will rise to leadership in the party organization and in policy making? Who will become senators and governors? To the extent that styles help to explain career advancement over the long term, they have value for our understanding of the origins of ambition, as well as the ways in which individual preferences interact with institutional structures to affect congressional careers.

Compared to the analyses above, our approach here is more descriptive, digging into the data to trace the trajectories of MCs from different styles across their careers. We use legislators' sophomore term styles as our anchoring point. As we know from earlier chapters, most MCs start out as party soldiers in the freshman term, but, by the second term, they have settled in, and the distribution of sophomore styles approximates the distribution of styles overall. Thus, MCs' stylistic differences in the second term should be better indicators of what they "are like" as legislators. More practically, focusing on sophomore styles enables us to include additional MCs who were elected in 1986 or 1987 and are in their second term during our first congress of data collection (the 101st Congress, 1988–1990), as well as MCs for whom their first term was a partial term and we were not able to collect sufficient data to calculate a style.

In all, we have a total of 550 unique individuals to track across their careers. Three-quarters (419) of these MCs left the House of Representatives between the 102nd and 114th Congresses, due to retirement, electoral loss, or progressive ambition, while another 131 continue to serve in the chamber. Our explorations of career exits focus on the MCs who have departed, while our examinations of the rise to leadership include MCs still serving, but with the recognition that some without positions to date may still gain them in the future.

Early Styles and Leadership

We begin with the big stakes—who becomes a "major leader" in the House of Representatives (Speaker of the House, Majority or Minority Leader, or Majority or Minority Whip)? In our sample, there are seven MCs for whom we observe sophomore term styles and who went on to become major leaders. They include eventual Speakers of the House Nancy Pelosi (D-CA), John Boehner (R-OH), Dennis Hastert (R-IL), and Paul Ryan (R-WI); House Majority Leader Eric Cantor (R-VA); and House Majority Whips Roy Blunt (R-MO) and James Clyburn (D-SC).[17] Of these, Boehner, Pelosi, Cantor, and Blunt had all become party builders by their second terms. Ryan and Clyburn were both party soldiers as sophomores and Hastert a policy specialist, though all eventually gravitated to the party builder style. In other words, the majority of major leaders were already party builders by their sophomore terms—a style held by only 6.5% of MCs in the sample at that stage of their careers. Additionally, among the other thirty sophomore party builders who did not go on to hold one of the top five positions in the chamber are such high-profile legislators as Rahm Emanuel (D-IL), Chair of the DCCC and the House Democratic Caucus before becoming Chief of Staff to Barack Obama and then Mayor of Chicago; Kay Granger (R-TX), who served as Deputy Whip and Vice Chair of the House Republican Conference; Tom Price (R-GA), former Chair of the Republican Study Committee and Republican Policy Committee and current Chair of the House Budget Committee; and Debbie Wasserman Schultz (D-FL), former Chief Deputy Whip and Chair of the Democratic National Committee (DNC).

The relatively early ascendance to the builder style by future Speakers Pelosi and Boehner as compared to Hastert and Ryan accords with common understandings of the context in which these MCs reached the Speakership. Pelosi, the daughter of a congressman, had spent her childhood steeped in politics and devoted her entire career to the Democratic Party, serving as a staff member of the Democratic National Committee (DNC) and Democratic Senate Campaign Committee (DSCC) even before entering Congress. Boehner, though from a more modest upbringing, was similarly committed to his party, and like Pelosi, once in office was focused on the House and uninterested in moving up to the Senate. As Draper (2012) described it:

Boehner had never bothered to conceal his ambitions. But they were limited to the institution of the House.... Boehner didn't want to break out of the pack. He just wanted to be leading it. From 1995 onward, he was riding the leadership escalator. (43–44)

In contrast, Hastert, who, as indicated by the opening quote to this chapter, was surprised to learn that Pelosi and Boehner had assiduously planned their rise to power, was more of an accidental Speaker, who had been "well down the leadership chain in early 1999, when scandal brought down Gingrich and Bob Livingston and suddenly thrust the Republican deputy whip into the Speaker's chair" (Draper 2012, 43). Paul Ryan, in turn, had perhaps the most varied ambitions of the group, starting out his life in Congress as an economic policy wonk and then the Republicans' budget guru, serving as Mitt Romney's running mate in the 2012 presidential election and eventually becoming, potentially somewhat reluctantly, the Speaker of the House after Boehner's resignation in the fall of 2015.

The relationship between MCs' early styles and their propensity to rise in the leadership becomes even clearer when we move beyond a sole focus on major leadership positions. If we examine whether an MC attains any type of leadership position (i.e., using the four category division from previous chapters of major leaders, party leaders, campaign leaders, and committee leaders), we find that 76% of sophomore builders eventually became leaders,[18] compared to just 36% of MCs from other styles ($t = 5.0$, $p < .05$).[19] The proportion of nonbuilder sophomores who ascend to positions of leadership ranges from 17% for ambitious entrepreneurs to 43% for policy specialists, with party builders and district advocates both coming in at about 30%. Thus, while these positions are not solely the province of "early" builders, they are much more likely than others to attain them.

The specific type of leadership position MCs achieve is also linked to their sophomore styles. Figure 8.4 presents the distribution of sophomore styles overall (the first set of columns) and then the relative distribution of sophomore styles among MCs who eventually rose to each type of leadership position.[20] This figure shows two results of interest. First, the tallest bar for each leadership type indicates where most of the leaders in that category "came from" in terms of style. For example, most major leaders were sophomore party builders, most party leaders were

[Bar chart showing percentages for District Advocate, Party Builder, Ambitious Entrepreneur, Party Soldier, and Policy Specialist across categories: Overall, Major Leader, Party Leader, Campaign Leader, and Committee Leader]

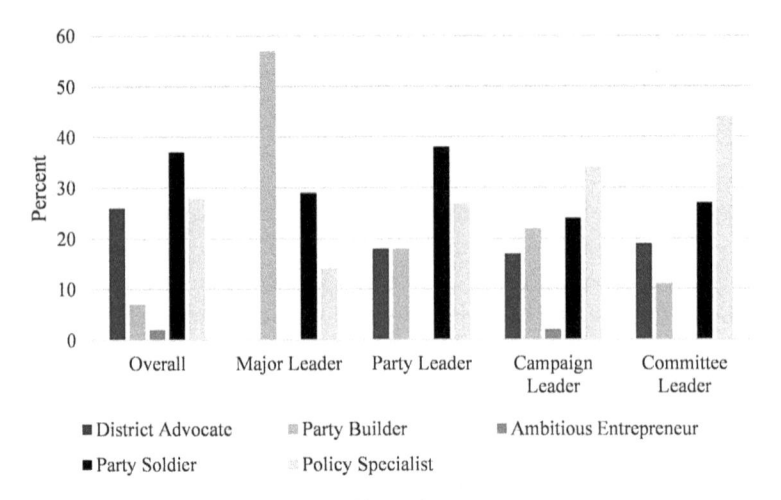

FIGURE 8.4 Sophomore styles and leadership attainment
Note: Distribution of styles among sophomore MCs in our sample (the first set of columns), and then the distribution of sophomore styles among MCs who attained each type of leadership position.

party soldiers, and most campaign leaders and committee leaders were policy specialists. Second, comparing each subcategory bar to the overall distribution bar for a style illustrates how over- or underrepresented MCs from that sophomore style are in later leadership positons. Party builders are overrepresented in all types—although they comprise just 7% of the sample, they are 57% of major leaders, 18% of party leaders, 22% of campaign leaders, and 11% of committee leaders. In contrast, district advocates are underrepresented in every form of leadership. Twenty-seven percent of sophomore MCs are district advocates, but no district advocate in the sample went on to become a major leader, and they comprise just 17–19% of the other leadership categories. Similarly, NO sophomore entrepreneurs become major leaders, party leaders, or committee leaders, and just two became campaign leaders (Democrats Joseph P. Kennedy II of Massachusetts and Adam Schiff of California). Party soldiers are slightly underrepresented in the major, campaign, and committee leadership categories, though they are on par with their overall distribution for party leadership. Finally, policy specialists become leaders at higher rates than we might expect given our characterization of them, but this is due in large part to their substantial (and not at all unexpected, given their focus on policy) overrepresentation as committee leaders.

In sum, then, early styles are indeed predictive of whether an MC is on, as Draper put it, "the leadership escalator." Party builders, and, to a lesser extent, party soldiers and policy specialists, go on to become leaders on various dimensions in the chamber, while district advocates and ambitious entrepreneurs are less likely to do so.

Style and Tenure in the House of Representatives

A second question of interest is whether early styles are linked to the longevity of MCs' House careers. In other words, can we predict how long legislators are likely to serve on the basis of their sophomore styles? If we combine the cross-sectional findings from earlier in this chapter—that, for example, district advocates and ambitious entrepreneurs tend to retire and run for higher office at greater rates—they suggest that MCs who start out in these styles may have shorter careers on average. Indeed, this is what we find. Sophomore district advocates serve an average of 11.6 years, ambitious entrepreneurs 12.3 years, party soldiers 13.2 years, party builders 14.6 years, and policy specialists 15.2 years.[21] These differences hold up with controls for leadership position, exclusive committee status, and the like, with district advocates having significantly shorter careers than their peers and policy specialists significantly longer. They also remain if we limit the sample to MCs who changed their styles at least once after the sophomore term. Thus, it is not just that MCs tend to remain in their sophomore styles—those sophomore styles are predictive of career longevity even if legislators subsequently transition to different styles.

The length of MCs' careers is linked, of course, to their reasons for departing. In our sample, retirees (across styles) have the longest mean years of service (eighteen), compared to ten years for the progressively ambitious and eleven years for those who leave office due to losing a re-election bid. When we calculate the rates of loss, retirement, and progressive ambition by sophomore styles, we find that, as illustrated in figure 8.5, the modal eventual mode of exit from the House for sophomore district advocates is electoral loss; for ambitious entrepreneurs, it is a run for higher office; and for party builders and policy specialists it is retirement. Party soldiers are split fairly evenly across modes of exit. Importantly, these patterns again hold after controlling for whether MCs

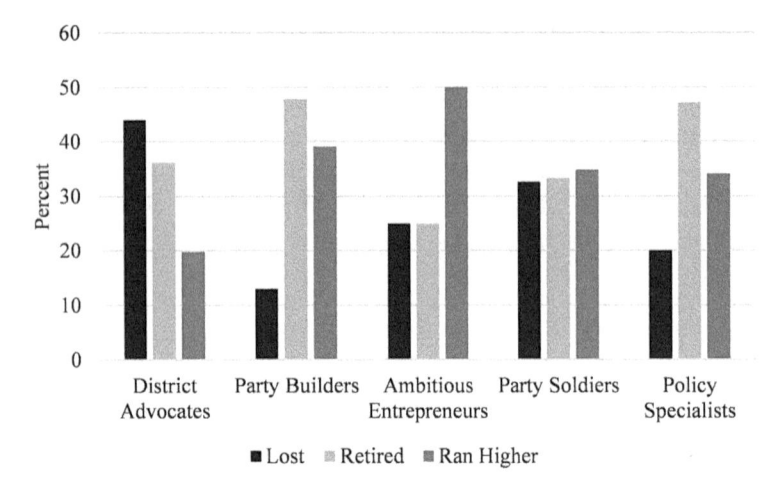

FIGURE 8.5 Career exits by sophomore styles
Note: Distribution of House exit modes by each sophomore style.

change styles after the sophomore term, so these early styles themselves are informative. If we want to predict how long an MC's House career will be and how he or she will eventually exit the House, knowing sophomore styles helps us to do so.

Predicting Progressive Ambition

For our final exploration of the dynamics of styles and careers, we target progressive ambition in more detail. As indicated by the results above, MCs who were ambitious entrepreneurs as sophomores run for office at the highest rates of any style—50% of sophomore entrepreneurs will eventually launch a bid, compared to 39% of party builders, 35% of party soldiers, 34% of policy specialists, and 20% of district advocates. However, given wide variation in the modes of career exits across styles, these differences are not statistically significant.

It is important to note that these across-career patterns differ from the cross-sectional results in table 8.3. There, we asked how likely it was, in a given year, that MCs who currently were in each style would run in the next election. Here, we ask how likely it is that MCs with each style as sophomores will eventually run at some point in their careers. Together, these patterns indicate both that early styles are suggestive of progressive ambition, and that MCs may shift to the ambitious entrepreneur style in advance of an impending run for higher office.

This is in line with literature on congressional careers that concludes that ambition often brings about behavioral changes. Most of this work has highlighted roll call voting, demonstrating that MCs with their eyes on a statewide constituency shift their positions away from the preferences of the district and, typically, toward those of the state (Francis and Kenny 1996; Hibbing 1986).[22] Ambition may affect other realms of activity as well. Herrick and Moore (1993) showed, for example, that progressively ambitious MCs become more legislatively active and specialized, although that specialization may drop off once an MC is actually running for the higher office (Victor 2011).

There is also considerable anecdotal evidence of shifts in behavior preceding a run. Recall, for example, David McIntosh (R-IN), whose arrival in Congress in 1995 was chronicled by Fenno (2007). Fenno continued to visit McIntosh during the early years of his House career, noting:

> Between my 1996 and 1998 visits, he had begun to entertain a new set of ambitions. When a U.S. Senate seat had opened up in Indiana for 2000, there had been Capitol Hill speculation about a possible McIntosh candidacy. When queried about that possibility, he had said "You never say never." And in a February 1998 *Roll Call* interview about his new role in CATS, he had denied having leadership aspirations in the House. Being in the leadership, he noted, is "much less valuable than it used to be." He had, however, offered an alternative. "Where I see myself is taking a shot" at the governor's race. (260)

These changing ambitions manifested themselves in the choices McIntosh made about how to spend his time. During Fenno's 1998 visit, he spoke with McIntosh's staffers about his schedule, noting:

> Another top campaign aide chipped in, "David is dividing his time—one-third to Washington business, one-third to state business, one-third to campaign business." And he added that when scheduling conflicts arose, primacy was always given to fund-raising activity. It all sounded very much like groundwork for a statewide campaign. (261)

And indeed it was, with McIntosh throwing his hat into the ring for the governor's race soon after, winning the Republican nomination with

70% of the vote, but losing badly to the incumbent Democrat, Frank O'Bannon, on Election Day.[23]

Across this time period, McIntosh evolved in his style from a party soldier in his first two terms to an ambitious entrepreneur in the term leading up to his race for governor. In that congress, he increased his legislative activity but decreased his specialization; increased his fundraising and redistribution to fellow copartisans; and broke from the party more often in roll call voting—all hallmarks of the ambitious entrepreneur style.

Given the low number of ambitious entrepreneurs in our sample that are trackable from the beginning of their careers, our ability to draw firm conclusions about the relationship between the timing of adopting the entrepreneur style and the run for higher office is limited. However, if we calculate the rates of progressive ambition among MCs who had *ever* been an entrepreneur[24] versus those who had not, we find a significantly higher probability of running for office among the former than the latter (33% vs. 19%, $t = 2.1$; $p < .05$). This result holds if we limit the sample to MCs who were *not* entrepreneurs as sophomores.

It is important to keep in mind that a minority of ambitious entrepreneurs actually runs for office, and, given their relatively low numbers, most MCs who do run for Senate or governor were not ambitious entrepreneurs, either as sophomores or at other times. Accordingly, we also look more broadly at whether *any* changes in style are associated with progressive ambition. Our hypothesis is that, in line with the findings of Francis and Kenny (1996) and others, the decision to run for higher office comes slowly for many MCs, with concomitant changes in behavior and style across time. An MC who plans a long career in the House of Representatives may see little need to change his or her style, while one who is strategizing about other opportunities may mix things up a bit more.

For example, Lindsey Graham, who, like McIntosh, was also chronicled by Fenno in the early years of his career, noted that he "didn't care" whether he became a committee chair and had "no interest" in moving up in the House of Representatives, but, in looking to his future career, recognized that a higher office might be of interest:

> I don't think you'll find many people going back to where they were. I'm 39, and that's about the average of my class. After 12 years, we'll still be in the prime of life. What will we do? Won't we have been away too long to pick up

where we left off? Will we go into lobbying or some private interest group? That's not much to look forward to. . . . I tell people that if I want to stay in politics, I'll run for the Senate or come back home and run for county council. I'm creating a farm team of my own in the district. If I ever want to run for another office, I will have a team in place. (2007, 225)

Graham eventually did run (successfully) for the Senate in 2002 and also shifted styles relatively frequently during his four terms in the House. He was a party soldier in his freshman and sophomore terms before becoming a policy specialist and then a district advocate.

He is not alone in this behavior. We find that the total number of shifts in style experienced by MCs is a significant ($p < .05$) predictor of the decision to run for higher office (controlling for the number of congresses in which an MC served, and limiting the analysis to MCs who entered Congress after the start of our data collection). For example, an MC who had served five terms and had maintained his or her original style from the beginning would have a 14% probability of exiting the House via a run for higher office, compared to a 19% probability for an MC who had shifted once and a 25% probability for an MC who, like Graham, had shifted twice. While these effects are, once again, not overwhelming in magnitude, they do suggest that strategic MCs change their behavior and styles to match their goals. As a result, styles, and transitions therein, can serve as signals about ambition.

Conclusions

Throughout this chapter, we have seen that MCs' styles are inextricably linked to their advancement in the House of Representatives and beyond. The styles MCs adopt are associated with gaining leadership positions and committee seats in their next terms, and they help to predict who will rise to positions of power within the chamber over the long term. Early styles also indicate the paths MCs' careers will take, including how long they will serve in the House and how they will exit it—via electoral loss, retirement, or progressive ambition.

The basic story to come from this chapter is that party builders and ambitious entrepreneurs are both ambitious, but in different ways. The builder style puts one on a path to institutional influence, while entrepreneurs move up and out of the House of Representatives. District advocates, while not as explicitly progressively ambitious as their entrepreneur peers, share their lack of devotion to House service, opting for retirement or to move up when those choices present themselves. Most often, though, they leave the House involuntarily through electoral loss. Party soldiers fall in the middle of the pack, due in large part to their relative youth. But, as we saw in chapter 5, many soldiers become builders down the road (two-thirds of "eventual" builders began as party soldiers), putting soldiers on the path to leadership within the House. Finally, policy specialists are perhaps the most committed House members—they are unlikely to run for higher office and have the longest tenures of any style, ending their careers by retiring after lengthy service. This commitment is rewarded, as these MCs are more likely to attain their preferred committee assignments and rise to roles as committee leaders.

As with other measures of success we have explored, we are careful not to make strong causal claims. For example, does wanting to run for higher office make one an ambitious entrepreneur, or does being an ambitious entrepreneur lead one to realize that a run for higher office is a feasible option? The most likely scenario is that some of both is at work. Nonetheless, this does not dampen the predictive power of early styles, and it suggests that the roots of leadership and ambition begin early. Styles, then, are central to understanding congressional careers.

CHAPTER NINE

Legislative Styles and Evaluations of Congress

It is an institution that is often demeaned, usually during campaigns. But it is an institution composed of people who pride themselves on being public servants, and I'm pleased to tell you that most of the members who come here do so to serve and look after people and do important things. — John Dingell, welcoming incoming freshman to the 112th Congress, as quoted by Draper (2012, 11)

We began this book with a straightforward premise—that members of Congress differ from one another in how they approach their jobs. They arrive in Washington, DC with varying experiences, interests, and goals, and these combine to influence their priorities and the day-to-day choices they make about how to pursue their careers. We theorized that such differences across MCs would be measurable and systematic, with common patterns of behavior coalescing into a small set of distinct legislative styles.

Our results have demonstrated the value of this gestalt approach to legislative behavior. We have shown that, based on their activity, MCs fall into one of five predictable and stable styles. These styles are, as expected, "sticky," but when stylistic changes do occur, the shifts are generally explicable. Legislators' patterns of behavior and, hence, their styles, evolve as they gain experience, take on new opportunities, and face new challenges. MCs' styles, in turn, affect their career prospects, and as such, are central to understanding a variety of phenomena of interest to congressional scholars, from the nature of the electoral connection, to individual and aggregate legislative success, to leadership pathways within the House, to progressive ambition beyond it.

In this final chapter, we revisit what we have learned about each of the styles that populate the halls of Congress—district advocates, party builders, ambitious entrepreneurs, party soldiers, and policy specialists. We focus not just on what characterizes each, but also on what we now know about their correlates and consequences, and thus how each style contributes to the functioning of Congress.

We conclude with a discussion of what our findings mean for normative evaluations of the House of Representatives and for the prospects of congressional reform.

The Styles, Revisited

To identify MCs' styles, we relied upon an inductive, data-centered approach, using cluster analysis to group legislators by their behavior. Our input variables included eight indices of legislators' activity: *home front* (proportion of district staff, number of district offices), *showboating* (number of one-minute speeches, number of bylines), *money* (total receipts), *lawmaking* (number of introductions, cosponsorships, and amendments; proportion of roll call votes for which the MC was present), *party voting* (percentage of the time the MC voted with his or her party on roll calls that split the parties, percentage of the time the MC voted with the leadership), *party giving* (dollars to the hill committee, dollars to copartisans), *bipartisanship in coalitions* (percentage of an MC's cosponsorships that were of measures introduced by the other party), and *policy focus* (the number of issues on which an MC introduced bills, the proportion of his or her introduced legislation that was referred to a committee on which he or she sat).

Our clustering algorithm takes into account MCs' scores across all of the indices, identifying groups of observations that are both similar to one another and distinct from those in other groups (see Sewell et al. 2016). The results indicated that a scheme with five clusters provided a particularly good fit with the data. This was in line with our prediction that a small number of clusters would emerge, and, combined with the intuitive matches between the styles and what we know of differences across legislators, provided confidence that our clusters validly capture legislators' styles.

These styles then became the starting point for our analyses of where legislators begin (i.e., their freshman term styles), what explains transitions in style across time, and how styles affect MCs' immediate successes and failures and their long-term career trajectories. Our results demonstrate that all five styles have advantages and disadvantages from the perspective of the MCs who adopt them, for the constituents they represent, and for the operation of the House as a policy-making institution.

District Advocates

We begin with district advocates. Twenty-six percent of the observations (i.e., MC-congresses) in our sample fall into this cluster. It is the style of 25% of new freshmen, and about 37% of the 1,011 MCs we observe between the 101st and 110th Congresses were a district advocate in at least one term. Thus, regardless of the nature of comparison, a sizable proportion of MCs are district advocates. As shown in chapter 3, this style is the most stable of the five, with over 90% of MCs who were district advocates in one term continuing it into the next.

As the name implies, district advocates are focused homeward, prioritizing the cultivation of their constituencies. Perhaps as a result, they tend not to be as invested in their parties. Indeed, through their moderation in voting and willingness to cross the aisle in cosponsorship coalitions (as well as their tendency to operate below the radar, not seeking out publicity beyond the district), they may perform a valuable role in bridging partisan gaps between Democrats and Republicans. The flip side, though, is that district advocates are not often the heavy lifters in policy making.[1] Compared to the other styles, their volume of lawmaking activity (i.e., introductions, cosponsorships, amendments, and presence on roll call votes) is the lowest, and their agendas are not particularly focused, with their introductions of bills spread across issue areas.

In reflecting on the inordinately high volume of media attention surrounding the death of Representative Joe Moakley (D-MA) in 2001, Fenno (2007) summarized his career in a way that highlights well both the strengths and weaknesses of district advocates:

> As a lifelong observer of Congress, however, I knew with near certainty that Representative John Joseph (Joe) Moakley was not a national hero. He was not a nationally known member of the House. He had registered no visible national accomplishments in Washington. He had never been pursued by the national media. He had never claimed national prominence, nor had anyone

else ever made that claim on his behalf. Joe Moakley was not a national figure. He was, by any national measure, an obscure member of the House. (1–2)

Why, then, did Moakley's passing attract such notice? Fenno argued that the answer was to be found both in an affable personality that endeared him to colleagues and in his deep and lasting connections with his constituency.[2] Moakley (a district advocate, at least in the congresses we observe at the end of his career) was not, Fenno concluded, "a memorable congressman but he *was* a memorable representative" (3).

The list of district advocates in our sample includes many such members, unassuming and modest contributors to congressional life, with a strong sense of duty to their districts. Some district advocates arrive at this style motivated by a fundamental belief that the appropriate role of a representative is to prioritize the home front. Our results suggest, though, that for many, the adoption of the style is strategic—a way of managing heterogeneous or unfriendly constituencies.[3] Recall, for example, how Phil Sharp (D-IN) was able to hold on to his (increasingly) Republican-leaning district by taking on an advocate style, aiming for a moderate approach that balanced the competing interests within his district and cultivated various important subconstituencies (Fenno 2007, 205–6). This is not to say that the behavior of advocates such as Sharp is somehow insincere or merely symbolic, as his efforts brought very real benefits to his constituents. But it does suggest that the necessity of adopting an advocate style means that these MCs often focus on reelection at the expense of contributing to lawmaking in a substantial way. Perhaps as a result, district advocates do not stand out in terms of legislative effectiveness, are less likely to attain their preferred committee assignments, and are less prone to rise to leadership positions. Thus, from the perspective of representation, devotion to the district can be a double-edged sword, as it often comes at the expense of distinction in Washington, DC.

This outside-the-beltway orientation also appears to manifest itself in advocates' level of commitment to long-term service in the House. As we observed in chapter 8, MCs who are early-career (i.e., sophomore term) district advocates have the shortest average tenures of any of the styles (eleven to twelve years in the House). Although the modal mode of eventual exit for early district advocates is electoral loss, MCs who are advocates in a particular congress are also among the most likely to voluntarily opt out of House service. Thus, while district advocates produce benefits for their districts and, through their bipartisanship, for the operation of Congress as a whole, their shorter careers may limit the extent of these contributions.

Policy Specialists

Among the three large styles (i.e., district advocates, policy specialists, and party soldiers), policy specialists provide a sharp contrast with district advocates. Although neither district advocates nor policy specialists tend to seek out public visibility or to focus on fund-raising, specialists are loyal partisans in both their roll call voting and in their cosponsorship coalitions and distinguish themselves legislatively by their policy focus (though not by their volume of activity). Their agendas are narrow in scope, and they tend to target issues related to their committee assignments.

Thus, the attention of policy specialists falls within the chamber, and they reap rewards accordingly. Compared to MCs from other styles, policy specialists are the most likely to see their bills progress through the legislative process and more often get their first-choice committee assignments. Early-career policy specialists also tend to rise over time to committee leadership positions. These successes no doubt contribute to their satisfaction with life in the House of Representatives, and as a result, we see less evidence of progressive ambition among specialists. Instead, these MCs appear content to serve out their careers in the House before eventually retiring from public life. Specialists have the longest average tenure in the House of Representatives of all the styles—over fifteen years.

As a group, policy specialists probably come closest to Mayhew's (1974) "hero of the Hill . . . the lonely gnome who passes up news conferences . . . in order to devote his time to legislative 'homework'" (147), and to the archetypal House "work horse." Thus it should be reassuring that such a sizable proportion of MCs fall into this style. Close to one-third of our total observations are policy specialists, and 43% of the MCs we study were policy specialists in at least one of the congresses in the sample period. On the other hand, if one values moderation, policy specialists do not generally provide that. They are good partisans and more ideologically extreme than their peers (with the highest mean absolute value NOMINATE score of any of the styles), and as a result, may have a difficult time compromising and working across the aisle. They also do not face much electoral pressure to adapt, as they have among the highest mean vote shares of the five styles (edged out just slightly by party builders). Therefore, the price of the policy entrepreneurship and legislative skill that specialists bring to the table may be polarized policy preferences and insulation from electoral pressure.

For example, Henry Waxman was a particularly effective lawmaker, but he was definitely not a moderate, with a NOMINATE score that places him in the top ten percent (i.e., more "liberal" than 90% of the other MCs in our sample).[4] Waxman achieved his legislative victories because of his tenacity and command of the policy-making process, not his advocacy of middle-of-the-road policies. Indeed, many of his signal accomplishments—the Affordable Care Act, the Children's Health Insurance Program, the Ryan White Care Act, and efforts to combat climate change and enhance the powers of the Food and Drug Administration and the Environmental Protection Agency—are decidedly left of center, and some remain sources of contention, used by Republicans as "cudgels" in their campaigns (Weisman 2014). Many congressional observers argue that the trade-off for getting "Waxmans" on both sides of the aisle is worth it, as these MCs have the skills to break through gridlock and get policy made. It is clear, though, that specialists are driven to pursue their own agendas, and their preferences on the policies they care about seldom approximate those of the median member of the House.

Party Soldiers

The third and final of the large stylistic groups is the party soldiers. Fifty-six percent of the MCs in our sample were party soldiers in at least one of the congresses we observe, though for many that reflects only a brief stop in the soldier style as freshmen. However, the style is not solely the province of new MCs—22% of more senior MCs (i.e., sophomores and beyond) are party soldiers. Like policy specialists, soldiers are party stalwarts, both in their in voting and in their cosponsorship coalitions, and tend to be DC- rather than district-oriented. Unlike them, they engage in considerably more showboating and more fund-raising (though neither engage in much redistribution of their funds to copartisans), and they have broad rather than specialized agendas.

The depiction of party soldiers that has emerged over the course of our analyses is of a group of MCs who define themselves as part of the party team and as adherents to the party philosophy. This partisan identity motivates them more than being "of" their district or pursuing particular policy goals. Their sense of party "teamness" is, of course, latent, and so we cannot point to a particular activity that encapsulates it. The pattern of behavior of party soldiers seems to, though, and it comes through clearly in anecdotes about how they approach their work. As Fenno (2007) described his visit to David McIntosh's Indiana district during his first term:

> He was recognized as a leader of the class, and his team-playing persona was central to his presentation of self to his constituents—and to our casual conversation as well. The local newspapers had primed people at home to think of him that way, by describing him as "a player," "a star," a "kid in a candy store," a "GOP poster boy," "the substance guy"—with emphasis on his access to Speaker Gingrich and his inner circle. (191–92)

Party soldiers, perhaps especially freshman soldiers, bring with them a characteristic energy and commitment to the party. However, this does not necessarily translate to satisfaction with the traditional ways of doing party business. In his discussions with Fenno, for example, McIntosh frequently made reference to his problems with the "older generation" of copartisans (192), whom he saw as out of touch and not sufficiently committed to the party's goals. And, in time, McIntosh grew disenchanted with Gingrich as well, contributing to efforts to push him out of the Speakership.

Though it may not always be welcomed by the incumbent leadership, soldiers' zeal for party principles and taste for reform may perform a useful role for parties by serving to continually reinvigorate them and keep them competitive. This has likely been particularly true over the past three decades, when majority control of the House of Representatives has been constantly in play. Indeed, it is impossible to consider the role of party soldiers without also taking into account increased polarization and party competition since the 1980s (see Lee 2016). In fact, the existence of party soldiers as a distinct and relatively widespread style may have been created by these phenomena. With the majority finally within the grasp of Republicans, there has been an incentive for MCs in both parties to prioritize the party team, with concomitant internal battles about which strategies best put the party on the path to gaining or maintaining control. In contrast, had we conducted these analyses on MCs in the 1970s, when parties were in many ways at their nadir (see Mayhew 1974), we expect that we would find many fewer party soldiers.[5]

In terms of their districts, party soldiers can provide good policy representation to homogenous constituencies. It is clear where they stand on issues, and to the extent that their districts' preferences line up with theirs, there will be strong policy congruence. However, given soldiers' relatively low levels of legislative effectiveness, constituents cannot count on these MCs passing their own legislation on topics of concern. Other types of connection with the constituency may also be weaker, as they are simply not a priority of the typical party soldier. And, of course, true believers who are unwilling to compromise on policy leave outpartisan constituents with little voice.

Party soldiers are part and parcel of contemporary congressional politics. It is important to underscore, though, that they do not dominate, and in fact, their numbers drop off a bit in the final few congresses in our sample period.[6] The other central point to remember about party soldiers is that most (though not all) move on from that style. It may be that freshmen's initial zeal for the party team is tempered as they gain experience and insight, that they invest more in policy as they settle into their jobs, or that they become focused on goals that require them to broaden their perspective or soften their edges. As we saw in previous chapters, many party soldiers become policy specialists, and most eventual party builders began their careers as party soldiers. Thus, it would be a mistake to assume that partisan competition and ideological polarization mean that Congress is populated mostly by party soldiers.

Ambitious Entrepreneurs

In addition to the three large stylistic categories, we also identify two smaller ones. The least prevalent style is ambitious entrepreneurs. These MCs comprise about 4% of the observations, and about 9% of the legislators we follow demonstrate this style at least once between the 101st and 110th Congresses. The behavior of these legislators probably comes closes to the classic "show horse" style. Ambitious entrepreneurs have the highest showboat score of any style (i.e., they make the most floor speeches/write the most editorials); raise the most money overall and come in second only to party builders in redistributing money to the party; and are legislatively active generalists, but are not effective in moving that legislation through the process (or, maybe more accurately, are not interested in doing so). As a group, these MCs also devote staff resources to their districts, and they are idiosyncratic in their voting and cosponsorship patterns, often breaking from the party line.

As the name suggests, these MCs are ambitious, and, we argue, their relationships with their parties and their orientation toward lawmaking are more instrumental, designed to help them further their career goals. Of course, this is not necessarily a bad thing, as these MCs may have sincere desires to "do good" at higher levels, and many of them have. Among the ambitious entrepreneurs in our sample are future governors Nathan Deal (R-GA) and Bobby Jindal (R-LA) and future senators Barbara Boxer (D-CA), Joe Donnelly (D-IN), Jeff Flake (R-AZ), Kirsten Gillibrand (D-NY), Bernie Sanders (I-VT), and Chuck Schumer (D-NY).

From the perspective of representation of their House constituents, these MCs' interest in moving up (or out) may be a mixed bag. They do focus staff resources at home, and many are skilled at attending to heterogeneous constituencies. On the other hand, compared to their colleagues in many other styles, their focus is really not on long-term service in the House of Representatives. Their modal path of exit from the House is a run for higher office, and, like their district advocate colleagues, they are also comparatively willing to walk away from House service through retirement. Not surprisingly, they have among the shortest average tenures (about twelve years).

And, despite the many honorable MCs who have been ambitious entrepreneurs, the style also has more than its fair share of scoundrels. Building on Basinger's (2013) data on legislators' involvement in scandals, we calculated the rate of scandal[7] for MCs who had been an ambitious entrepreneur at least once versus those who had never displayed this style,[8] and we found a significant difference—54% of entrepreneurs had been implicated in scandal (broadly conceived) versus 39% of others ($t = 2.9$; $p < .05$). Indeed, the ambitious entrepreneurs in our sample include such well-known former House members as Rod Blagojevich (D-IL), who became governor of Illinois and was ousted from office and convicted for corruption and soliciting bribes; Tom DeLay (D-TX), convicted (but later acquitted) of conspiracy to violate election law; Bob Menendez (D-NJ), currently under indictment for corruption; Dan Rostenkowski (D-IL), involved in the House Post Office scandal; Jim Traficant (D-OH), charged with racketeering before his House service and charged and convicted of corruption during it; and Enid Greene Waldholtz (R-UT), whose one term in the House was marred by accusations of campaign finance violations by her then-husband Joe Waldholtz.

When citizens and pundits think about what is wrong with Congress, it is often examples like these that come to mind. But it should be underscored that the behavior of these members was extreme and not typical of the average ambitious entrepreneur. More generally, although entrepreneurs' show horse approach to legislative life may not be popular from a normative perspective, they can perform some valuable functions in Congress. In particular, their willingness to break from the party line in voting may serve as a useful counterbalance to the many party soldiers and policy specialists who toe it faithfully. It should also be noted that, like party soldiers, the entrepreneur style is among the least stable—only half of MCs with that style in one congress will continue with it in the next, with most becoming either district advocates or party builders.[9]

For some MCs, a move to the entrepreneur style comes late in the game as they actively gear up for a run for higher office. We saw this with David McIntosh (R-IN) as he transitioned from a soldier to an entrepreneur in his final term before running for governor, and it holds true as well for MCs such as Chuck Schumer (D-NY) and Bill McCollum (R-FL), who had been long-term party builders before the former ran successfully for senator and the latter unsuccessfully for governor. Thus, from the perspective of constituents and the parties, individual ambitious entrepreneurs tend to be an ephemeral phenomenon, with MCs briefly taking on this style before transitioning to another style, running for higher office, or departing the House through retirement.

Party Builders

The final style is that of the party builders. We have described this style as the "movers and shakers" in the House and indeed they are, with many formal leaders and other party and chamber elites displaying this style. Not unexpectedly, it is relatively small—about 12% of the observations in the sample are party builders, and about 17% of the MCs were builders at some point between the 101st and 110th Congresses.

Not surprisingly, party builders share with their party soldier and policy specialist colleagues a focus on party loyalty. They have the highest mean scores on party voting and among the lowest on coalition bipartisanship. Where they truly stand out on this dimension, however, is in their redistribution of campaign contributions to their party hill committees and to copartisans. Party builders receive by far the highest mean scores of any group on party giving.

In terms of their other activity, builders are perhaps best characterized as both work horses and show horses. They are active in the lawmaking process and are publicly quite visible, coming in second to ambitious entrepreneurs in their showboat scores and in their volume of legislative activity. In some ways, then, party builders and ambitious entrepreneurs are alike, but a major difference is that party builders are committed to careers within the institution. Their ambition is not to rise beyond the House, but to rise within it. On that front, they enjoy considerable success. Three-quarters of early-career builders will go on to attain leadership positions of some type, including becoming the very top leaders in the chamber. However, the style appears both to precipitate and to anticipate the rise to leadership (i.e., being a builder makes it more likely that an MC will gain a leadership position in the next term, and gaining a leadership position makes it more likely that one will become a builder).

Party builders, then, govern their parties and the House of Representatives. It is no doubt of value to the chamber to have MCs who are willing to invest in it in this fashion. In considering the downside of the electoral connection and reelection incentive, Mayhew (1974) noted:

> What is needed is a system of "selective incentives" to induce at least some members to work toward keeping the institution in good repair. And it is just such a system that has evolved over the decades. What happens is that prestige and power within the Congress itself are accorded to upholders of the institution; the Capitol Hill pecking order is geared to the needs of institutional maintenance. (146)

In our formulation, party builders fulfill this role. Their motivation is not selfless—it is ambition that drives the styles of legislators like Nancy Pelosi and John Boehner. Neither is it nonpartisan. The MCs who pursue the builder style are among the strongest partisans, and so, at least in the contemporary period, the institutional maintainers and the party stalwarts are one in the same. Thus, the reemergence of parties and partisanship in the 1980s may have made these maintainers less of a contributor to the smooth operation of the institution now than they were at the time of Mayhew's writing.

From the perspective of representation, builders present both advantages and disadvantages. Constituents no doubt reap benefits from being represented by powerful MCs, and builders tend to be good ideological fits with their districts, so they can provide strong policy congruence through their roll call votes. The flip side, though, is that these members are focused on DC rather than their districts (with the lowest mean score of any style for home front attention) and may be too preoccupied with congressional business to focus their energy on policy making, even on issues of interest to their constituents. As we saw in chapter 6, party builders do not seem to suffer electoral harm as a result of their styles, suggesting that constituents believe that the benefits of being represented by a builder outweigh the costs. Nonetheless, that value that party builders bring to their parties and the chamber may come at the cost of attentive representation of their constituents.

Considering Congressional Reform

In sum, then, there is no single perfect style, but each of the five contributes something of potential value to the functioning of the legislature. The portrait of Congress that emerges is of a body of members doing more or less what we expect MCs to do—making policy, representing their constituents, working for their parties, and promoting their careers. Some are more focused on one or more of these dimensions of congressional life than others (and/or are more successful in it), but we see a broad distribution of styles, with no one type dominating. Thus, a critique that, for example, no one in the House is focused on policy or that no one attends to their districts is simply not true.

While the goals of members in the 1990s and 2000s remain in line with those posited by Fenno (1973) over four decades ago, public views of the legislative branch have changed dramatically since the 1970s. Although Congress could never be characterized as popular, levels of approval of and trust in the institution are now at historical lows. Indeed, at the time of this writing (late 2016), approval of Congress hovers in the low teens. Although several congresses have passed since our data collection ended, the increased dissatisfaction that we observe today took root during the time period we study.

Why do Americans currently hold Congress in such low regard? Partisan polarization is typically identified as the main culprit, both by scholars of the institution itself and by political scientists who study public opinion. Mann and Ornstein (2006) argue, for example, that the move from decentralized committee government to centralized party and leadership control has led to an inability of Congress to govern effectively, making it the "broken branch." At the mass level, Hetherington and Rudolph (2015) show that citizens' feelings about their own party and the opposite party have changed. Democrats and Republicans today not only have differing policy preferences, but also simply do not like each other. Accordingly, they have difficulty trusting institutions such as Congress that make so visible the clashes between the parties.

Legislators' styles do, of course, reflect the partisan context in which they serve, and it is true that the typical representative today is more ideologically extreme in his or her voting than were his or her peers from decades past. However, that most legislators are good partisans does *not* mean that their behavior in other realms is identical. As we described above, party builders, party soldiers, and policy specialists—all party loyalists—differ from one another in their attentiveness to lawmaking, their policy focus, their fund-raising habits, the extent to which they seek out visibility, and the amount of resources they devote to the home front. It is also important to underscore that, even with the increase in polarization between 1989 (when our data collection begins) and 2008 (when it ends), the proportion of district advocates (i.e., the style held by MCs who break from the party line) does not change much—ranging from about 25–30% of MCs per congress.

Nonetheless, the sense that "something has to change" has led to discussions of potential reforms to improve the performance of Congress and voters' trust in it as an institution. Some target congressional procedures, others the nature of political rhetoric outside Congress, and still others members of the House (and Senate) themselves. We focus here on "member" reforms, as they have the clearest connections to style. Such reforms include proposals to increase electoral competition at the district level, to impose term limits, and to introduce stricter campaign finance rules. In our closing pages, we consider style as a lens for evaluating the likely effects of such reforms.

Increasing Electoral Competition

Although concerns about incumbency advantage are far from new, over the past several decades districts have grown increasingly homogenous (ideologically or otherwise) and safe for one party. The MCs who represent these districts are therefore insulated from electoral pressures and face little incentive to compromise on policy with the other party. This, many claim, contributes to polarization in the chamber. Scholars have found that this is often the case, but only at the margins, as the effects are small and not sufficient to explain the entirety of polarization (Abramowitz, Alexander, and Gunning 2006; Carson, Crespin, et al. 2007; McCarty, Poole, and Rosenthal 2009; Theriault 2008). Nonetheless, pundits and other observers often propose utilizing redistricting to make districts more heterogeneous and competitive. For example, Michael Bloomberg, Mayor of New York City and one-time potential presidential hopeful, issued a report calling for nonpartisan redistricting to increase competition (Bloomberg 2010), and several states utilize nonpartisan commissions to draw district lines.

Putting aside the question of whether there would be sufficient political will to make widespread redistricting happen (probably not, as those currently in power are advantaged by the status quo), what effect would it have? Increased competition, whether it arose from redistricting or other causes, would likely lead MCs to take more moderate positions and increase their efforts to reach across the aisle, as their electoral futures would depend upon building reelection coalitions that included copartisans, independents, and outpartisans. There would also be increased incentive to devote time and resources to the home front as MCs attempted to cultivate their constituencies. In other words, increased competition at the district level would probably create more district advocates.

From the perspective of decreasing levels of polarization, having a higher proportion of district advocates in Congress would be a good thing. Importantly, though, unless the majority of MCs were district advocates, it would not necessarily solve the problems associated with polarization. Our results in chapter 8 demonstrated that advocates face difficulty climbing the leadership ladder, and even with more district advocates in Congress, it is still likely that positions of power would be reserved for the remaining "good partisans." There could also be a downside for lawmaking, as many district advocates simply cannot afford to focus on policy entrepreneurship and instead need to devote their efforts to reelection. Thus, increasing electoral competition would likely mean replacing policy specialists with district advocates, which could solve some problems, but would generate others.

Institute Term Limits

Another common proposal for reform is to impose term limits on congressional service. Proponents argue that limiting time in Congress would encourage a body of "citizen legislators" who remained connected to their districts, would provide for an influx of new ideas, and would encourage legislators to solve problems in the here and now rather than focusing on the long-term consequences for their parties and their careers. Opponents, on the other hand, argue that limiting terms deprives Congress of the expertise of its senior members, that the system of reelection already works to promote accountability, and that term limits would shift the balance of power away from the legislature toward the executive (for summaries, see Carey 1998; Kousser 2005).

Legislative styles provide an interesting angle from which to assess these arguments. Of course, in a situation where all MCs were term limited, incentive structures would change greatly, and so too might the styles legislators adopt. In assessing the general value of term limits as a proposal, though, we should consider whether, under the current system, the types of legislators who serve the longest terms also have the most "objectionable" behavior. Recall from chapter 8 that, although the average tenures of the various styles do not differ greatly, advocates and entrepreneurs are on the low end and party builders and policy specialists are on the high end. Holding all else equal, then, builders and specialists would be most likely to be term-limited out, with advocates and entrepreneurs less so. Thus, were term limits to be imposed under the current distribution of styles, we would lose more strong partisans, but would also lose legislators with a commitment to the institution and to policy making. And, importantly, if the results from chapter 4 on freshman styles held post-term limits, the MCs who replaced those departing builders and specialists would not be relatively moderate, bipartisan district advocates, but would instead be party soldiers, as that is the style where most MCs start out.

It is not clear how the presence of term limits would shape the long-term strategizing of MCs, but the effect might be bimodal. Some newly elected MCs, the classic "citizen legislators," would likely focus on their districts and short-term policy goals and, after a period of congressional service, would return to private life. Term limits might lead others, however, to accelerate their progressive ambition, knowing that a long career in public life requires that they move up to the Senate or governorship. Thus, term limits could also incentivize the ambitious entrepreneur style, which, ironically, is perhaps the most normatively at odds with the vision of what proponents of term limits want to accomplish.

In sum, then, term limits are likely to have *some* effect on legislators' strategies, and hence their styles, but it is not clear whether that effect would be beneficial or deleterious. On this point, we are in agreement with Mayhew (2000), who argued:

> To limit House and Senate members to, say, twelve years in office—the reform that seems most likely to win approval, if any does—might, for better or worse, alter or eliminate certain career-related features of congressional performance. Exactly so, and for the better, the advocates of term limits would claim—but we cannot be sure of that. (187)

In other words, if the goal is to produce a "better" distribution of types of legislators (whatever that may look like), term limits are not necessarily the solution.[10]

Money

Perhaps the biggest change in congressional politics that occurred across the time period we study is the role of money and fund-raising.[11] Not only has the cost of campaigning increased, legislators are now expected to raise and redistribute funds to their copartisans and party organizations, with proficiency at fund-raising and generosity in redistribution now a prerequisite for climbing the leadership ladder (see, for example, Heberlig and Larson 2012; Pearson 2015).[12]

How then might curtailing the role of fund-raising affect legislative styles?[13] Or, put another way, "what are the 'action' implications of the fact that MCs seem to be increasingly drawn from two atypical slices of the population—multimillionaires and *willing* round-the-clock fund-raisers?" (Mayhew 2000, 233). One possibility is that it would result in broadening the types of MCs who are considered viable candidates for high-level leadership positions. If prowess at fund-raising is no longer viewed as a necessary skill in a leader, then some MCs who were formerly left out due to an unwillingness or inability to fund-raise might be more likely to rise through the hierarchy. And, freed from hours spent on raising money, all MCs would also have more time to spend on lawmaking and district attention.

In all, though, we anticipate that restrictions on money in politics would have minimal effects on the distribution of legislative styles. We would still expect to see some MCs who prioritize their districts, some who are motivated by policy making, some who want to become leaders, some with their eyes on a higher prize, and some with combinations of these goals. And, while fund-raising might become less important in the rise to leadership, MCs who are tapped for these positions are still likely to be strong partisans with a taste for public visibility. In other words, there is not a clear causal link between reducing the role of money in politics and having, say, district advocates rather than party builders rise to chamber leadership positions. This is in line with studies of leadership careers that have found that, over the past forty to fifty years, advancement has become less about gaining seniority and more about the strategies of party elites and individual members (see, for example, Loomis 1984; Ehrenhalt 1991; Meinke 2016). Thus, reforms that reduce the role of money in Congress may have potentially normatively desirable effects, but by themselves are unlikely to change the basic styles that members adopt.

Conclusions

The study of legislative styles we have undertaken makes several important contributions to understandings of congressional politics. First, and most fundamentally, we have demonstrated that, based on their activity, legislators can indeed be classified into one of a small number of distinct styles. These styles, while more complicated than indicated by the classic "show horse/work horse" distinction, map on to common intuitions and the conventional wisdom about how MCs navigate their jobs. Thus, it is possible to quantify the sorts of stylistic differences that, at least since Fenno (1978),[14] have been of interest to political scientists.

Moreover, not only is it possible to classify MCs in this way, it is valuable as well. Legislative styles offer new insight into a variety of fundamental questions about legislative behavior and about Congress as an institution. For example, we have seen that styles help to explain the path to party and chamber leadership. Future leaders distinguish themselves from their peers quite early. Taking styles into account also offers a richer conception of how MCs manage heterogeneous constituencies, how shocks such as majority shifts do (and do not) influence behavior, why some MCs enjoy more legislative success than do others, and whether MCs leave the House via electoral loss, retirement, or progressive ambition. Congress thus appears to work to provide legislators with ways to pursue their careers while also contributing to the good of their constituents, the chamber, or the nation as a whole.

Finally, although we have focused here on the modern US House of Representatives, our approach is easily transportable to different eras and different settings. Scholars interested in the history of the House or the Senate, state legislatures, or comparative legislatures could all utilize a clustering approach to legislative styles. Styles can be analyzed in any situation in which there is sufficient data on what legislators do and theory to guide expectations about differences across members. Although we do not expect the *same* styles to emerge in all contexts (e.g., in parliamentary systems, the tendency of MPs to be party loyalists in voting will not usefully distinguish members), we predict that stylistic differences themselves will emerge. The correlates and consequences of these styles are central to understanding the puzzle that lies at the heart of legislative politics, regardless of the setting: how the goals of elected members interact with the incentives and constraints imposed by the institution to affect the nature and quality of lawmaking and democratic representation.

Notes

Chapter One

1. As we will show, these impressionistic categories map well onto the styles that emerge from our analyses.
2. Equally important, the broader literature on congressional politics gravitated away from the sociological approaches that had dominated work in the 1940s and 1950s and toward rational choice models of legislative behavior and institutions (see Polsby and Schickler 2002).
3. It is true that some MCs expend more effort overall than others, so their choices about allocation of resources are not strictly zero-sum—e.g., introducing more bills does not always necessitate being less active in another area. Some activities, however, do present zero-sum choices (i.e., to vote with or against their party majority on a roll call).
4. The book, although ostensibly about the politics of foreign trade, offers many broader lessons to students of agenda-setting and legislative behavior.
5. This expectation is in line with work on MCs' presentational styles, which shows that such styles are stable over the electoral cycle and change only slowly across careers (see, for example, Fenno 2000; Grimmer 2013).
6. See, for example, Grimmer and Powell's (2013) work on the effects of committee exile (i.e., when a member is involuntarily removed from a committee due to changes in his or her party's seat share) on MCs' decisions about allocation of effort in the district versus Washington, DC.

Chapter Two

1. Fenno also offered a fourth goal—a career beyond the House—which he said would be treated only peripherally as it was not among the most consequen-

tial for committee behavior (1973, 1). From the perspective of legislative styles, however, this goal is on par with the first three.

2. In later work, Fenno puts more focus on the balancing of goals, arguing that "most members of Congress develop, over time, a mix of personal goals.... This complex view of House member goals is, we think, a realistic view. And it is the job of empirical political science to describe and explain the various mixes of goals, and the conditions under which they are adopted or altered" (1978, 221; see also Fenno 2000).

3. Of course, this choice is not without risk, and most MCs are particularly cautious about their reelection prospects.

4. Roll call voting sometimes comes close, though even there MCs have considerable power to explain and justify their choices, and constituents may grant them significant leeway to vote as they see fit (Bianco 1994; Grimmer 2013).

5. This may be the reason that few studies of the electoral connection have identified strong linkages between MCs' electoral vulnerability and their behavior. If there are many possible reelection-oriented behaviors and legislators choose those that either help them also to achieve other goals and/or that resonate particularly well with their constituents, then we should not necessarily expect a strong relationship between vote shares and any single activity. This would only hold true if vulnerable MCs did more of *everything* that could promote reelection.

6. Our approach thus serves as a useful complement to those that seek to identify and explain the *extraordinary* actions of members (see, most notably, Mayhew 2000).

7. Given the nature of our algorithm, we must have data on a measure for all congresses in order to include it.

8. Prior to the 104th Congress, these funds were not lumped into a single allowance. Nonetheless, we see the same amount of variation in offices and staff assignment in the 101st–103rd Congresses as we see in the 104th–110th. For regulations on how MCs can use their allowances, see http://cha.house.gov/handbooks/members-congressional-handbook.

9. Most MCs have about fifteen staff members paid for from their MRAs.

10. A Lexis-Nexis search for "missed roll call votes" during the sample period turns up nearly one thousand articles.

11. Those who miss substantial numbers of votes tend to be those who suffer from a serious illness or accident during the term. While we do not exclude these MCs from the analysis, we do limit our investigations to those who serve a full term (or enough of one to generate a record on all of the measures that comprise style) during a particular congress, so MCs who retire early or pass away are not included.

12. We focus on the introduction and cosponsorship of (public) bills and joint resolutions (i.e., omitting simple and concurrent resolutions). Bills and joint res-

olutions both carry the force of law if passed and are functionally equivalent to one another.

13. Andrews was also a prolific sponsor in earlier congresses, introducing approximately one hundred bills in the 106th, 107th, and 108th Congresses as well.

14. For example, William Dannemeyer (R-CA) once recited a poem about offshore oil drilling (concluding "oil's well that ends well"), and Thomas Downey (D-NY) offered a (satirical) proposal to lower the minimum age requirement in the House to fifteen years (Lacey 1996).

15. Ideally, we would include as a third indicator some measure of an MC's television interviews (on Sunday morning talk shows or news networks), but these data are not available. One could also examine the number of news stories *about* each legislator as a measure of visibility, but we choose not to, as such coverage is, at best, only partially controlled by an MC him- or herself.

16. The correlation between vote share going into a congress and amount of money raised in that congress is $-.24$ ($p < .01$), a result that holds even after controlling for congress.

17. The party organizations set giving thresholds for rank-and-file members, party and committee leaders, and so on, though these are not strictly enforced.

18. While giving to the hill committee and giving to colleagues is highly correlated ($r = .63$), these are distinct decisions. About two hundred MCs in the sample give to the hill committee but not colleagues, and about nine hundred redistribute funds to colleagues but do not give to their hill committee.

19. It is not uncommon for state-specific bills to be introduced by one MC and cosponsored by all or most of the state delegation, regardless of party.

20. The categories include agriculture, budget, campaign finance, children's issues, civil rights, consumer issues, corporate regulation, crime, defense and foreign policy, education, environment, government operations, health, jobs and infrastructure, Medicare, moral issues, Social Security, taxes, and welfare.

21. King and Latham were also seen as potential candidates for the Republican nomination, but they too declined to enter the race.

22. In our case, the observations are of each MC's behavior in each of the 101st–110th Congresses. We exclude congresses where an MC served only a partial term (i.e., for those who enter Congress after a special election, or for those who leave before the end of their last term), for a total of 4,276 observations.

23. For readers familiar with the commonly used R-factor analysis, the basic logic is the same, as both are data reduction techniques. However, in most factor analysis, the goal is to reduce the number of variables to a few underlying factors. In cluster analysis, the goal is to group cases in the appropriate number of categories (see Filho et al. 2014, 2409).

24. Indeed, as discussed above, the correlation between these two variables in the raw data is .63.

25. Using summary variables as the inputs in a clustering analysis is appropri-

ate. Ahlquist and Breunig (2012), for example, advocate using principal components analysis to create input variables.

26. These decisions are necessarily based on judgment, and there are some variables that one might argue should fall into another category. (For example, do cosponsorships belong under lawmaking and should overall fund-raising be rolled into party giving?) We ran the analyses several ways and found the resulting clusters to be robust. Before proceeding, we also examined the correlation matrix of all of the input variables to confirm that our indices "worked" empirically (i.e., that the constituent variables were related to one another in the expected fashion).

27. We calculate the z-scores separately by Congress because, for some indicators, such as spending, the overall trend shows an increase or decrease across time. In dividing MCs into clusters, we are interested in how they compare to their current peers.

28. The model can disregard the temporal aspect of the data, allowing MCs to belong to different clusters at each time point with no regard to what clusters the MCs belonged to previously. The fact that the estimates did not give a large value of λ or similar rows of the transition probability matrix strongly indicates that the data do not support relaxing the assumption of temporal dependence.

29. For example, an MC's electoral vulnerability may shape her behavior, and hence, her style. But whether or not an MC is vulnerable is not a part of his or her style.

30. Two clusters did not turn out to be a good fit for the data, offering more evidence against the work horse/show horse distinction.

31. Another way to view this is to suppose that $\lambda = 1$. Then any two MCs belonging to the same style have the same probability distribution over their behaviors; the MC's past behaviors provide no additional insight into their current behaviors. In contrast, having $0 < \lambda < 1$ implies that two MCs belonging to the same style will act similarly to each other, but looking at the MC's past behavior will still help to make more accurate predictions of current and future behavior.

Chapter Three

1. We conducted robustness checks to confirm that our clusters held with slight tinkering to the inputs (e.g., rolling the cosponsorship variable into the party voting index) and to different numbers of congresses. While there are, as expected, some small differences, the same general pattern of clusters emerges.

2. It is likely that in the congresses after our data collection ends, Ryan's ascent up the leadership ladder and increasingly public persona corresponded to a transition in style. We explore evolutions in style in later chapters.

NOTES TO PAGES 47–58

3. Ideally, we would have access to data on pork and other district benefits delivered by each representative. Unfortunately, such data are not available for our time frame. However, anecdotal evidence does suggest that district advocate MCs are active in efforts to bring money to their districts.

4. We have data on these four MCs for nine or ten of the congresses in the sample. With the exception of Smith, who falls into another cluster in one of the congresses, all maintain the district advocate style in every congress for which we have information.

5. Because Sanders caucused with the Democrats, we consider him a Democrat for purposes of our analyses.

6. Although related to the questions of model fit addressed in chapter 2, this is a different question, targeting individual observations rather than the clustering model as a whole.

7. Our clustering algorithm, which assumes a Markov process, induces some stickiness as well. However, the results from that model indicate that the data support the assumption of temporal dependence.

8. The proportion of party soldiers is unusually high (and the proportion of policy specialists unusually low) in the 101st Congress. Some of this may be an artifact of our model, which takes into account prior behavior in assigning current cluster assignments. Because the 101st is the first congress for which we have data, there is no prior activity to include. In our analyses of the correlates of style, we include controls for congress to address this issue. We also ran models excluding the 101st Congress, but found no substantial differences.

9. Based on the mean scores on the indices of activity, it is apparent that the policy specialist and party soldier styles are where back bencher party loyalists congregate.

10. Young's particular focus was on defense, and he served on the Subcommittees on Defense (which he chaired) and Military Construction, Veterans Affairs, and Related Agencies. He was also well-known for his prowess at earmarking.

11. They are also the smallest group, so a shift of a handful of MCs can result in large percentage shifts. Not surprisingly, they have the highest standard deviation on consistency of any group.

12. The table also reveals some other interesting patterns in transitions—e.g., ambitious entrepreneurs never transition (directly) to the policy specialist style and policy specialists never transition to become ambitious entrepreneurs. We also see that party soldiers who change style from one congress to the next tend to become policy specialists, while ambitious entrepreneurs become district advocates or party builders. We devote chapter 5 to explaining the nature of shifts in style.

13. Akin claimed that conception was impossible in cases of "legitimate rape" (Moore 2012).

Chapter Four

1. And some, such as Wes Cooley (R-OR), Duke Cunningham (R-CA), Jesse Jackson, Jr. (D-IL), and William Jefferson (D-LA), would go to jail.

2. We are agnostic about whether career experiences themselves shape MC interests or whether there is selection (e.g., Does being a doctor make one interested in health policy? Do those with interests in health become doctors? Or are both at work?). Regardless of the causal dynamics, prior experiences should help us to explain MCs' styles.

3. In these and the analyses to follow, we focus on the 567 freshmen elected to the 101st–110th Congresses who served a full term (i.e., omitting those who came to office after a special election, or those who left office before the end of the term).

4. There is some variation in the proportion of freshman soldiers across time (from about 50–65%), but this actually peaks in the middle congresses of our time frame (the 105th and 106th Congresses). Thus, there is no evidence that our aggregate patterns are due to a cohort effect, with increasing polarization producing greater numbers of new party soldiers as senior members from other styles retire or move to higher office.

5. Also not surprisingly, given Fenno's description of how the party leadership had targeted McIntosh as a future player, he had a bit of party builder thrown in as well. McIntosh's "soft probabilities" in his freshman term were .63 party soldier and .37 party builder. He was also one of the smaller group of MCs who maintained the soldier style into his sophomore term.

6. Recall, for example, Henry Waxman's (D-CA) early decisions to focus on health and environmental policy, and then to continue to pursue these issues once elected to Congress.

7. NOMINATE scores are calculated from legislators' roll call votes (the algorithm reflects how often MCs vote with other MCs) and, as a result, are not in place prior to the start of their freshman terms. Nonetheless, NOMINATE is often interpreted as a measure of MCs' latent ideology, which *does* exist upon their entry to Congress, and, in many cases, is observable through their campaign appeals and in their prior political records. Accordingly, we feel comfortable using it to explain style.

8. Along these lines, Grose (2011) finds that African American constituents prefer a districted-oriented representational style, and that their MCs respond accordingly.

9. Even though policy specialists tend to vote with their parties, their overall legislative (and, likely, presentational) styles do not highlight their sense of "teamness" with the party in the manner of party soldiers.

10. In the long run, however, such prestigious committees may be populated more by policy specialists.

11. Of course, there are issues of causality—are certain types of MCs (who

were destined to be party soldiers anyway) more likely to be given exclusive assignments? Or does the assignment lead them to be more likely to adopt patterns of activity that look like those of other party soldiers? With first-term legislators, we are not able to disentangle these possibilities.

12. There are no sizable differences across groups in the mean Sullivan Index scores, but if we look at the proportion of MCs in each style who come from districts that score above the median on this measure, nearly 70% of policy specialists do versus 55–56% of party soldiers and district advocates.

13. The combination of these patterns—that builders and entrepreneurs are the most likely to be tapped for exclusive assignments, but also differ from their peers in myriad other ways, increases confidence that the stylistic differences we see across groups are not just a function of institutional positions. These MCs differ in ways beyond the prestige of the committee assignments they receive.

14. Although soldiers are more likely to receive exclusive assignments in the freshman term, we find that, among the full sample, policy specialists and party builders are more likely than soldiers to have exclusive committee seats.

15. We explore the effects of gender, along with race, in more nuanced analyses later in the chapter.

16. Her Republican counterpart, John Boehner (R-OH), was first elected to the 102nd Congress, where he began as a party soldier. In the 103rd Congress, he too became a party builder.

17. A more qualitative assessment of the nonpolitical precongressional careers of party builders and ambitious entrepreneurs yields no clear patterns either.

18. In fact, Latino MCs adopt the district advocate style at slightly higher rates than Caucasian MCs, and all five Asian American MCs are party soldiers as freshmen.

19. This difference also emerged as significant in the multinomial logit analyses in table 4.2.

20. While this may appear to contradict Grose's (2011) findings that Black representatives pursue a district-oriented style, their tendency to be classified as policy specialists is due to the fact that they are, as a group, good partisans. It is also likely that their policy focus aligns with their efforts at descriptive representation for their largely minority districts (i.e., in pursuing issues of interest to those constituents).

21. However, with an N of only eight, we should be very cautious about drawing firm conclusions.

Chapter Five

1. Interior and Public Works has jurisdiction over coal-related issues, and Rahall chaired the subcommittee on Mining and Natural Resources.

2. In analyzing the dynamics of style for senior members, we face potentially

thorny selection issues, as the MCs who stay for twenty-plus years likely differ in important ways from those who lose reelection, who move up to a more prestigious office, or who opt out for other nonelected opportunities. In chapter 8, we investigate the relationships between styles and MCs' career decisions.

3. The latter two measures may differ from one another. Consider, for example, two MCs who each shifted style three times. If the first changed from a party soldier to a policy specialist to a district advocate to a party builder, that is a qualitatively different pattern from one who started as a party soldier and then oscillated back and forth from that style to another one.

4. The "whole career" group is not fully representative of the population of MCs—most notably, it excludes the small proportion of legislators who serve more than twenty years in the House.

5. Of course, these percentages are affected by the fact that most MCs appear in our sample for only about four terms, and the maximum number of possible transitions is therefore limited. However, even if we target the analyses on MCs who served more than five of the ten terms, the numbers do not change drastically—about 60% have experienced zero or one shift in style and 72% display just one or two styles.

6. If we examine the styles of freshmen who did *not* return to Congress in the second term (either voluntarily or involuntarily), we there are no party builders among that group and about twice the proportion of ambitious entrepreneurs relative to the group that does return. However, the proportions of the three largest styles—district advocates, party soldiers, and policy specialists—remain constant.

7. Among the full sample, the median seniority is seven years, or four terms, and the mean is nine years.

8. This does not necessarily mean they maintained this style without interruption in the interim, though many of them did.

9. Importantly, this underestimates the propensity of soldiers to become builders, as some may do so beyond the fifth term, and others might have done so earlier and changed styles and/or exited office.

10. Later in this chapter, we explore whether these transitions in style reflect small or large changes in underlying patterns of behavior.

11. This seems to explain Nick Rahall's (the West Virginia Democrat whose behavior was the focus of our opening example) apparent shifts between the district advocate and policy specialist styles in the 107th–110th Congresses. In the 107th, Rahall, a long-time district advocate, displayed a change in behavior (linked, perhaps, to becoming the ranking member of the Resources Committee) that resulted in a drop in probability of being an advocate to .46. However, he remains categorized as an advocate because he is one of the very few truly hybrid MCs, with a .46 probability of being an advocate, a .23 probability of being a soldier, and a .30 probability of being a specialist. By the 108th Congress, the

probability of being a specialist rose to .53, and the probability of being an advocate remained relatively constant at .46, resulting in Rahall being categorized as a specialist. Over the next congresses, his relative probabilities of being an advocate and specialist fluctuate back and forth between .45 and .55, producing the transition in style we observe. We should underscore, though, that Rahall is a unique case, as most transitions are more clear-cut.

12. Our measures here consist of two dummy variables indicating whether an MC gained or lost more than three points in vote share. The comparison category is legislators who maintained relatively constant vote share. We use these dummies rather than the raw change in vote share to account in a straightforward way for unopposed MCs.

13. This includes committee leadership (as the full chair or ranking member), as a part of the chamber and party leadership, or as an officer in the party's congressional campaign committee. We provide more detail on these assignments below.

14. We focus just on gaining leadership or exclusive assignments (i.e., rather than gaining or losing them) for a couple of reasons. First, it is rare to lose such a position absent a majority shift, and often, a "loss" of such a position does not really reflect a downgrade. For example, an MC might move off of one committee in exchange for seats on two other committees of particular interest to him or her, or might give up a seat to take on a leadership position. In measuring leadership, there is also substantial variation across time in how the parties structure leadership opportunities, particularly for whips and in the congressional campaign committees. Again, then, there is reason to believe that losing one of these positions does not often amount to a real loss in status.

15. This variable is drawn from Charles Stewart and Jonathan Woon's "Modern Standing Committees" data. It reflects whether any of the committee assignments an MC had in congress t did not continue in congress $t + 1$.

16. We obtained these data from Brian Gaines. His dichotomous indicator of redistricting indicates whether district lines were redrawn in a way that changed the constituency represented by the MC. It is therefore a rather blunt measure of change, but this should make it more difficult for us to uncover effects.

17. Most party builders have at least some "status," but this is not an unrealistic scenario—there are thirty-seven observations in the sample of builders without majority status, an exclusive committee assignment, or a leadership position.

18. We calculate these probabilities using CLARIFY (Tomz, Wittenberg, and King 2003), where all characteristics of MCs are held at their means (for continuous variables) or their modes (for dichotomous variables like gender, race, and age).

19. Just gaining leadership increases the probability from .78 to .90, and just gaining an exclusive committee increases it from .66 to .97.

20. Hyde would maintain the specialist style through the 104th Congress, be-

fore shifting back to the party builder style and then to the ambitious entrepreneurs. This suggests that for minority party builders who are not clear fits with their leadership, the transition to majority status may bring transitions and instability in style.

21. Henry Hyde had also been a policy specialist in the early years of his career, before ascending to party builder status.

22. These changes should also dampen the effects of gaining a position, but it still seems likely that having a new, named position may affect behavior and, hence, styles.

23. There is some variation in the number of party and campaign leadership positions across time as the parties expand, contract, and reorganize their leadership structures (Meinke 2016). Nonetheless, as these positions go to only a small proportion of MCs, it seems reasonable to assume that gaining one remains prestigious.

24. These groupings parallel those used by other scholars. See, for example, Heberlig and Larson (2012), who differentiate between elected positions (Speaker, floor leaders, whips, and caucus/conference officers); "extended" leadership positions, which are chairs and vice chairs; and members of party committees (including steering committees, policy and research committees, and campaign committees) (171).

25. This dynamic may have contributed to Nick Rahall's changes in style. He became the ranking member of Resources in the 107th, and, perhaps as a result, his probability of being a district advocate dropped relative to his level in the 106th Congress. It was not until the 108th, however, that the policy specialist style became dominant for him.

26. The patterns of results are very similar if we use a more stringent cutoff (i.e., a maximum soft probability of .90, where 40% of MCs have probabilities lower and 60% higher). However, it makes little sense in this context to say that we "expect" a change in style in the next term for an MC whose behavior gives him or her a probability of, say, .88 of fitting into his or her current style. Thus, we opt for the .75 cutoff.

27. As shown in table 5.2, gaining an exclusive committee assignment in the sophomore term is associated with a transition from the soldier to specialist style.

Chapter Six

1. He later noted, for example, that "obeying the electoral incentive does not necessarily bar a politician from being autonomous" (2000, 14).

2. These regional divisions come from ICPSR, where states are classified as New England, Middle Atlantic, East North Central, West North Central, Solid South, Border, Mountain, Pacific, or External.

3. Sulkin, Testa, and Usry (2015) show, for example, that copartisan constituents of MCs reward policy activity, while outpartisans do not. Even more notably, district attention (as indicated by the number of offices and proportion of staff in the district) is rewarded by outpartisans and independents, but punished by copartisans.

4. When Sharp was first elected in 1974, he represented the 10th district. Following the 1980 redistricting, his constituency became the 2nd district.

5. In this term, McIntosh launched an unsuccessful bid for governor of Indiana. As we show in chapter 8, such progressive ambition is often presaged by a transition in legislative style.

6. Winning the election is, of course, conditional on deciding to run again versus retire or make a bid for higher office. As with progressive ambition, retirement can also be strategic and based on electoral considerations (see, for example, Groseclose and Krehbiel 1994; Hall and Van Houweling 1995). We explore the dynamics of these career choices and their relationship with styles in chapter 8.

7. Our general pattern of results is robust to different methods of calculating fit between an MC and his or her district (e.g., normalized presidential vote share). We opt for our approach because we are most interested in testing hypotheses about ideological fit.

8. We get the same pattern of results if, rather than splitting the sample, we interact fit with style. For ease of presentation of results, we opt for splitting the sample.

9. For the vote share model, we get the same general pattern of findings if we include all MCs who ran. However, excluding losers allows us to more precisely test two different hypotheses—for the win/loss models, it is whether style is associated with reelection success, and for the vote share models it is whether, for winners, style is associated with variation in the magnitude of victory.

10. Poor-fitting builders, entrepreneurs, and specialists also perform better than soldiers.

11. The only significant difference is for ambitious entrepreneurs, who outperform party soldiers.

12. There may also be asymmetric valence effects. For example, if a district is relatively liberal, constituents may still prefer a very liberal MC to a slightly conservative one, and so identical distance scores may not be functionally equivalent. (For a similar argument about citizens and issue voting, see Rabinowitz and MacDonald 1989.) Exploring these possibilities is beyond the scope of our analyses here, but would be a useful extension.

13. Dingell's "next vote share" in the nine congresses in our data set for which he was a party builder range from 59.8 to 88%. Coburn appears once as a party builder, after which he gets 55.5% of the vote, and then transitions to the party soldier style for two terms before running for the Senate.

14. The loss rate is just 8% for ambitious entrepreneurs, though there are so few observations for entrepreneurs that we are hesitant to generalize.

15. In the models where the dependent variable is whether MCs are unopposed in the next election, we control for whether they were unopposed in the *previous* election. Similarly, in the challenger quality models, we control for the previous challenger's quality. This enables us to capture patterns in competition in the district across time, and also makes it more difficult to uncover relationships with style, providing for a conservative test.

16. A handful of MCs also die in the middle of a term or resign from office due to scandal or by being appointed to an executive position by the President. Replacements for these MCs are either elected in special elections or appointed by the state's governor. For the sake of comparability, we limit our analyses to cases in which the previous MC finished his or her last time and retired, ran for higher office, or lost the election.

17. In general, losing and being replaced by a copartisan means a loss in the primary, but there are also cases of run-offs and post-redistricting situations in which two incumbents run against one another.

18. Due to redistricting between the 1970s and 1990s, Flynt's former district had evolved and split such that Collins and Gingrich served concurrently.

Chapter Seven

1. Although they can have slightly different meanings, we use legislative "success," "effectiveness," and "productivity" interchangeably here, with success and effectiveness most often referring to individuals and productivity to aggregate units such as committees and congresses.

2. To be reported out of committee generally entails receiving a positive vote there. It is also possible for bills to be "pulled" from recalcitrant committees onto the floor via a discharge petition, although these are rare (see Pearson and Schickler 2009).

3. Which calendar it appears on depends on the bill's content, particularly whether or not it is a spending bill.

4. This is perhaps particularly surprising given our findings from chapter 3 that Andrews was among the most prolific introducers of legislation in the House. Throughout most of the period we observe, he was a party builder.

5. For this illustration, we opt for a dummy variable measure rather than the mean count of bills because the averages for substantive and significant and commemorative bills are so small. However, the pattern of results is relatively invariant to how we measure the prevalence of different types of bill introductions across styles.

6. As Volden and Wiseman note, stories in the *CQ Almanac* do not constitute

"ex ante measures of bill significance, as bills that move farther through the lawmaking process are much more likely to be mentioned" (2014, 20).

7. Volden and Wiseman's category of commemorative bills includes those for "private relief of an individual" (2014, 21). Private bills focus on providing a service or decision to a particular individual, as in, for example, an immigration case, and as a result do not really fall into the realm of public policy.

8. We also ran OLS models with the proportion of successful bills at each stage as the dependent variable, and we obtain the same pattern of results. We opt for the count models as, given the low denominator for success rates (i.e., the substantive bills introduced), the percentages tend to jump around quite a bit.

9. Due to data availability issues, our measure of cosponsorship coalition size is based on all public bill introductions, not just substantive measures.

10. This is achieved by Duncan Hunter (R-CA) in the 108th House and Howard Coble (R-NC) in the 109th. At the time, Hunter was a party soldier and Coble was a policy specialist. Coble also had the most substantive bills move beyond committee, at twenty-five.

11. Bill success models that do explain a substantial amount of variation either include past success as a predictor of current success or use dependent variables that include the volume of introductions (which are more readily predictable by the usual suspect variables).

12. For these analyses, we combine chamber and party leaders into one category, as some styles have no chamber leaders (i.e., Speaker of the House, Minority Leader, Whip).

13. We get the same pattern of results when the number of substantive bills passed is used as the dependent variable.

14. The results in table 7.1 do not change with the inclusion of these more nuanced leadership variables. For the sake of parsimony, we opted for the simpler measure in the initial models.

15. This wide range is connected to variation in the number of new MCs per congress, as freshmen tend to flock to the party soldiers style, but is also a function of the large number of party soldiers we observe in the 101st Congress.

16. In the next chapter, we explore whether styles affect whether MCs obtain seats on exclusive committees.

17. Historically, there have been three classes of House standing committees—exclusive, semiexclusive, and nonexclusive. These categories are linked to decision rules about the number and type of committees on which individual MCs can serve and (roughly) approximate the desirability of particular committees. The most recent Congressional Research Service report on the subject just divides into two categories—exclusive and nonexclusive. Although these categorizations are subject to change over time and variation within parties, for purposes of analysis, we classify exclusive committees as Appropriations, Financial Services, Energy and Commerce, Rules, and Ways and Means.

18. The District of Columbia committee does not deal with district issues for any representative in our sample, as we do not include delegates, and hence no MCs in our analyses hail from DC.

19. In the interest of space, we do not report them here.

20. "Better" could mean more thoughtfully written, more politically feasible, or some combination thereof.

Chapter Eight

1. Previously, we explored whether having an exclusive committee assignment as a freshman was related to initial style, and how gaining such an assignment shaped MCs' subsequent styles. Here, we turn things around to ask whether particular styles precipitate different types of committee assignments.

2. Palmer and Simon (2003), for example, examine the career choices of "congressional widows," who are appointed to fill out their husbands' terms after their deaths, and find meaningful differences between those who step down (the discretely ambitious) and those who choose to run for reelection (the statically ambitious).

3. 1,049 individuals served in Congress across our time frame. However, there is a subset of members who served just one partial term, and for these, we do not have sufficient data on legislative activity to calculate styles.

4. In the "left the House" category, we also include MCs who have announced their intentions to retire or run for higher office in 2016, at the end of the 114th Congress.

5. This "loss" percentage differs from that reported in chapter 6—there, we focused on what happened to an MC at the end of each term in which he or she served. Here, we ask how each MC's career ended.

6. For our purposes, we consider a member to have retired if he or she left the House (voluntarily) and did not immediately run for another office. A handful of representatives leave office and then run later for the Senate or a governorship.

7. Among the 1,011 MCs, there are three groups—647 who ended their service during our period of study (up through the 110th Congress, or 2008), 201 whose House careers have ended, but did so after our period of study, and 163 who are still serving. For our calculations of the career finales of MCs, we collected additional data on whether MCs in the middle group lost, retired, or ran for higher office.

8. The results sum to more than 100 because MCs can (and many do) hold more than one category of position over the course of their careers.

9. If we limit the analyses to MCs who have completed their careers, that figure is slightly lower, at 35%. This is because MCs who started their careers during our period of data collection but who are still serving have been in office for

at least five terms, and so have exceeded the median House career. As a group, these long-serving members are more likely to have risen to leadership positions.

10. These calculations may underestimate the proportion of MCs who hold such positions, as some members of the sample served for part of their careers (and may have held leadership roles) before our data collection began. However, if we limit our analyses to MCs who entered our data set as freshmen, we find similar proportions across leadership categories, with the exception of committee leadership positions, which are fewer in number since MCs for whom we observed the beginning of their careers are, on average, lower in seniority than those whose careers started earlier.

11. Because we are interested in assessing how style in one term leads to attaining positions at the start of the next, we necessarily exclude freshmen from these analyses.

12. In our analyses of attaining exclusive committee assignments, we also control for whether an MC had such an assignment in the previous term. While MCs generally can hold just one assignment at a time, some request switches from one exclusive committee to another. Slight changes in the definitions of particular committees as exclusive or not have also occurred across time.

13. Lowey would later become the chair of the DCCC, the first woman to hold the post.

14. In addition, Volden and Wiseman (2014) show that freshmen who are not effective legislatively retire earlier than their peers. This could be due to dissatisfaction with their performance in Congress, or it could be a reflection of the fact that MCs from particular styles are less focused on legislative success AND less committed to a long career in the House of Representatives.

15. Derrick was actually a party soldier rather than a district advocate in the terms for which we observe his behavior, but this quote indicates that, given the choice between becoming a district advocate or retiring, he chose to exit.

16. Given the low Ns once the progressively ambitious are broken out by style, systematic regression analyses with multiple independent variables are not appropriate.

17. These MCs are listed by the highest office attained; all had climbed the leadership ladder in steps over time.

18. Nine sophomore builders never attained a leadership position. One (Sheila Jackson Lee, D-TX) remains in office and so, conceivably, could attain a position in the future. Three (Wayne Allard, R-CO; Tom Campbell, R-CA; and Charlie Melancon, D-LA) ran unsuccessfully for the Senate. Two (Jerry Costello, D-IL, and Ruben Hinojosa, D-TX) settled into long careers as district advocates after a single term as party builders. One (Mike Kopetski, D-OR) retired after his second term to become a trade consultant. Two (John Sweeney, R-NY, and Anthony Weiner, D-NY) left office after scandals, Sweeney by electoral loss and Weiner through resignation.

19. Importantly, less than 10% of sophomore MCs held a leadership position, so this difference is not a function of sophomore builders already having such positions. And, even among sophomore leaders, there is substantial variation in styles—the majority are actually party soldiers.

20. MCs can and do hold more than one type of position, especially across a career, so some legislators appear in multiple columns.

21. These calculations likely underestimate the range of years served, as they include MCs who are still in office. For these MCs, we calculated their career length assuming that they leave after the next congress, which provides a very conservative estimate.

22. However, there is disagreement in the literature about the extent of ideological "shirking" in roll call voting. See, for example, Rothenberg and Sanders (2000) and Carson, Crespin, et al. (2004).

23. McIntosh launched a bid again in 2004, but withdrew after President George W. Bush endorsed another candidate, Mitch Daniels, who had served as his budget director (Fenno 2007, 263).

24. For this reason, we limit the sample to MCs who entered Congress beginning or after the 101st, when our data collection begins.

Chapter Nine

1. The existence and prevalence of this style offers further evidence against the work horse/show horse divide. District advocates are neither legislative work horses nor publicity-seeking show horses.

2. Moakley reflected on his goals for representation thusly: "The politicians, when I was a kid, put you to work, put oil in your cellar, put food on your table, helped you get a job, get to school. That was how I was brought up" (Zitner 2001).

3. This does not appear to be the case for Moakley, who was a good fit for his district (a distance score of zero), and who received between 80% and 100% of the vote during the elections of his House career that we observe.

4. Nor was he particularly focused on his district, mentioning in his memoir how the "luxury of a safe seat" freed him to focus on matters beyond reelection (Waxman and Green 2009, 33).

5. Unfortunately, given data availability issues and the sheer enormity of the task of collecting complete data about MCs' behavior, it is not possible to extend our data collection back past the 101st Congress.

6. Previously, we speculated that this might be because increases in polarization mean that more MCs are stalwarts in voting, and so an identity centered solely on being part of the team may no longer be as distinctive or pay off as much for MCs.

7. We define scandal as occurring when an MC has been investigated by the Ethics Committee, been charged with a crime, has personal issues (e.g., infidelity) that have attracted the attention of the media, and/or is mentioned by CREW (Citizens for Responsibility and Ethics in Washington) as one of the year's "most corrupt."

8. This is likely to be a conservative estimate of the differences between the groups, as some MCs may have been ambitious entrepreneurs before the congresses of our data collection.

9. MCs sometimes make brief forays into the ambitious entrepreneur style before returning to a previous style. In chapter 5, we described how a shift in majority control moves some leaders (e.g., Richard Gephardt [D-MO], Newt Gingrich [R-GA], Richard Armey [R-TX]) temporarily to the entrepreneur style, though these MCs tend to settle back into a party builder style.

10. Mayhew also points out that the ability of MCs to have long careers in the House has meant that junior, senior, and midcareer legislators coexist in the chamber, with these groups potentially displaying different patterns of behavior and aiming toward different goals (2000, 211).

11. Recall that we normalize fund-raising (and other variables) by congress to take into account inflation and the increased focus on raising money across time.

12. However, our results for ambitious entrepreneurs suggest that skills in this area also enable legislators to build independent reputations and to launch campaigns for higher office without first rising through the party hierarchy.

13. It is important to note that any reforms aimed at reducing the role of money in Congress would address not just the behavior of members, but also the ability of outside interests to donate large sums in the first place. However, our focus here is on the fund-raising activity of individual MCs.

14. Though, importantly, research on styles extends back even further, to the works of Barber (1965) and Davidson (1969).

Works Cited

Abramowitz, Alan, Brad Alexander, and Matthew Gunning. 2006. "Incumbency, Redistricting, and the Decline of Competition in U.S. House Elections." *Journal of Politics* 68(1): 75–88.

Adler, E. Scott, and John S. Lapinski. 1997. "Demand-Side Theory and Congressional Committee Composition: A Constituency Characteristics Approach." *American Journal of Political Science* 41(3): 895–918.

Adler, E. Scott, and John Wilkerson. *Congressional Bills Project*. NSF 00880066 and 00880061.

Ahlquist, John S., and Christian Breunig. 2012. "Model-based Clustering and Typologies in the Social Sciences." *Political Analysis* 20(1): 92–112.

Aleman, Eduardo, Ernesto Calvo, Mark P. Jones, and Noah Kaplan. 2009. "Comparing Cosponsorship and Roll-Call Ideal Points." *Legislative Studies Quarterly* 34(1): 87–116.

Anderson, William D., Janet M. Box-Steffensmeier, and Valeria Sinclair-Chapman. 2003. "The Keys to Legislative Success in the U.S. House of Representatives." *Legislative Studies Quarterly* 28(3): 357–86.

Ansolabehere, Stephen, and James Snyder. 2000. "Campaign Warchests in Congressional Elections." *Business and Politics* 2(1): 9–33.

Ansolabehere, Stephen, James M. Snyder Jr., and Charles Stewart III. 2001. "The Effects of Party and Preferences on Congressional Roll-Call Voting." *Legislative Studies Quarterly* 26(4): 533–72.

Arnold, R. Douglas. 1990. *The Logic of Congressional Action*. New Haven: Yale University Press.

Baker, Ross K. 1989. *House and Senate*. New York: W. W. Norton and Company.

Barber, James David. 1965. *The Lawmakers: Recruitment and Adaptation to Legislative Life*. New Haven: Yale University Press.

Barone, Michael, and Richard E. Cohen. 2001. *The Almanac of American Politics 2002*. Washington, DC: National Journal Group.

———. 2007. *The Almanac of American Politics 2008*. Washington, DC: National Journal Group.

Barone, Michael, and Grant Ujifusa. 1989. *The Almanac of American Politics 1990*. Washington, DC: National Journal.

———. 1993. *The Almanac of American Politics 1994*. Washington, DC: National Journal.

———. 1995. *The Almanac of American Politics 1996*. Washington, DC: National Journal.

———. 1997. *The Almanac of American Politics 1998*. Washington, DC: National Journal.

Basinger, Scott. 2013. "Scandals and Congressional Elections in the Post-Watergate Era." *Political Research Quarterly* 66(2): 385–98.

Bauer, Raymond Augustine, Lewis Anthony Dexter, and Ithiel de Sola Pool. 1963. *American Business and Public Policy: The Politics of Foreign Trade*. New York: Prentice-Hall.

Berkman, Michael B. 1994. "State Legislators in Congress: Strategic Politicians, Professional Legislatures and the Party Nexus." *American Journal of Political Science* 38(4): 1025–55.

Bernhard, William, and Tracy Sulkin. 2013. "Commitment and Consequences: Reneging on Cosponsorship Pledges in the U.S. House." *Legislative Studies Quarterly* 38(4): 461–87.

Bianco, William T. 1994. *Trust: Representatives and Constituents*. Ann Arbor: University of Michigan Press.

Bishin, Benjamin. 2009. *Tyranny of the Minority: The Subconstituency Politics Theory of Representation*. Philadelphia: Temple University Press.

Bond, Jon R. 1985. "Dimensions of District Attention Over Time." *American Journal of Political Science* 29(2): 330–47.

Bonica, Adam. 2013. "Ideology and Interests in the Political Marketplace." *American Journal of Political Science* 57(2): 294–311.

Bowman, Bridget. 2014. "New Members Orientation Welcomes New Class of Lawmakers." *Roll Call*, November 10. Accessed April 1, 2016.

Box-Steffensmeier, Janet M. 1996. "A Dynamic Analysis of the Role of War Chests in Campaign Strategy." *American Journal of Political Science* 40(2): 352–71.

Box-Steffensmeier, Janet M., David C. Kimball, Scott R. Meinke, and Katherine Tate. 2003. "The Effects of Political Representation on the Electoral Advantages of House Incumbents." *Political Research Quarterly* 56(3) 259–70.

Brace, Paul. 1985. "A Probabilistic Approach to Retirement from the U.S. Congress." *Legislative Studies Quarterly* 10(1): 107–23.

Broder, David. 1993. "Party Loyalty Loses Out to Committee Clout." *Chicago Tribune*, June 13. Accessed April 1, 2016. http://www.rollcall.com/news/home/new-member-orientation-welcomes-new-class-of-lawmakers.

Browne, William. 1985. "Multiple Sponsorship and Bill Success in U.S. State Legislatures." *Legislative Studies Quarterly* 10(4): 483–88.
Burden, Barry C. 2007. *Personal Roots of Representation*. Princeton: Princeton University Press.
Burns, Robert, and Richard Burns. 2008. *Business Research Methods and Statistics Using SPSS*. London: SAGE.
Cain, Bruce, John Ferejohn, and Morris Fiorina. 1987. *The Personal Vote: Constituency Service and Electoral Independence*. Cambridge: Harvard University Press.
Canes-Wrone, Brandice, David W. Brady, and John F. Cogan. 2002. "Out of Step, Out of Office: Electoral Accountability and House Members' Voting." *American Political Science Review* 96(1): 127–40.
Cann, Damon M. 2008. *Sharing the Wealth: Member Contributions and the Exchange Theory of Party Influence in the U.S. House of Representatives*. Albany: State University of New York.
Canon, David T. 1999. *Race, Redistricting, and Representation: The Unintended Consequences of Black Majority Districts*. Chicago: University of Chicago Press.
Carey, John. 1998. *Term Limits and Legislative Representation*. New York: Cambridge University Press.
Carnes, Nicholas. 2013. *White-Collar Government: The Hidden Role of Class in Economic Policy Making*. Chicago: University of Chicago Press.
Carson, Jamie L. 2005. "Strategy, Selection, and Candidate Competition in U.S. House and Senate Elections." *Journal of Politics* 67(1): 1–28.
———. 2008. "Electoral Accountability, Party Loyalty, and Roll-Call Voting in the U.S. Senate." In *Why Not Parties? Party Effects in the United States Senate*, edited by Nathan Monoe, Jason Roberts, and David W. Rohde, pp. 23–38. Chicago: University of Chicago Press.
Carson, Jamie L., Michael H. Crespin, Charles J. Finocchario, and David W. Rohde. 2007. "Redistricting and Party Polarization in the U.S. House of Representatives." *American Politics Research* 35(6): 878–904.
Carson, Jamie L., Michael H. Crespin, Jeffery A. Jenkins, and Ryan J. Vander Wielen. 2004. "Shirking in the Contemporary Congress: A Reappraisal." *Political Analysis* 12(2): 176–79.
Carson, Jamie L., Erik J. Engstrom, and Jason M. Roberts. 2007. "Candidate Quality, the Personal Vote, and the Incumbency Advantage in Congress." *American Political Science Review* 101(2): 289–301.
Carson, Jamie L., Gregory Koger, Matthew J. Lebo, and Everett Young. 2010. "The Electoral Costs of Party Loyalty in Congress." *American Journal of Political Science* 54(3): 598–616.
Clapp, Charles. 1963. *The Congressman: His Work As He Sees It*. Washington, DC: Brookings.

Congressional Management Foundation. 2013. *Life in Congress: The Member Perspective*. Washington, DC.

Cook, Timothy E. 1988. "Press Secretaries and Media Strategies in the House of Representatives: Deciding Whom to Pursue." *American Journal of Political Science* 32(4): 1047–69.

Cooper, Joseph, and William West. 1981. "The Congressional Career in the 1970s." In *Congress Reconsidered*, edited by Lawrence C. Dodd and Bruce I. Oppenheimer, pp. 83–106. Washington, DC: Congressional Quarterly Press.

Copeland, Gary W. 1989. "Choosing to Run: Why House Members Seek Election to the Senate." *Legislative Studies Quarterly* 14(4): 549–65.

Cox, Gary W., and Mathew D. McCubbins. 1993. *Legislative Leviathan: Party Government in the House*. Berkeley: University of California Press.

Currinder, Marian. 2009. *Money in the House: Campaign Funds and Congressional Party Politics*. Boulder: Westview.

Davidson, Roger. 1969. *The Role of the Congressman*. New York: Pegasus.

Davidson, Roger H., Walter J. Oleszek, Frances E. Lee, and Eric Schickler. 2014. *Congress and Its Members*. 14th ed. Thousand Oaks: CQ Press.

———. 2016. *Congress and Its Members*. 15th ed. Washington, DC: CQ Press.

Dempster, Arthur P., Nan M. Laird, and Donald B. Rubin. 1977. "Maximum Likelihood from Incomplete Data via the EM Algorithm." *Journal of the Royal Statistical Society* 39(1): 1–38.

Draper, Robert. 2012. *Do Not Ask What Good We Do: Inside the U.S. House of Representatives*. New York: Free Press.

Dumain, Emma. 2012. "Orientation Staffers Prep for Freshman Class." *Roll Call*, November 8.

Ehrenhalt, Alan. 1991. *The United States of Ambition: Politicians, Power, and the Pursuit of Office*. New York: Times Books.

Fahrenthold, David A. 2014. "Andrews Proposed 646 bills, Passed 0: Worst Record of Past 20 Years." *Washington Post*, February 4.

Fenno, Richard F. 1973. *Congressmen in Committees*. Boston: Little, Brown.

———. 1978. *Home Style: House Members in Their Districts*. Boston: Little, Brown.

———. 1986. "Adjusting to the U.S. Senate." In *Congress and Policy Change*, edited by Gerald C. Wright, Leroy N. Rieselbach, and Lawrence C. Dodd, pp. 123–47. New York: Agathon Press.

———. 2000. *Congress at the Grassroots: Representational Change in the South, 1970–1998*. Chapel Hill: University of North Carolina Press.

———. 2003. *Going Home: Black Representatives and Their Constituents*. Chicago: University of Chicago Press.

———. 2007. *Congressional Travels: Places Connection, and Authenticity*. London: Routledge.

Filho, Dalson Britto Figueredo, Enivaldo Carvalho da Rocha, Jose Alexandre da Silva Junior, Ranulfo Paranhos, Mariana Batista da Silva, and Barbara Sofia Felix Duarte. 2014. "Cluster Analysis for Political Scientists." *Applied Mathematics* 5(15): 2408–15.

Fiorina, Morris P. 1974. *Representatives, Roll Calls, and Constituencies*. Lexington, MA: Lexington Books.

———. 1981. "Some Problems in Studying the Effects of Resource Allocation in Congressional Elections." *American Journal of Political Science* 25(3): 543–67.

Fitch, Bradford. 2015. "The Cures to Freshman Office Headaches." *Roll Call*, May 26.

Fowler, James. 2006. "Connecting the Congress: A Study of Cosponsorship Networks." *Political Analysis* 14(4): 456–87.

Fox, Richard, and Jennifer Lawless. 2005. "To Run or Not to Run for Office: Explaining Nascent Political Ambition." *American Journal of Political Science* 49(3): 659–76.

Francis, Katherine A. 2014. "Pathways to Congress: Precongressional Careers and Congressional Behavior." PhD diss., Department of Political Science, University of Illinois at Urbana-Champaign.

Francis, Wayne L., and Lawrence W. Kenny. 1996. "Position Shifting in Pursuit of Higher Office." *American Journal of Political Science* 40(3): 768–86.

Frantzich, Stephen E. 1978. "Opting Out: Retirement from the House of Representatives, 1966–1974." *American Politics Quarterly* 6(3): 251–73.

Frisch, Scott A., and Sean Q. Kelly. 2006. *Committee Assignment Politics in the U.S. House of Representatives*. Norman: University of Oklahoma Press.

Gan, Guojun, Chaoqun Ma, and Jianhong Wu. 2007. *Data Clustering: Theory, Algorithms, and Applications*. Alexandria: SIAM.

Gilmour, John B., and Paul Rothstein. 1993. "Early Republican Retirement: A Cause of Democratic Dominance in the House of Representatives." *Legislative Studies Quarterly* 18(3): 345–65.

Godbout, Jean-Francois, and Bei Yu. 2009. "Speeches and Legislative Extremism in the U.S. Senate." In *Do They Walk Like They Talk?*, edited by L. M. Imbeau, pp. 185–205. New York: Springer.

Goodliffe, Jay. 2001. "The Effect of War Chests on Challenger Entry in U.S. House Elections." *American Journal of Political Science* 45(4): 830–44.

———. 2007. "Campaign War Chests and Challenger Quality in Senate Elections." *Legislative Studies Quarterly* 32(1): 135–56.

Greenfield, Meg. 2001. *Washington*. New York: PublicAffairs.

Griffin, John D., and Patrick Flavin. 2007. "Racial Differences in Information, Expectations, and Accountability." *Journal of Politics* 69(1): 220–36.

Grimmer, Justin. 2013. *Representational Style in Congress: What Legislators Say and Why It Matters*. New York: Cambridge University Press.

Grimmer, Justin, and Eleanor Neff Powell. 2013. "Congressmen in Exile: The

Politics and Consequences of Involuntary Committee Removal." *Journal of Politics* 75(4): 907–20.

Grimmer, Justin, Sean Westwood, and Solomon Messing. 2014. *The Impression of Influence: Legislator Communication, Representation, and Democratic Accountability.* Princeton: Princeton University Press.

Grose, Christian R. 2011. *Congress in Black and White: Race and Representation in Washington and at Home.* New York: Cambridge University Press.

Groseclose, Timothy, and Keith Krehbiel. 1994. "Golden Parachutes, Rubber Checks, and Strategic Retirements from the 102d House." *American Journal of Political Science* 38(1): 75–99.

Gugiu, Mihaiela Ristei, and Miguel Centellas. 2013. "The Democracy Cluster Classification Index." *Political Analysis* 21(3): 334–49.

Hall, Richard L. 1996. *Participation in Congress.* New Haven: Yale University Press.

Hall, Richard, and Robert P. Van Houweling. 1995. "Avarice and Ambition in Congress: Representatives' Decisions to Run or Retire from the U.S. House." *American Political Science Review* 89(1): 121–36.

Harbridge, Laurel. 2015. *Is Bipartisanship Dead? Policy Agreement and Agenda-Setting in the House of Representatives.* New York: Cambridge Univesrity Press.

Harden, Jeffrey J. 2016. *Multidimensional Democracy: A Supply and Demand Theory of Representation in American Legislatures.* New York: Cambridge University Press.

Harward, Brian M., and Kenneth W. Moffett. 2010. "The Calculus of Cosponsorship in the U.S. Senate." *Legislative Studies Quarterly* 35(1): 117–43.

Hasecke, Edward B., and Jason D. Mycoff. 2007. "Party Loyalty and Legislative Sucess: Are Loyal Majority Party Members More Successful in the U.S. House of Representatives?" *Political Research Quarterly* 60(4): 607–17.

Heberlig, Eric S., and Bruce A. Larson. 2012. *Congressional Parties, Institutional Ambition, and the Financing of Majority Control.* Ann Arbor: University of Michigan Press.

Herrick, Rebekah. 2001. "The Effects of Political Ambition on Legislative Behavior: A Replication." *Social Science Journal* 38(3): 469–74.

Herrick, Rebekah, and Michael K. Moore. 1993. "Political Ambition's Effect on Legislative Behavior: Schlesinger's Typology Reconsidered and Revised." *Journal of Politics* 55(3): 765–76.

Hess, Stephen. 1986. *The Ultimate Insiders: The Senate and the National Press.* Washington, DC: Brookings.

Hetherington, Marc, and Thomas Rudolph. 2015. *Why Washington Won't Work.* Chicago: University of Chicago Press.

Hibbing, John R. 1982. "Voluntary Retirement from the U.S. House of Representatives: Who Quits?" *American Journal of Political Science* 36(3): 824–28.

———. 1986. "Ambition in the House: Behavioral Consequences of Higher Office Goals Among U.S. Representatives." *American Journal of Political Science* 30(3): 651–65.

———. 1991. *Congressional Careers: Contours of Life in the U.S. House of Representatives*. Chapel Hill: University of North Carolina Press.

Hoyle, Sam. 2013. "Braley Endorsed: Loebsack Supports Run." *WHOTV.com*, February 16. Accessed April 1, 2016. http://whotv.com/2013/02/16/braley-endorsement-loebsack-supports-run/.

Jacobson, Gary C. 1990. "The Effects of Campaign Spending in House Elections: New Evidence for Old Arguments." *American Journal of Political Science* 34(2): 334–62.

———. 2001. *The Politics of Congressional Elections*. New York: Longman.

Jacobson, Gary C., and Michael A. Dimock. 1994. "Checking Out: The Effects of Bank Overdrafts on the 1992 House Elections." *American Journal of Political Science* 38(3): 601–24.

Jacobson, Gary C., and Samuel Kernell. 1983. *Strategy and Choice in Congressional Elections*. 2nd ed. New Haven: Yale University Press.

Jang, Jaewon, and David B. Hitchcock. 2012. "Model-Based Cluster Analysis of Democracies." *Journal of Data Science* 10(2): 321–43.

Johannes, John. 1984. *To Serve the People: Congress and Constituency Service*. Lincoln: University of Nebraska Press.

Johannes, John R., and John C. McAdams. 1981. "The Congressional Incumbency Effect: Is It Casework, Policy Compatibility, or Something Else? An Examination of the 1978 Election." *American Journal of Political Science* 25(3): 512–42.

Kedrowski, Karen. 1996. *Media Entrepreneurs and the Media Enterprise in the U.S. Congress*. Cresskill: Hampton Press.

Kernell, Georgia. 2009. "Giving Order to Districts: Estimating Voter Distributions with National Election Returns." *Political Analysis* 17(3): 215–35.

Kessler, Daniel, and Keith Krehbiel. 1996. "Dynamics of Cosponsorship." *American Political Science Review* 90(3): 555–66.

Kiewiet, D. Roderick, and Langche Zeng. 1993. "An Analysis of Congressional Career Decisions, 1947–1986." *American Political Science Review* 87(4): 928–41.

Kingdon, John W. 1973. *Congressmen's Voting Decisions*. New York: Harper and Row.

———. 1984. *Agendas, Alternatives, and Public Policies*. Boston: Little, Brown.

———. 1989. *Congressmen's Voting Decisions*. Ann Arbor: University of Michigan Press.

Koger, Gregory. 2003. "Position Taking and Cosponsorship in the U.S. House." *Legislative Studies Quarterly* 28(2): 225–46.

Kousser, Thad. 2005. *Term Limits and the Dismantling of State Legislative Professionalism*. New York: Cambridge University Press.

Krehbiel, Keith. 1990. "Are Congressional Committees Composed of Preference Outliers?" *American Political Science Review* 84(1): 149–63.

Krook, Mona Lena, and Diana Z. O'Brien. 2012. "All the President's Men? The Appointment of Female Cabinet Ministers Worldwide." *Journal of Politics* 74(3): 840–55.

Krutz, Glen S. 2005. "Issues and Institutions: 'Winnowing' in the U.S. Congress." *American Journal of Political Science* 49(2): 313–26.

LaForge, Chera. 2012. "On to Bigger and Better Things: The Behavioral Consequences of Ambition in the U.S. House of Representatives." PhD diss., University of Illinois, Urbana-Champaign.

Langbein, Laura I., and Lee Sigelman. 1989. "Show Horses, Work Horses, and Dead Horses." *American Politics Quarterly* 17(1): 80–95.

Lawless, Jennifer, and Richard L. Fox. 2005. *It Takes a Candidate: Why Women Don't Run for Office*. New York: Cambridge University Press.

Lawless, Jennifer L., and Sean M. Theriault. 2005. "Will She Stay or Will She Go? Career Ceilings and Women's Retirement from the U.S. Congress." *Legislative Studies Quarterly* 30(4): 581–96.

Lazarus, Jeffrey. 2008. "Incumbent Vulnerability and Challenger Entry in Statewide Elections." *American Politics Research* 36(1): 108–29.

Lee, Frances. 2016. *Insecure Majorities: Congress and the Perpetual Campaign*. Chicago: University of Chicago Press.

Livingston, Steven G., and Sally Friedman. 1993. "Reexamining Theories of Congressional Retirement: Evidence from the 1980s." *Legislative Studies Quarterly* 18(2): 231–53.

Loomis, Burdett. 1984. "Congressional Careers and Party Leadership in the Contemporary House of Representatives." *American Journal of Political Science* 28(1): 180–202.

Maestas, Cherie D., Sarah Fulton, L. Sandy Maisel, and Walter J. Stone. 2006. "When to Risk It? Institutions, Ambitions, and the Decisions to Run for the U.S. House." *American Political Science Review* 100(2): 195–208.

Maltzman, Forrest, and Lee Sigelman. 1996. "The Politics of Talk: Unconstrained Floor Time in the U.S. House of Representatives." *Journal of Politics* 58(3): 819–30.

Mann, Thomas E. 1978. *Unsafe at Any Margin: Interpreting Congressional Elections*. Washington, DC: American Enterprise Institute for Public Policy Research.

Mann, Thomas E., and Norman J. Ornstein. 2006. *The Broken Branch: How Congress Is Failing American and How to Get It Back on Track*. New York: Oxford University Press.

Martin, Joe, and Robert J. Donovan. 1960. *My First Fifty Years in Politics*. New York: McGraw-Hill.

Matthews, Donald R. 1959. "The Folkways of the U.S. Senate: Conformity to

Group Norms and Legislative Effectiveness." *American Political Science Review* 53(4): 1064–89.

———. 1960. *U.S. Senators and Their World*. New York: Alfred A. Knopf.

Matthews, Donald R., and James A. Stimson. 1975. *Yeas and Nays: Normal Decision-Making in the U.S. House of Representatives*. New York: Wiley.

Mayhew, David. 1974. *Congress: The Electoral Connection*. New Haven: Yale University Press.

———. 2000. *America's Congress: Actions in the Public Sphere, James Madison through Newt Gingrich*. New Haven: Yale University Press.

McCarty, Nolan, Keith T. Poole, and Howard Rosenthal. 2009. "Does Gerrymandering Cause Polarization?" *American Journal of Political Science* 53(3): 666–80.

McLachlan, Geoffrey J. 1992. *Discriminant Analysis and Statistical Pattern Recognition*. Hoboken: Wiley.

Meinke, Scott. 2016. *Leadership Organizations in the House of Representatives: Party Participation and Partisan Politics*. Ann Arbor: University of Michigan Press.

Miler, Kristina C. 2010. *Constituency Representation: The View from Capitol Hill*. New York: Cambridge University Press.

Miller, Warren E., and Donald E. Stokes. 1963. "Constituency Influence in Congress." *American Political Science Review* 57(1): 45–56.

Minta, Michael. 2011. *Oversight: Representing the Interests of Blacks and Latinos in Congress*. Princeton: Princeton University Press.

Miquel, Gerard Padro I., and James M. Snyder. 2006. "Legislative Effectiveness and Legislative Careers." *Legislative Studies Quarterly* 31(3): 347–81.

Mooi, Erik, and Marko Sarstedt. 2011. *A Concise Guide to Market Research*. Berlin: Springer-Verlag.

Moore, Lori. 2012. "Rep. Todd Akin: The Statement and the Reaction." *New York Times*, August 20.

Moore, Michael K., and John R. Hibbing. 1992. "Situational Dissatisfaction in Congress: Explaining Voluntary Departures." *Journal of Politics* 60(4): 1088–1107.

Morris, Jonathan. 2001. "Reexamining the Politics of Talk: Partisan Rhetoric in the 104th House." *Legislative Studies Quarterly* 26(1): 101–21.

Nyhan, Brendan, Eric McGhee, John Sides, Seth Masket, and Steven Green. 2012. "One Vote Out of Step? The Effects of Salient Roll Call Votes in the 2010 Election." *American Politics Research* 40(5): 844–79.

Obama, Barack. 2014. "Statement on Representative Robert E. Andrews's Decision Not To Seek Reelection." February 4. https://www.whitehouse.gov/the-press-office/2014/02/04/statement-president-retirement-congressman-rob-andrews.

Ornstein, Norman. 1983. "The Open Congress Meets the President." In *Both*

Ends of the Avenue, edited by Anthony King, pp. 185–211. Washington, DC: American Enterprise Institute.

———. 2014. "Henry Waxman: A Relic of the Era When Congress Used to Work." *The Atlantic*, February 6.

Palmer, Barbara, and Dennis Simon. 2003. "Political Ambibtion and Women in the U.S. Houseof Representatives, 1916–2000." *Political Research Quarterly* 56(2): 127–38.

Parker, David C. W., and Craig Goodman. 2009. "Making a Good Impression: Resource Allocation, Homestyles, and Washington Work." *Legislative Studies Quarterly* 34(4): 493–524.

———. 2012. "Our State's Never Had Better Friends: Resource Allocation, Home Styles, and Dual Representation in the Senate." *Political Research Quarterly* 66(2): 370–84.

Parker, Glenn R. 1986. *Homeward Bound: Explaining Changes in Congressional Behavior*. Pittsburgh: University of Pittsburgh Press.

Payne, James. 1980. "Show Horses and Work Horses in the United States House of Representatives." *Polity* 12(3): 428–56.

Pearson, Kathryn. 2015. *Party Discipline in the House of Representatives*. Ann Arbor: University of Michigan Press.

Pearson, Kathryn, and Logan Dancey. 2011. "Elevating Women's Voices in Congress: Speech Participation in the House of Representatives." *Political Research Quarterly* 64(4): 910–23.

Pearson, Kathryn, and Eric Schickler. 2009. "Discharge Petitions, Agenda Control, and the Congressional Committee System, 1929–76." *Journal of Politics* 71(4): 1238–56.

Polsby, Nelson W., and Eric Schickler. 2002. "Landmarks in the Study of Congress since 1945." *Annual Review of Political Science* 5:333–67.

Poole, Keith T., and Howard Rosenthal. 2007. *Ideology and Congress*. New Brunswick: Transaction Publishers.

Price, David E. 1973. *The Congressional Experience: A View from the Hill*. Boston: Little, Brown.

———. 2004. *The Congressional Experience: Transforming American Politics*. Boulder: Westview Press.

Rabinowitz, George, and Stuart Elaine MacDonald. 1989. "A Directional Theory of Issue Voting." *American Political Science Review* 83(1): 93–121.

Ragsdale, Lyn, and Timothy E. Cook. 1987. "Representatives' Actions and Challengers' Reactions: Limits to Candidate Connections in the House." *American Journal of Political Science* 31(1): 45–81.

Ranney, Austin. 1983. *Channels of Power: The Impact of Television on American Politics*. New York: Basic Books.

RealClearPolitics. 2009. *10 Candidates Who Spent Giant Sums of Their Personal Wealth: Michael Huffington*. July 9.

Rivers, Douglas, and Morris P. Fiorina. 1992. "Constituency Service, Reputation and the Incumbency Advantage." In *Home Style and Washington Work: Studies in Congressional Politics*, edited by Morris P. Fiorina and David W. Rohde, pp. 17–45. Ann Arbor: The University of Michigan Press.

Rocca, Michael S. 2007. "Non-Legislative Debate in the House of Representatives." *American Politics Research* 35(4): 248–505.

Rocca, Michael S., and Stacy Gordon. 2010. "The Position-taking Value of Bill Sponsorship in Congress." *Political Research Quarterly* 63(2): 387–97.

Rocca, Michael S., and Gabriel Sanchez. 2008. "The Effect of Race and Ethnicity on Bill Sponsorship and Cosponsorship in Congress." *American Politics Research* 36(1): 130–52.

Rohde, David W. 1979. "Risk-Bearing and Progressive Ambition: The Case of Members of the United States House of Representatives." *American Journal of Political Science* 23(1): 1–26.

———. 1988. "Studying Congressional Norms: Concepts and Evidence." *Congress and the Presidency* 15(2): 139–45.

Romesburg, H. Charles. 2004. *Cluster Analysis for Researchers*. Raleigh, NC: Lulu Press.

Rothenberg, Lawrence S., and Mitchell Sanders. 2000. "Severing the Electoral Connection: Shirking in the Contemporary Congress." *American Journal of Political Science* 44(2): 316–25.

Rui, Xu, and Donald Wunsch. 2005. "Survey of Clustering Algorithms." *IEEE Transactions on Neural Networks* 16(3): 645–78.

Sarlin, Benjamin. 2009. "Freshman Terror." *The Daily Beast*, August 3. Accessed April 1, 2016. http://www.thedailybeast.com/articles/2009/08/03/freshman-terror.html.

Schansberg, D. Eric. 1994. "Moving Out of the House: An Analysis of Congressional Quits." *Economic Inquiry* 32(3): 445–56.

Schiller, Wendy. 1995. "Senators as Political Entrepreneurs." *American Journal of Political Science* 39(1): 186–203.

Schlesinger, Joseph A. 1966. *Ambition and Politics: Political Careers in the United States*. Chicago: Rand McNally.

Schneider, Judy. 2013. *One-Minute Speeches: Current House Practices*. Washington, DC: Congressional Research Service.

Schneier, Edward V. 1988. "Norms and Folkways in Congress: How Much Has Actually Changed?" *Congress and the Presidency* 15(2): 117–38.

Sewell, Daniel K., Yuguo Chen, William Bernhard, and Tracy Sulkin. 2016. "Model-Based Longitudinal Clustering with Varying Cluster Assignments." *Statistica Sinica* 26(1): 205–33.

Shepsle, Kenneth A., and Barry R. Weingast. 1987. "The Institutional Foundations of Committee Power." *American Political Science Review* 81(1): 85–104.

Sinclair, Barbara. 1986. "The Role of Committees in Agenda Setting in the U.S. Congress." *Legislative Studies Quarterly* 11(1): 35–45.

Smith, Steven S. 1989. *Call to Order: Floor Politics in the House and Senate.* Washington, DC: Brookings.

Spirling, Arthur, and Kevin Quinn. 2010. "Identifying Intraparty Voting Blocs in the UK House of Commons." *Journal of the American Statistical Association* 105(490): 447–57.

Squire, Peverill. 1989. "Challengers in U.S. Senate Elections." *Legislative Studies Quarterly* 14(4): 531–47.

Stewart, Charles III, and Jonathan Woon. Congressional Committee Assignments, 103rd to 112th Congress, 1993–2011.

Stone, Walter J., Sarah A. Fulton, Cherie D. Maestas, and L. Sandy Maisel. 2010. "Incumbency Reconsidered: Prospects, Strategic Retirement, and Incumbent Quality in U.S. House Elections." *Journal of Politics* 72(2): 179–90.

Stratmann, Thomas. 2000. "Congressional Voting over Legislative Careers: Shifting Positions and Changing Constraints." *American Political Science Review* 94(3): 665–76.

Sulkin, Tracy. 2005. *Issue Politics in Congress.* New York: Cambridge University Press.

———. 2011. *The Legislative Legacy of Congressional Campaigns.* New York: Cambridge University Press.

Sulkin, Tracy, Paul Testa, and Kaye Usry. 2015. "What Gets Rewarded? Legislative Activity and Constituency Approval" *Political Research Quarterly* 68(4): 1–13.

Sullivan, John L. 1973. "Political Correlates of Social, Economic, and Religious Diversity in the American States." *Journal of Politics* 35(1): 70–84.

Swers, Michele L. 2002. *The Difference Women Make: The Policy Impact of Women in Congress.* Chicago: University of Chicago Press.

———. 2013. *Women in the Club: Gender and Policy Making in the Senate.* Chicago: University of Chicago Press.

Tate, Katherine. 2003. *Black Faces in the Mirror: African Americans and Their Representatives in the U.S. Congress.* Princeton: Princeton University Press.

Theriault, Sean M. 1998. "Moving Up or Moving Out: Career Ceilings and Congressional Retirement." *Legislative Studies Quarterly* 23(3): 419–33.

———. 2005. *The Power of the People: Congressional Competition, Public Attention, and Voter Retribution.* Columbus: Ohio State University Press.

Thomsen, Danielle M. 2015. "Why So Few (Republican) Women? Explaining the Partisan Imbalance of Women in the U.S. Congress." *Legislative Studies Quarterly* 40(2): 295–323.

Tibbetts, Ed. 2013. "Loebsack Not Interested in Harkin's Seat." *Waterloo-Cedar Falls Courier*, January 29. Accessed April 1, 2016. http://wcfcourier.com/news/local/govt-and-politics/loebsack-not-interested-in-harkin-s-seat/.

Toeplitz, Shira. 2011. "McCarthy Unveils Gun-Control Bill." *Politico*, January 13. Accessed April 1, 2016. http://www.politico.com/story/2011/01/mccarthy-unveils-gun-control-bill-047565.

Tomz, Michael, Jason Wittenberg, and Gary King. 2003. "CLARIFY: Software for Interpreting and Presenting Statistical Results." *Journal of Statistical Software* 8(1): 1–30.

Victor, Jennifer Nicoll. 2011. "Legislating Versus Campaigning: The Legislative Behavior of Higher Office Seekers." *American Politics Research* 39(1): 3–31.

Volden, Craig, and Alan E. Wiseman. 2014. *Legislative Effectiveness in the United States Congress: The Lawmakers*. New York: Cambridge University Press.

Voorhis, Jerry. 1947. *Confessions of a Congressman*. Garden City: Doubleday and Company.

Wallace, Gregory. 2012. "Ryan: 'Wonk' Is a Compliment." *CNN*, November 13. Accessed April 1, 2016. http://politicalticker.blogs.cnn.com/2012/11/13/ryan-wonk-is-a-compliment/.

Wawro, Gregory J. 2001. *Legislative Entrepreneurship in the U.S. House of Representatives*. Ann Arbor: University of Michigan Press.

Waxman, Henry, and Joshua Green. 2009. *The Waxman Report: How Congress Really Works*. New York: Hachette.

Weingast, Barry R. 1979. "A Rational Choice Perspective on Congressional Norms." *American Journal of Political Science* 23(2): 245–62.

Weisman, Jonathan. 2014. "Henry Waxman, Key Democrat and Force for Health Care Law, Is to Retire." *New York Times*, January 30.

Wilson, Rick K., and Cheryl D. Young. 1997. "Cosponsorship in the U.S. Congress." *Legislative Studies Quarterly* 22(1): 25–43.

Wolak, Jennifer. 2007. "Strategic Retirements: The Influence of Public Preferences on Voluntary Departures from Congress." *Legislative Studies Quarterly* 32(2): 285–308.

Woon, Jonathan. 2008. "Bill Sponsorship in Congress: The Moderating Effect of Agenda Positions on Legislative Proposals." *Journal of Politics* 70(1): 201–16.

———. 2009. "Issue Attention and Legislative Proposals in the U.S. Senate." *Legislative Studies Quarterly* 34(1): 29–54.

Wu, C. F. Jeff. 1983. "On the Convergence Properties of the EM Algoritm." *Annals of Statistics* 11(1): 95–103.

Zitner, Aaron. 2001. "Rep. Joseph Moakley; Longtime Lawmaker." *Los Angeles Times*, May 29.

Index

Affordable Care Act, 48, 156, 210
African American Representatives, 70, 84–86, 181, 228
agriculture, 18, 81, 167–69, 172, 225
Akin, Todd, 58
Allard, Wayne, 237
ambitious entrepreneurs: characteristics of, 48–49, 169, 190, 202, 212, 214; elections and, 137–40, 45; freshman as, 70–75, 79–80, 98, 230; leadership positions, 113, 121, 179, 181, 197; minority shift and, 113, 117; progressive ambition and, 191–94, 200–201; retirement, 186–88; tenure of, 199; transition patterns of, 55–56, 92, 97, 105, 112, 227
Andrews, Robert, 21–22, 156, 225, 234
appropriations committee, 122, 168–69, 172, 235
Armey, Dick, 112, 129, 239

Bass, Charles, 78, 129
beltway mentality: inside, 64; outside, 71, 193, 208
Bishop, Sanford, 129
Blagojevich, Rod, 213
Blunt, Roy, 196
Boehner, John: Hobson similarity, 2–4; leadership positions, 103, 113, 175, 181, 229; as party donor, 25; political ambition, 196–97, 215
Boswell, Leonard, 31–32, 57–58, 121–22
Boxer, Barbara, 213
Braley, Bruce, 31–33, 57–58, 121

Burton, Dan, 46
Bush, George H. W., 238

campaign leadership positions: advocate style, 182–83; entrepreneur style, 115, 117, 164; policy specialists, 115, 164
Campbell, Tom, 79, 237
Cantor, Eric: leadership position, 103, 196; as party builder, 48, 52–53, 129; as party donor, 25
centralization of power, 50, 87
Cheney, Dick, 26
Children's Health Insurance Program, 210
Citizens Against Government Waste, 47
Clinton, Bill, 64, 80, 181
Clyburn, James, 25, 48, 196
CMF. *See* Congressional Management Foundation (CMF)
coalition bipartisanship, 26–27, 214
Coburn, Tom, 79, 139, 233
Cole, Tom, 48
Collins, Cardiss, 22
Collins, Mac, 150–51, 234
Congressional Management Foundation (CMF), 9
Conte, Silvio, 26
Conyers, John, 48
Cooley, Wes, 228
Costello, Jerry, 237
CQ Almanac, 158–59, 234
Cramer, Bud, 47, 129
Culberson, John, 103
Cunningham, Duke, 228

Daniels, Mitch, 238
Dannemeyer, William, 225
Davis, Robert, 20
DCCC. *See* Democratic Congressional Campaign Committee (DCCC)
Deal, Nathan, 213
decision calculus, 12, 186
DeLauro, Rosa, 45
DeLay, Tom, 3, 25, 112, 129, 213
Democratic Congressional Campaign Committee (DCCC): financing of, 25; leadership structure, 114, 178, 182
Democratic National Committee (DNC), 48, 196
Democratic Senate Campaign Committee (DSCC), 196
Derrick, Butler, 186, 237
Dingell, John, 139, 153, 205, 233
discrete ambition, 176, 188
district advocates: careers, 81–83; characteristics of, 46–47, 57–58, 207–9; committee representation, 167–69, 173; elections and, 145–49; freshmen as, 65, 70–78, 89, 98, 102, 152; as ideologues, 86, 101; legislative success, 157–65, 238; minorities as, 84–86; polarization and, 218–19; progressive ambition and, 115, 121, 183, 190–99, 206, 221; retirement, 186–88; stability, 55–56, 92, 98, 118, 217
district attention, 7, 20–21, 34, 126, 220, 233
DNC. *See* Democratic National Committee (DNC)
Donnelly, Joe, 79, 213
Downey, Thomas, 225
DSCC. *See* Democratic Senate Campaign Committee (DSCC)
Duncan, John, 28, 235

electoral success: fit and, 134–39; indicators of, 131–33; style and, 14, 98, 128–31, 139–46, 152–53; vote margins, 134, 136–37
Emanuel, Rahm, 25, 79–80, 186
Energy and Commerce Committee, 67, 72, 103, 235
Ernst, Joni, 33, 58
Evans, Lane, 28

Federal Election Commission, 24
female representatives: agendas, 70; as district advocates, 74, 85; as freshmen, 70, 83–86; as party builders, 74–75; as party soldiers, 75, 85; style difference from males, 84–86, 106, 185
Flake, Jeff, 22, 213
Flynt, Jack, 150–51, 234
Foley, Tom, 27
Frank, Barney, 129
freshmen MCs: appointments, 44, 103; initial styles, 4, 11, 15, 73–81; majority status, 87–89; as party soldiers, 59, 94, 119, 147, 152, 186; previous careers, 81–83; race and gender, 2, 83–86; transition from freshman term, 96–100; transition to Congress, 61–73
fund-raising: ambitious entrepreneurs and, 115–17, 190; disadvantages of, 9, 201, 220; experience and, 97; leadership roles and, 45–46, 115, 221; measurements of, 24–25; party soldiers and, 210, 217

Gaydos, Joseph, 20
Gephardt, Richard, 24–25, 239
Gibbons, Jim, 23
Gifford, Gabrielle, 47
Gillibrand, Kirsten, 48–49, 79, 213
Gingrich, Newt: challenges, 64, 151, 211, 234; Contract with America, 2, 112; editorials, 23; entrepreneur style, 112, 239; as fund-raiser, 24
Goode, Virgil, 79–80
Goodlatte, Bob, 113
Graham, Lindsey, 64, 186, 202–3
Granger, Kay, 196
Greenfield, Meg, 64

Hall, Ralph, 26, 49
Harkin, Tom, 33, 58
Harris, Katherine, 79–80
Harvard University, 62
Hastert, Dennis, 24–25, 175, 196–97
Hayden, Carl, 1
Hayworth, J. D., 100
Heritage Foundation, 62
Hinojosa, Ruben, 237
Hobson, David, 2–3
House Administration Committee, 61, 167–69, 171–72
House Budget Committee, 45, 196

House Democratic Caucus, 80, 196
Hoyer, Steny, 25, 48
Huffington, Michael, 79–80
Hunter, Duncan, 235
Hyde, Henry, 112–13, 231–32

ideologues, 86, 101, 105–6
Intelligence Committee, 80, 168, 172–73

Jackson, Jesse, Jr., 228
Jefferson, William, 228
Jindal, Bobby, 49, 79–80, 213
Johnson, Nancy, 129
joint resolutions, 30–31, 156, 224
Judiciary and Homeland Security Committee, 113, 168–69, 171–72

Kasten, Bob, 45
Kennedy, Joseph P., 198
Kennedy, Patrick, 129
Kennedy, Ted, 153
Kennedy School of Government, 62
Kildee, Dale, 46
King, Steve, 31, 57–58, 122, 225
Kopetski, Mike, 237
Kucinich, Dennis, 46, 52–53

LaHood, Ray, 23
Latham, Tom, 31–33, 57–58, 122, 225
Latino representatives, 70, 84–86, 229
Lee, Sheila Jackson, 237
legislative behavior: bill progression, 155–57; constituencies and, 6; electoral effects of, 125–31; gestalt view of, 37, 205; measurements of, 29; polarization and, 4; reelection and, 124; scholarly understanding of, 7, 13, 54
legislative styles: aggregate patterns in, 49–56; careers and, 56–60, 81–83, 175–222; choices of, 19–29; gender and, 83–86; history of, 5–9; identifying, 33–37; initial styles explained, 73–81; nature of, 11–12; productivity, 165–73; race and, 83–86; shifts in, 104–6; shocks effect on, 106–18; success, 134–39, 154–65; trade offs of, 9–11
Lewis, Jerry, 25
Lewis, John, 23
Loebsack, David, 31–33, 57–58, 121
Lowey, Nita, 182, 237

majority shift: as behavioral influence, 221–22; freshmen MCs and, 89; partisanship and, 110–13; as style change cause, 11, 59, 93, 231
majority status: changes in, 12, 92, 109–12, 232; electoral effects of, 101, 115; leadership positions and, 185; legislation and, 161–64, 180; style shape and, 72, 75
Margolies-Mezvinsky, Marjorie, 64
Markey, Edward, 46
Martin, Joe, 5
McCarthy, Carolyn, 44–45
McCollum, Bill, 214
McCotter, Thaddeus, 45
McDermott, Jim, 20
McIntosh, David: as ambitious entrepreneur, 202, 214; early career, 68, 87, 129–30, 201–2; vs. Gingrich, 68–69, 211; as party soldier, 69, 202, 211, 214, 228; vs. Sharp, 129–30, 135, 146
Melancon, Charlie, 237
Member Representational Allowance (MRA), 20, 62, 224
Menendez, Bob, 213
military experience, 2, 81–83
minority party: freshmen in, 2, 81; party builders, 108–9, 232; party soldiers, 90; party specialists, 111; progressive ambition and, 189, 192
Moakley, Joe, 207–8, 238
Mollohan, Alan, 47, 91
Morella, Constance, 26
MRA. *See* Member Representational Allowance (MRA)
Murtha, John, 49

National Republican Congressional Committee (NRCC), 25, 113–14, 178
new member orientation, 61
nonpolitical careers, 81–83
NRCC. *See* National Republican Congressional Committee (NRCC)

Obama, Barack, 80, 103, 156
Obamacare. *See* Affordable Care Act
Oberstar, James, 49
Otter, Butch, 23

partisans, good, 209, 217–18, 229
party builders: characteristics of, 47–48, 129,

party builders (*continued*)
185, 214–16; committee appointments, 172–73, 229; electoral success of, 137, 139–41, 145–46; freshmen as, 70–75, 79–80; leadership positions, 114–15, 180–81, 221; legislation and, 157–58, 160–65, 217; majority status and, 111–12, 232; progressive ambition and, 190–94, 199–200, 203; retirement, 186–88, 199; transition patterns, 55–56, 97, 110, 186, 212

party giver, 35, 42

party giving: by district advocates, 46–47; explanation of, 45–46; by party builders, 47–48, 215; as style factor, 206

party soldiers: careers and, 81, 93; characteristics of, 45–46, 85, 157, 210–12; electoral success of, 145–48, 150; freshmen as, 59, 65–79, 89, 119, 195; leadership positions, 179, 204; legislation and, 158, 160, 163–65; majority status and, 87, 111; progressive ambition, 179, 204; retirement, 186; transition patterns, 55–56, 92–97, 227

party voting: freshmen and, 65; as loyalty demonstration, 25–26, 214; as style indicator, 34, 206

Pascrell, William, 23

Paul, Ron, 49

Pelosi, Nancy: as bill sponsor, 27; fundraising, 25; as party builder, 48, 80, 215; Speaker of the House, 175, 196–97

polarization: bipartisan coalitions vs., 26–27; districts advocates and, 217–18; freshmen and, 65; gerrymandering and, 218; party soldiers and, 211–12, 228; policy specialists and, 51

Policy Agendas and Congressional Bills Project, 28

policy specialists: careers and, 74, 83; characteristics of, 44–45, 83, 103, 180, 209–10; electoral success of, 137–39, 141, 145–50; freshmen as, 65, 70–71, 73, 76, 98; leadership positions, 109–10, 169, 197–99; legislation and, 154, 157–65; majority status and, 87, 111–12, 115; polarization and, 49–51; progressive ambition, 181–83, 191–94, 200; retirement and, 186–88, 199; transition patterns, 55–56, 97–102, 105, 120, 227

Price, David, 10, 16, 62–63, 67, 183

Price, Tom, 48, 79–80, 101
primary challenger, 133, 141–42
progressive ambition: careers and, 195–203; definition, 176; electoral considerations and, 233; styles and, 184–94, 209; term limits and, 219
Pryce, Deborah, 113
Public Works Committee, 91, 168, 172, 229

Quayle, Dan, 68

Rahall, Nick, 91, 96, 229–32
Rangel, Charles, 25
redistricting: electoral success and, 190, 234; entrepreneur style and, 109; as macro-level shock, 11, 108, 187; progressive ambition and, 191–92; reasons for, 218; retirement and, 187
Republican Policy Committee, 48, 80, 113, 196
Republican Study Committee, 48, 80, 196
retirement: considerations for, 184–85, 213, 233; copartisans and, 148–49; forced, 177; progressive ambition and, 94, 184, 188–95; by style, 186–88, 199, 203–4
Reynolds, Tom, 113
risk aversion, 63, 189
Rogers, Mike, 79–80, 101
Romney, Mitt, 45, 197
Rostenkowski, Dan, 49, 213
Rules Committee, 155
Ryan, Paul, 45, 113, 196–97, 226
Ryan White Care Act, 210

Sanders, Bernie, 4, 49, 79–80, 213
Saxton, James, 23
Schakowsky, Janice, 79
Schiff, Adam, 79, 198
Schroeder, Patricia, 9
Schumer, Charles, 4, 213, 214
seniority: electoral success and, 136–37, 141; leadership position and, 180–83, 221; legislative success, 151, 154; norms, 114; progressive ambition, and, 191; retirement and, 187; style distribution by, 56; style shifts by, 94, 97, 104–5
Shadegg, John, 100
showboating: as activity, 20, 23, 34–35, 206; by ambitious entrepreneurs, 48, 212; by district advocates, 46; by freshmen, 65;

INDEX 259

    by party builders, 47, 215; by policy soldiers, 45, 210; by policy specialists, 44
Shuler, Heath, 47
Smith, Christopher, 47, 227
Smith, Lamar, 23
Snowe, Olympia, 129
Solis, Hilda, 103
Southern Democrats, 47, 129, 135
State of the Union, 181
static ambition, 176
style changes, abrupt, 60, 119–20
Sullivan Index, 71, 73, 77, 229
Sweeney, John, 237

Tancredo, Tom, 23
Taylor, Gene, 47, 129
term limits, 64, 176, 217, 219–20
Terry, Lee, 78
Traficant, James, 23, 26, 219

Van Hollen, Chris, 48
Voorhis, Jerry, 5

vote share: contextual shock and, 107–20; decrease, 17, 58, 66, 108; electoral security and, 72; electoral success, 132, 136–37, 141, 161, 164; freshmen and, 73–77, 102; progressive ambition, 108, 119, 191; retirement and, 187–89; style and fit, 138–41; two-party vote, 132

Waldholtz, Enid Greene, 79, 214
Walker, Robert, 64
Walsh, James, 47
Wasserman Schultz, Debbie, 48, 79, 101, 196
Waxman, Henry, 44–45, 53–54, 115, 153, 210, 228
Ways and Means Committee, 72, 168–69, 171, 235
Weiner, Anthony, 237
Weller, Jerry, 79, 101

Young, C. W., 52–54, 113, 227

Chicago Studies in American Politics

A SERIES EDITED BY BENJAMIN I. PAGE, SUSAN HERBST, LAWRENCE R. JACOBS, AND ADAM J. BERINSKY

Series titles, continued from front matter:

THE AMERICAN WARFARE STATE: THE DOMESTIC POLITICS OF MILITARY SPENDING *by Rebecca U. Thorpe*

CHANGING MINDS OR CHANGING CHANNELS? PARTISAN NEWS IN AN AGE OF CHOICE *by Kevin Arceneaux and Martin Johnson*

TRADING DEMOCRACY FOR JUSTICE: CRIMINAL CONVICTIONS AND THE DECLINE OF NEIGHBORHOOD POLITICAL PARTICIPATION *by Traci Burch*

WHITE-COLLAR GOVERNMENT: THE HIDDEN ROLE OF CLASS IN ECONOMIC POLICY MAKING *by Nicholas Carnes*

HOW PARTISAN MEDIA POLARIZE AMERICA *by Matthew Levendusky*

THE POLITICS OF BELONGING: RACE, PUBLIC OPINION, AND IMMIGRATION *by Natalie Masuoka and Jane Junn*

POLITICAL TONE: HOW LEADERS TALK AND WHY *by Roderick P. Hart, Jay P. Childers, and Colene J. Lind*

THE TIMELINE OF PRESIDENTIAL ELECTIONS: HOW CAMPAIGNS DO (AND DO NOT) MATTER *by Robert S. Erikson and Christopher Wlezien*

LEARNING WHILE GOVERNING: EXPERTISE AND ACCOUNTABILITY IN THE EXECUTIVE BRANCH *by Sean Gailmard and John W. Patty*

ELECTING JUDGES: THE SURPRISING EFFECTS OF CAMPAIGNING ON JUDICIAL LEGITIMACY *by James L. Gibson*

FOLLOW THE LEADER? HOW VOTERS RESPOND TO POLITICIANS' POLICIES AND PERFORMANCE *by Gabriel S. Lenz*

THE SOCIAL CITIZEN: PEER NETWORKS AND POLITICAL BEHAVIOR *by Betsy Sinclair*

THE SUBMERGED STATE: HOW INVISIBLE GOVERNMENT POLICIES UNDERMINE AMERICAN DEMOCRACY *by Suzanne Mettler*

DISCIPLINING THE POOR: NEOLIBERAL PATERNALISM AND THE PERSISTENT POWER OF RACE *by Joe Soss, Richard C. Fording, and Sanford F. Schram*

WHY PARTIES? A SECOND LOOK *by John H. Aldrich*

NEWS THAT MATTERS: TELEVISION AND AMERICAN OPINION, UPDATED EDITION *by Shanto Iyengar and Donald R. Kinder*

SELLING FEAR: COUNTERTERRORISM, THE MEDIA, AND PUBLIC OPINION *by Brigitte L. Nacos, Yaeli Bloch-Elkon, and Robert Y. Shapiro*

OBAMA'S RACE: THE 2008 ELECTION AND THE DREAM OF A POST-RACIAL AMERICA *by Michael Tesler and David O. Sears*

FILIBUSTERING: A POLITICAL HISTORY OF OBSTRUCTION IN THE HOUSE AND SENATE *by Gregory Koger*

IN TIME OF WAR: UNDERSTANDING AMERICAN PUBLIC OPINION FROM WORLD WAR II TO IRAQ *by Adam J. Berinsky*

US AGAINST THEM: ETHNOCENTRIC FOUNDATIONS OF AMERICAN OPINION *by Donald R. Kinder and Cindy D. Kam*

THE PARTISAN SORT: HOW LIBERALS BECAME DEMOCRATS AND CONSERVATIVES BECAME REPUBLICANS *by Matthew Levendusky*

DEMOCRACY AT RISK: HOW TERRORIST THREATS AFFECT THE PUBLIC *by Jennifer L. Merolla and Elizabeth J. Zechmeister*

AGENDAS AND INSTABILITY IN AMERICAN POLITICS, SECOND EDITION *by Frank R. Baumgartner and Bryan D. Jones*

THE PRIVATE ABUSE OF THE PUBLIC INTEREST: MARKET MYTHS AND POLICY MUDDLES *by Lawrence D. Brown and Lawrence R. Jacobs*

THE PARTY DECIDES: PRESIDENTIAL NOMINATIONS BEFORE AND AFTER REFORM *by Marty Cohen, David Karol, Hans Noel, and John Zaller*

SAME SEX, DIFFERENT POLITICS: SUCCESS AND FAILURE IN THE STRUGGLES OVER GAY RIGHTS *by Gary Mucciaroni*

Lightning Source UK Ltd.
Milton Keynes UK
UKHW022107291019
352543UK00007B/241/P